BLOOD LINES

HOW THE FBI TOOK ON MEXICO'S MOST VIOLENT DRUGS CARTEL

MELISSA DEL BOSQUE

JOHN BLAKE

First published in Great Britain by John Blake Publishing,
an imprint of Kings Road Publishing
Suite 2.25, The Plaza,
535 Kings Road,
London, SW10 0SZ

www.johnblakebooks.com

www.facebook.com/johnblakebooks ⓕ
twitter.com/jblakebooks ⓔ

First published in the USA in 2017, by Ecco Press, an imprint of HarperCollins
This edition published by John Blake Publishing in 2018

ISBN: 978 1 78606 952 8

British Library Cataloguing-in-Publication Data:

A catalogue record for this book is available from the British Library.

Design by www.envydesign.co.uk

Printed and bound in Great Britain by Clays Ltd, Elcograf S.p.A.

1 3 5 7 9 10 8 6 4 2

Papers used by John Blake Publishing are natural, recyclable products made from wood
grown in sustainable forests. The manufacturing processes conform to the environmental
regulations of the country of origin.

Every attempt has been made to contact the relevant copyright-holders, but some were
unobtainable. We would be grateful if the appropriate people could contact us.

John Blake Publishing is an imprint of Bonnier Publishing
www.bonnierpublishing.com

ONE

SPECIAL AGENT SCOTT LAWSON PULLED INTO THE EMPTY PARKING LOT AND KILLED the engine. He could hear the muffled cadence of automatic rifle fire – *pop, pop, pop, pop* – echoing from across the river in Mexico. He rolled down his driver's side window, shielding his eyes from the South Texas sun with his left hand.

Lawson was new to Laredo, Texas and he'd come to the park by the river because it was as close to Nuevo Laredo as he could get without entering Mexican territory, which was out of his jurisdiction. The Mexican city was less than a quarter of a mile from where he sat in his beat-up Chevy Impala but it felt a world away. He surveyed the wide expanse of the Rio Grande as it flowed languidly underneath the international bridge towards the Gulf of Mexico.

He'd heard that the river's calm could be misleading, that there were hidden undercurrents. The Mexicans called it the Rio Bravo – the fierce river. Lawson got out of his car and walked to the edge. From the riverbank, he could see a chaotic jumble of telephone lines and electric wires, Spanish billboards and crumbling white colonial-style buildings similar to the ones in downtown Laredo. The two cities could have been as one if it weren't for the river.

He winced instinctively as the staccato of rapid gunfire rang out again across the river. A pillar of black smoke rose in the sky. Something was burning. He couldn't tell what. A Mexican flag – the largest flag he'd ever seen – billowed in the warm afternoon breeze near the customs office on the other side of the bridge. He realised he couldn't have been further from home in Tennessee. But as a rookie, he'd had no choice where the FBI sent him. And after six weeks on the border, he was still trying to make sense of where he'd landed.

Every day at his desk he read about the carnage and saw the grisly photos on websites like Borderland Beat, which obsessively reported every twist and turn in the drug war in Mexico. But it still felt abstract to him. That's why he'd left his office and driven to the edge of the river when he'd heard that another gun battle had broken out in Nuevo Laredo. But as he stood on the riverbank, a tall and blond gringo in cowboy boots so obviously out of place – *like some fool target*, he thought – he could see nothing of the Zetas or the Gulf Cartel, who had declared war against one another only a few days ago. He could only hear the percussive echo of automatic gunfire and see traces of smoke as the two factions fought for territory, the violence spilling out across Nuevo Laredo.

All around him, life carried on as usual on the American side of the river. The region was already seven years into the drug war and it had all taken on a surreal normality. A block away from where he'd parked his squad car, people went about their shopping in the downtown stores, while Mexicans – some of them innocent bystanders – died in the city across the river. The FBI's sources in Mexico had already predicted that this war would be even more vicious than the last, when the two former allies had battled the Sinaloa Cartel for the city five years earlier. Back then, in 2005, Nuevo Laredo's police force had been wiped out, their bodies quartered and decapitated and left in plastic bin bags by cartel gunmen. The Mexican army had patrolled the streets in armoured personnel carriers and people had called the city 'Little Baghdad'.

Lawson had been told his first week in Laredo that it would be their job to make sure the violence didn't spill across the river. But so far, he'd spent most of his time sitting in a grey-carpeted cubicle, studying an FBI policy manual the size of a phone book and writing up reports, which they called 1023s, for the FBI's intelligence analysts on any information he could gather about the escalating violence south of the Rio Grande.

He missed working the streets as a deputy outside Nashville. As he stood at the edge of the river, thirty years old and with the new gold FBI badge clipped to his belt beneath his shirt, he wondered whether he'd made a mistake. Growing up, he'd idolised small-town cops like his dad. But his dad had insisted on something more for him than a cop's meagre salary. He had drilled into him from an early age the idea of joining the FBI. But what was the point of being part of an elite federal agency if he was stuck behind a desk? *Nuevo Laredo is on fire,* he thought darkly, *and I'm writing reports about it.*

AT THE TRAINING ACADEMY, no one had bothered to tell Lawson that Laredo was considered a hardship post. Very few agents volunteered because it was too close to the drug war in Mexico for agents with families and many felt isolated there if they didn't speak Spanish. As a rookie, he was the perfect candidate because he had to go where the bureau sent him. Even better, he had no wife or kids to consider in the equation. Since it was a hardship post, he had to commit to staying for five years. But there was a payoff. If he stuck it out, he could choose his next city and most agents didn't get that privilege until they'd been in the FBI for more than a decade. He was still young, he thought, and in five years he could be back home in Tennessee.

He'd arrived a week before Christmas in 2009, with a few duffel bags filled with clothes and a cowboy hat he'd bought in San Antonio. From San Antonio, he'd driven south through mostly empty ranch land. As he started to worry he'd gone too far, with signs on the interstate pointing towards Mexico, he arrived in the outskirts of Laredo. With a population of less than 240,000, it wasn't a big city. Laredo splayed out along a bend in the Rio Grande. On the other side of the river was Mexico and a sprawling Nuevo Laredo that was twice as large as its American sister city. Maybe that's why Laredo felt so rootless. Four vehicular bridges and a railroad bridge linked the two cities. The traffic pulsed back and forth across the bridges at all hours of the day, most of it tractor-trailers carrying cargo south into Mexico or north towards other parts of the United States or Canada. When he'd researched Laredo, he'd learned it was called 'America's truck stop' because it was the largest inland port in the country. Every day, more than twelve thousand semi-trucks travelled through the border city. Their diesel fumes left a blue haze that gave the air a metallic taste.

He wondered why the FBI had chosen to send him to the border. Maybe it was the five weeks of Spanish in Mexico, which he was now struggling to remember. Maybe it was because he'd worked narcotics. On the Rutherford County drug interdiction task force, he'd arrested his share of dealers and helped seize kilos of meth, marijuana and black-tar heroin on the interstate. He'd interviewed smugglers after seizing their drug loads and seen real fear in their eyes when they told him about their relatives back in Mexico who would die because they'd lost the load. He'd thought he understood.

But before he'd left the FBI's training academy in Quantico, Virginia, he'd been pulled aside for a special briefing after the others had gone home. He remembered the gory images, one after another, of beheadings, dismembered torsos with the letter Z carved into them, flickering across the instructor's computer screen. The Zetas were a new kind of cartel, hyperviolent and military-trained, the instructor told him. Formed in 1999 by deserters from Mexico's elite Special Forces, the Grupo Aeromóvil de Fuerzas Especiales, or GAFE, they'd started off as bodyguards and enforcers for the Gulf Cartel but had turned into a cartel in their own right, spurring unprecedented violence and brutality in the drug war. The Zetas were fighting for control of the US-Mexico border, his instructor said, and they were killing people in Laredo too. 'You have no idea what you're getting into,' he'd warned. 'Every day your life will be on the line.'

But much to his surprise, he'd found that Nashville had a higher homicide rate than Laredo, though no one believed him back home. Yet from the riverbank, he could hear grenades exploding and automatic gunfire less than a quarter mile away. How could two cities, so much alike, have six murders a year in one and three hundred in the other?

His first week in Laredo, the special supervisory agent, David Villarreal, had given him the rundown and what was expected of him: 'The Zetas are what we focus on in this squad. That's what we do. And you need to learn as much as you can about them.' So Lawson had accompanied other agents while they met with their sources, typing up the 1023s for them afterwards, just so he could learn whatever he could about the Zetas. What he'd found out so far was that Heriberto Lazcano, known as Z-3, was the cartel's leader and Miguel Ángel Treviño Morales, or Z-40, his second in command. And that Treviño ruled over Nuevo Laredo like a feudal lord along with his younger brother Omar, known as Z-42, who at thirty-four was three years younger than Miguel and served as his right-hand man. Lawson was told that the Z stood for their radio call sign and the number denoted when they'd joined the cartel. The Treviños had been some of the cartel's first recruits from Nuevo Laredo.

Miguel had come up fast in the Zetas on his reputation as a sadistic, cold-blooded killer whose appetite for violence verged on the psychopathic. In one story he'd heard, Miguel had killed the baby of a rival in a microwave; in another telling, it was a vat of boiling oil. Lawson didn't know whether the story was true but it seemed anyone who worked in law enforcement along the border had heard a variation of it and no one seemed to doubt Miguel was capable of it.

Between his research on the Zetas and studying the FBI policy manual he was going out on patrol with the Laredo cops who'd been assigned to his squad, just to get out of the office and feel like a street cop again. At least the bureau had put him on violent crimes, which was what he had requested. The FBI's Laredo Resident Agency, where he'd been assigned, was a small satellite office with its headquarters 160 miles away in San Antonio.

The Laredo RA was divided between two squads – white-collar and violent crimes. Each squad had eight agents assigned to it, and four Laredo police officers to help ease the friction that was always there between the feds and the locals.

Violent crimes was staffed mostly by Puerto Rican and Cuban agents transferred from Miami who complained that they'd been demoted to backwater Laredo because they spoke Spanish. They called the blond and six-foot-five Lawson *güero*, because of his pale complexion, and would laugh when he tried to speak Spanish in his thick Tennessee drawl. Lawson took it good-naturedly. He was the son of a cop. And he knew they were testing him, to see how and where he would fit in.

To ease his transition into the Laredo office, the FBI had assigned a more senior agent, Jason Hodge, to be his training agent. In his late thirties, Hodge still dressed like the accountant he'd once been and was full of nervous energy, his button-down shirts often stained with coffee. They sat back-to-back in their cubicles. Lawson noticed that Hodge had the habit of fidgeting with the rubber sole that had partially separated from one of his leather shoes. *Thwap, thwap, thwap,* he'd hear whenever Hodge was puzzling over something in one of his cases.

Hodge was dismayed that he'd been put on violent crimes. He preferred writing intelligence briefs or working on white-collar investigations. A stack of documents and an Excel spreadsheet would put a smile on his face. But the thought of going undercover or doing surveillance made him uneasy. His favourite topic of conversation was his impending transfer out of Laredo, which he hoped would come at the end of the year. He already had his remaining days figured down to the last hour.

They couldn't have been more different. But Hodge had also been one of the first to make him feel welcome in Laredo, inviting him over for his wife's home-cooked meals. Lawson appreciated the food and the company. The last thing he wanted was to return to his empty room at the extended-stay hotel, which backed up to a seedy trucker bar. He was supposed to be buying a house and settling in – the FBI would buy the house back if he couldn't sell it, since he was in a hardship post – but he hadn't even started to look. He was still struggling with the idea that for the next five years he would be calling Laredo, Texas, his home.

TWO

STILL WIRED FROM THE ADRENALINE, MIGUEL AND OMAR TREVIÑO WERE IN THE mood to celebrate. They'd narrowly escaped from a fierce fire-fight with the military in the centre of Nuevo Laredo. At least six men had died and the soldiers had shot up three police cars that had come to the cartel's defence. But the brothers had managed to shoot their way out of the ambush. By the time they regrouped on the outskirts of the city, nighttime had fallen and the only light on the deserted highway came from the headlights of their convoy.

It was late October 2009 and still four months away from the Zetas' declaration of war against the Gulf Cartel. But Miguel was someone who always planned ahead. For the last two years he'd been investing in quarter-horse racing, which not only indulged his passion but was also a sign of his growing status within the Zetas. In Mexico, quarter-horse racing had long been an obsession steeped in northern Mexico's proud ranching heritage, which was also deeply ingrained in its former territories of California and the American Southwest. Every cartel had its favourite jockeys, trainers and horse agents. Owning the best bloodlines signalled that Miguel's wealth and power were ascending in the drug world. And very soon, he knew that his place within that world would be tested.

His mind had begun forming around a plan after he'd received the good news from Texas two weeks earlier. A sorrel colt he owned, called Tempting Dash, had qualified for one of the most prestigious quarter-horse races in America. In the past, he hadn't thought much of the horse. The colt came from a top bloodline but he'd been so skinny and small they'd called him Huesos, 'Bones', on the racetracks in Mexico. But the horse had surprised them all with its speed. In two days, Tempting Dash would run in the Dash for Cash Futurity in Texas, one of the most lucrative races of the season, with a $445,000 purse. The race was held every October at the Lone Star Park racetrack in Grand Prairie, not far from where the brothers had spent their teenage years in status-conscious Dallas, with its luxury cars and gated mansions. Miguel had always liked Dallas, which had shown him a more enticing side of life than the poor, working-class *barrios* of Nuevo Laredo.

For the last two years, Ramiro Villarreal, a horse agent from Monterrey, had been buying and racing horses for Miguel in the States. And it was Villarreal who had delivered the good news about Tempting Dash. With so much money on the line, Miguel wasn't going to leave the outcome of the race solely up to fate and the horse's natural ability.

He instructed his younger brother to radio Villarreal on his Nextel to make sure everything was going to plan in Texas. Omar had come up with Miguel through the ranks of the cartel. His rounded cheeks and boyish face made him appear less menacing than his brother, who had fierce dark eyes and sharp cheekbones, but Omar, who always strived to be his elder brother's equal, was just as ruthless and prone to violence.

Villarreal picked up his Nextel to answer Omar's call. He was driving to a horse auction at Heritage Place in Oklahoma City, then on to Lone Star Park for the race on Saturday.

'What are you doing, Gordo? . . . ,' Omar asked the rotund horse agent. 'Talk to me . . . what's the forecast? . . . When is Chevo leaving?'

'After nine-forty . . . but he has to get there at the same time for the vet to check them out there . . .' Villarreal said.

'Did the batteries take?' It was an old trick. To win the race, Tempting Dash would be shocked with volts of electricity from a handheld device. The manoeuvre used by jockeys, called 'buzzing', had been outlawed on US tracks. But during a training session, they had used it on Tempting Dash to see the colt's reaction and whether the shock resulted in that extra surge of speed needed to win.

'It's done,' Villarreal said, meaning the experiment had worked. 'And where are you now?'

'I'm on the road between San Antonio and Austin.'

'You will win, Gordo, you're going to win,' said Omar. He instructed Villarreal to pose with Tempting Dash in the winner's circle and, when the photo was snapped, to make a sign with his hand that the brothers would recognise so that the true owner of the horse would be known. 'We're going to win,' said Omar.

'If I win what?' Villarreal said. The radio connection on his Nextel was beginning to break up.

'. . . We're going to win. You will see.'

MIGUEL'S RISE TO POWER had been an unlikely one. He had no political connections and he came from a poor neighbourhood on the margins of Nuevo Laredo. But he was a man of his time, very much shaped by Mexico's past. And as the Gulf Cartel and the

Zetas were on the brink of war in late 2009, he was poised to attain even greater power.

In many ways, politics had paved the way for Miguel's ascension. Over several decades, the semi-authoritarian Partido Revolucionario Institucional, or PRI, had ruled Mexico, and its leaders had amassed their wealth through *plata o plomo*, silver or lead, co-opting or threatening anyone who challenged their power monopoly and allowing cronyism and corruption to flourish.

As the illicit drug economy grew in Mexico, eventually generating as much as $35 billion or more annually, the PRI's leaders divided the country among the handful of organisations, including the Gulf and Sinaloa cartels. Generals, law enforcement and politicians took a cut from the cartels that worked the divided territories and, in return, they let them run their trafficking businesses without interruption. As part of the arrangement, cartel leaders pledged to keep the violence among themselves and not to call undue attention to their growing illicit empires. With 90 per cent of the cocaine and 70 per cent of the methamphetamines and heroin consumed in the United States – the biggest drug market in the world – either produced or passing through Mexico, it was a pragmatic plan of accommodation that also made the political elite extremely wealthy.

But by 2000, the old arrangements, already frayed, started to unravel after the PRI lost its bid for the presidency for the first time in more than seventy years. The new president, Vicente Fox, a former Coca-Cola executive, and his opposing political party, the Partido Acción Nacional, or PAN, promised to make the government less corrupt and more democratic. 'Mexico doesn't deserve what has happened to us. A democratic change is urgent,' he proclaimed.

It was a message Mexicans had been waiting to hear since the revolution but it was already too late. The cartels had become too powerful and the rule of law too weak. As the old arrangements with the PRI fell away under President Fox, the cartels saw an opening. They began to further exert control over their territories. Heavily armed and well financed, they wouldn't take orders from the politicians anymore. Now it would work the other way around. It was a terrible irony that, just as Mexico was being heralded around the world for its budding democracy, the country's first paramilitary drug organisation – the Zetas – was formed.

The cartel's military founders had been trained by the American military to combat the growing threat of narcotrafficking. But the drug lords paid better than the government. Osiel Cárdenas, leader of the Gulf Cartel, based in Matamoros in the border state of Tamaulipas, recruited the military deserters to be his bodyguards and to protect the Nuevo Laredo *plaza*, or smuggling territory, the most coveted in his vast drug empire, which ranged from the Texas-Mexico border down to the Gulf coast of Mexico. Cárdenas called their partnership 'the Company'. His enemies were legion. Paranoid and ruthless, he'd earned his nickname, El Mata Amigos, 'the Friend Killer', after enlisting one of the Zetas' founding soldiers, Arturo Guzmán Decena, to shoot a business partner in the back of the head.

In 2003, Cárdenas was arrested and sent to a high-security prison near Mexico City, where he continued to run the Company from behind bars. He sent his Zetas to tamp down any revolt in his territories in the eastern half of Mexico.

With the arrest of Cárdenas, the wily drug lord Joaquín 'El Chapo' Guzmán sensed weakness and an opportunity, and sent in his army of *sicarios*, or hit men, to take over the coveted *plaza* of Nuevo Laredo. Guzmán's Sinaloa Cartel, from the fertile golden triangle in the west of the country where most of the country's opium was grown, was the largest, most powerful drug organisation in Mexico. And El Chapo and his associates wanted all of Mexico for themselves.

Miguel and Omar aligned themselves with the Zetas, the Company's enforcers, to wage war against El Chapo and the Sinaloa Cartel. Their hometown of Nuevo Laredo had always been a coveted plaza in the drug trade. Trucks and trains continuously shuttled back and forth across the five international bridges. Nearly half of the trade between the two countries – at least $180 billion in imports and exports – passed through Nuevo Laredo every year. Among the thousands of semis packed with televisions, car parts and combustion engines there was other valuable cargo, including kilos of cocaine, heroin and methamphetamine cleverly concealed in false compartments or waved through by US customs agents on the cartel's payroll.

The brothers' job was to exterminate the Sinaloa Cartel's gunmen and workers in Nuevo Laredo, which the Company called *contras*. Miguel immediately excelled at his new vocation. He wasn't military-trained like the other Zetas but he was an experienced hunter. He saw no difference between killing *contras* and the deer he hunted in the empty ranch lands beyond the city. If he didn't kill someone every day, he felt he hadn't done his duty. If he was unable to apply the *tiro de gracia* to a *contra* himself, then his brother Omar, who always shadowed him everywhere, would finish the job for him.

Miguel's reputation for ferocity and violence grew. By 2006, the Zetas had repelled the Sinaloa incursion and preserved the Company's territory, and Miguel's rank within the Zetas was on the rise.

Heriberto Lazcano, a former Special Forces soldier, was now in charge of the Zetas. Lazcano was a pragmatic leader, ambitious and ruthless. He'd earned his nickname, El Verdugo, 'the Executioner', for his baroque torture methods, which included feeding his victims to lions and tigers he kept on one of his many ranches. In 2007, Mexico finally extradited Osiel Cárdenas to a high-security prison in the United States. The Friend Killer's grip on the Company was slipping and Lazcano sensed an opening. He began to think of independence and expansion. As a former military man, he had his own ideas about how the Zetas should be run. While the Gulf Cartel was content with smuggling drugs, the Zetas could instead demand a cut from every black-market transaction in their territories, whether it was oil stolen from the national monopoly Pemex, pirated CDs or prostitution. They could also levy a tax on legitimate businesses and commerce in exchange for protection.

In Miguel Treviño, Lazcano recognised a useful and equally cold-blooded ally. He sent his new second in command to conquer more territory. The Zetas, using their military training, gathered intelligence on rivals and government forces using a system of spies and informants, and they set up private communications networks. But their most effective tactic was spreading terror to subjugate their enemies and the communities they conquered. Corpses of members of rival drug gangs were left swinging from bridges, and garbage bags full of mutilated body parts were strewn along the highways. Bodies were stacked in piles outside police stations or at major intersections, their torsos carved with the letter Z. This was Miguel's specialty and his calling card.

By 2008, Lazcano had also tasked Miguel with national recruitment to expand their ranks. In a first for Mexico's drug trade, the Zetas set up military-style training camps, staffed by Colombian paramilitaries and Kaibiles, special-force commandos from Guatemala renowned for their jungle-warfare skills, to train recruits in the use of shoulder-fired missiles, .50-caliber machine guns and other military-grade weaponry smuggled in from the United States or Central America. The Zetas were training ordinary men to become mercenary soldiers. Miguel looked for recruits like himself, poor and with no education or future. He wanted to know if these men, most of them barely out of their teens, were cold-blooded enough to be Zetas. They were given a machete or a sledgehammer and told to kill a person tied up in front of them. The human targets were culled from kidnapped *contras* or the waves of migrants passing through their territories on their way to the United States. Those who felt no remorse after the slaughter were enlisted to be Miguel's personal bodyguards or soldiers for the front line. They accepted that their lives would be brief and violent. It was a pact made with the devil for money and to feel, for once, what it was like to have power.

As the Zetas grew in power and number, a new president of Mexico was elected in 2006, under the same business-orientated party, the PAN, as his predecessor, Vicente Fox. But President Felipe Calderón took a harsher, more militant stance against the growing power of the drug traffickers. His first year in office, Calderón turned the military out into the streets to fight the cartels, igniting Mexico's drug skirmishes into an all-out war. But by 2010, there was little he could call victory. All Calderón had was a mounting pile of bodies – as many as 120,000 – and a growing number of *desaparecidos*, casualties in the expanding drug war.

Even more troubling, the US military had issued a global security report in early 2009 warning that Mexico was at risk of a 'rapid and sudden collapse' if Calderón was unsuccessful in his military campaign. Incensed, the Mexican president told the US media, 'To say that Mexico is a failed state is absolutely false. I have not lost any part – any single part – of Mexican territory.' But the truth was far more complicated than Calderón would admit. Many of the soldiers, the police and even some of his own government ministers already worked for the other side.

MIGUEL AND THE ZETAS were making so much money that it had started to become a burden. As he made his plans on the deserted outskirts of Nuevo Laredo for the upcoming race in Texas, each brother carried duffel bags full of cash to bribe their way out of ambushes and military roadblocks. Most of their money was in US dollars but it wasn't good for anything but bribes until they could launder it through the banking system. A team of accountants and lawyers worked daily to devise new ways to make the dirty money clean.

The Zetas were a multi-billion-dollar, transnational business just like General Motors or ExxonMobil and there was no more lucrative and coveted territory for moving merchandise than their hometown. In one month, shipping between one thousand and three thousand kilos of Colombian cocaine to the United States, Miguel could make as much as $30 million. This was from just one city in an expanding territory under his control along the eastern half of Mexico.

With their new wealth, the brothers invested in cash-intensive businesses like casinos and bars, and bought up real estate, sports cars and coal mines. But Miguel remained fixated on horses, a passion he shared with his brothers and their father, who had managed ranches for wealthy landowners in northern Mexico.

If Tempting Dash won the futurity, with its $445,000 purse, Miguel would own a valuable commodity. Increasingly, it made sense to grow his racing business in the United States and get his money out of Mexico. The coming battle for territory and power between the Zetas and the Gulf Cartel had the potential to be more vicious, more deadly than anything seen before.

Up until then, the only wealth his family had ever known was in their numbers. They were a large and sprawling family of seven brothers and six sisters, with Miguel right in the middle, followed by Omar. Growing up on both sides of the US–Mexico border, they'd always lived on the margins because of poverty, especially after their father left when they were young.

If they were familiar with anything, it was hardship. The eldest, Juan Francisco, was locked up for twenty years in a US prison for marijuana smuggling. In Nuevo Laredo, a gunman from the Sinaloa Cartel had shot the youngest brother down in the street in front of his mother's home. These days she spent much of her time in Texas, where it was safer, along with his remaining brothers and sisters, away from the endless spiral of murder and vengeance in Mexico.

But the drug business had made Miguel wealthy beyond what any of them could have imagined. With his millions he could build a racing dynasty in the United States that would be his legacy and for his mother, Maria, who had always cared for them despite their struggles. Working with Villarreal, he'd learned how easy it was to purchase racehorses in the United States, where transactions were often in cash and sealed with nothing more than a handshake. He would use the horses to funnel more of his money through the US banks, where it would be safe from his enemies. He would recruit others to set up front companies in the United States to mask his involvement. They could bid on valuable horses, as Villarreal had been doing, and Miguel could put any name on the ownership document he wanted.

But who could he trust to run the operation? In the drug business, betrayal and double dealing were inevitable. He only had to look at the trail of bodies he'd left behind him on his quick rise to the top. He already suspected that Ramiro Villarreal had been padding his expenses. After two years, Villarreal knew too much about his business. Something would have to be done about the horse agent. The closest he came to something akin to trust was with his family. Lately he'd been thinking about his second-eldest brother, José, who was forty-three and still chasing the American dream in a suburb of Dallas. José was a US citizen and had a clean record. He'd never wanted anything to do with the drugs or Miguel and Omar's business. On a good year, he cleared $50,000 working as a brick mason. With four children to support, he barely made enough to keep the lights on at home.

His brother could use the money. And Miguel could convince him with the fact that he'd never have to touch a kilo of cocaine. It would all look perfectly legitimate. José would be his new front man. This way, he'd keep the money in the family. And the Treviño name would be associated with the finest champions, the best bloodlines the United States had to offer. The plan was nearly perfect. He'd deal with Villarreal when the time was right.

THREE

THE PALE-YELLOW AND RUST-COLOURED BUILDING THAT HOUSED THE FBI OVER-
looked the interstate less than a mile from the international
border. At six stories, it was one of the tallest buildings in Laredo
and it stood out against the flat and hazy skyline. The black iron
fence and a metal detector at the entrance were the only signs
the building housed several federal law-enforcement agencies,
including the FBI. In the pecking order of federal agencies
fighting the drug war at the border, the bureau was somewhere
in the middle. At the very top was the DEA, with twice as many
agents and resources, which occupied the top two floors of the
building. Some of the other agents called them the 'cowboys of
the DOJ' because they didn't hesitate to run roughshod over
other agencies when it came to drug investigations. Homeland
Security Investigations, or HSI, was the underdog. A part of the
Department of Homeland Security, it had existed for less than
a decade and was still finding its way as an investigative agency.
The FBI and the HSI shared a floor underneath the DEA.

Two months into his new job, Scott Lawson was still
daydreaming about getting in his truck and heading north for

Tennessee. But the thought of his father's disappointment kept him rooted in Laredo. Besides the massive FBI policy manual, the only thing on his desk was a framed photograph of his great-uncle, Bailey Howell, a six-time All-Star in the NBA, underneath the basket boxing out Wilt Chamberlain when he played for the Boston Celtics. Going pro had been Lawson's dream too but he'd been forced to accept in college that it was never going to happen. So he'd settled for Plan B, which was to become a cop like his old man.

Growing up, he'd sometimes ride along after school with his father to the scenes of car wrecks and burglaries. His parents had divorced when he was three and both had remarried. His dad was busy with a new wife and a baby at home. So he looked forward to those nights alone with his dad, patrolling the backcountry roads. There was rarely a murder in rural Hardeman County, Tennessee. His dad had done two tours of duty in Vietnam before he was twenty-one and seen enough of death already. By the time Lawson was fifteen, he was treated more like a fellow deputy. His dad would send him to check the pulses of car-crash victims to see whether they were alive or dead. He did whatever he was told, just so he could ride along with him at night. He loved the camaraderie his dad had with the other chain-smoking deputies on the force. The way he looked at it, they sacrificed themselves to protect the innocent. It made him feel as if he was part of a special brotherhood.

But no matter how hard his dad worked, he never made enough money. Like most cops, his father liked to joke that the feds left all the grunt work up to the locals while they sat in their air-conditioned offices 'in their suits and ties with their nice salary and benefits.' But being able to provide for your family and retire someday, especially in small-town Tennessee, was no joke, and so his father had encouraged him to become a federal agent – take the salary and the benefits – and do better than he had.

Having watched his father struggle to provide for them, Lawson knew he had a point. So after getting a college degree in criminal psychology, he became a deputy south of Nashville with the idea of joining the FBI as soon as he gained some law-enforcement experience. After four years as a deputy, he applied and was accepted into the FBI training academy in Quantico. The only thing that made his dad prouder was his graduation six months later. And now here he was in Laredo, a fully-fledged FBI agent and obedient son, wondering whether he'd been better off a deputy in Tennessee. With a sigh, he flipped open the policy manual and started on a new chapter.

His reading was interrupted by Hodge, who swung around in his office chair. 'I've got something for you,' he said, his voice lowering to a conspiratorial whisper. Lawson turned around in his chair to face Hodge with a look of puzzlement. 'I want you to go to Central Texas with me,' Hodge said, 'and help me flesh out a new investigation.'

Lawson nodded, waiting for the rest. He assumed Hodge was referring to the tip from Mexico that the FBI's McAllen office had received about a recent Oklahoma horse auction. An American had bid on some racehorses and set a public auction record of $875,000 for a horse named Dashin Follies. It made news in the Oklahoma papers but the source said the real buyer was a man named Miguel Treviño. When Hodge had mentioned it a couple of weeks ago, Lawson was already familiar with Treviño. He'd been immediately intrigued when Hodge had mentioned the Zeta cartel boss to him but his hope was just as quickly burst when Hodge mentioned he was working the lead with someone else.

He leaned in closer in his chair to hear what Hodge had to say.

Hodge explained that he and the other agent from the McAllen office had already visited with the American who'd bid on the horses. His name was Tyler Graham, he said, a young guy from a prominent family outside Austin who had made their fortune racing and breeding quarter horses.

Hodge had found the interview at Graham's farm tough going, which was why he needed Lawson's help now. It was difficult to strike up any kind of rapport with him, Hodge said. He didn't know a thing about horses. 'You're a country boy. You wear cowboy boots,' he said. 'I know you know something about horses.'

During one of the many dinners at Hodge's house, Lawson had mentioned how his mother kept several quarter horses at a stable near their home and insisted he learn how to ride. Someday he hoped to have a ranch of his own in Tennessee, with a few horses. Lawson felt foolish now having told them of his dream. It was a long way from the reality of a rookie agent living in a cheap extended-stay hotel near the interstate.

'So, what do you want me to do?' he asked.

Hodge explained that McAllen was handing off the investigation. The FBI had made some changes since the Zetas and the Gulf Cartel had split in February 2010, cleaving their territory in two. The McAllen office, 150 miles southeast of Laredo on the border, would have an AOR, or area of responsibility, focused solely on the Gulf Cartel now. Everything west of McAllen was now Zeta territory, which meant Laredo got the Treviños.

'I want you to meet Tyler Graham and try to get him to co-operate,' Hodge said. Lawson's job would be to be likable and establish a rapport with Graham and see whether he would work with them as a source. 'Why don't you see how you hit it off?' Hodge said, urging him on.

Lawson felt his mood lifting for the first time in days. He

was no expert on the Zetas but he did know something about horses. Right now they didn't have much, said Hodge, just Graham, who'd said very little during their first meeting, and the tip from Mexico.

Lawson wasn't sure he could get Graham to work with them. Graham came from a wealthy family and rich people had the tendency to disappear behind a wall of lawyers. But Lawson was willing to try if it got him out of the office and back on the streets.

FOUR

LAWSON COULD SEE THE RED SSS LOGO FOR SOUTHWEST STALLION STATION emblazoned on the side of a white barn as they approached the farm. It was mid-March 2010 and translucent green leaves had begun to bud from the skeletal branches of the pecan and hackberry trees that lined the long driveway. He could live here in a heartbeat, he thought.

Twenty years earlier, Southwest Stallion Station, in the small farming town of Elgin, thirty miles east of Austin, had been a premium stud farm, responsible for the breeding of some of quarter-horse racing's most celebrated champions.

As the years passed, though, some of the lustre had faded. A devastating drought and the Great Recession had done further damage. Lawson noticed that the paddocks looked half-empty, and the parched yellow grass had given way to dust. But with 1,300 acres of prime Central Texas real estate, it was still a jewel of a farm.

During their four-hour drive from Laredo, Lawson had peppered Hodge with questions from behind the wheel about Tyler Graham, collecting what information he could to be prepared for their meeting. Graham's grandfather Charles "Doc" Graham was a tough, persuasive character, a product of the Great Depression who had started with a fledgling veterinary clinic outside Austin and shrewdly invested in a cattle feedlot and several other successful businesses. These included Heritage Place in Oklahoma City, one of the pre-eminent auction houses for racehorses in the country and the place where his grandson Tyler had made the record-setting bid that had caught the FBI's attention. Doc's passion was quarter-horse racing. He'd been influential in getting the Texas Legislature to revive betting at racetracks in the 1980s. The move had reinvigorated the Texas racing industry. But then legalised casino gambling dealt another devastating blow in the 1990s. Now every state that bordered Texas had casinos at its racetracks and Texas was once again nursing a dying racing industry. A stubborn bloc of conservatives and Baptists in the Texas Legislature made sure that any effort to legalise gambling died before it ever reached the governor's desk.

Lawson had been to the Kentucky Derby several times to watch Thoroughbreds race but, even though he grew up riding quarter horses, he'd never seen them race. He knew the horses were famous for being lightning-fast sprinters, while Thoroughbreds were bred for endurance. There was nothing more American, more western, than quarter-horse racing. Bred from small, sturdy Spanish horses and larger-boned breeds brought over by English settlers, quarter horses were as common as cactus on the American frontier. Every rancher had a dependable quarter horse – wide-chested and short-legged but smart and agile – a horse that could work all day herding cattle, then race on the weekends at a makeshift track on the edge of town. In quarter-horse racing, even an ordinary ranch horse (and its owner) had a chance at becoming a champion. Thoroughbred racing was for the elite.

Tyler Graham was just breaking into the racing business in his own right. He had followed in his grandfather's footsteps and graduated from Texas A&M University, one of the best agriculture schools in the country. He'd majored in animal sciences and minored in economics so that he'd have the business sense to capitalise on his grandfather's legacy. Lawson thought about what a risky venture it was, trying to make a living in agriculture: drought, a dwindling water supply, high feed prices and marginal profits made the whole enterprise more a labour of love than a solid business prospect. Most in Graham's situation chose an easier path and parcelled off their valuable land to developers who'd turn their horse farms into suburban tract developments with names like Cowboy Acres and Heritage Ranch. Keeping his grandfather's legacy intact was a heavy responsibility for a twenty-six-year-old fresh out of college.

On the way to the ranch, Hodge told Lawson more about his first meeting with Graham, who had mentioned a racehorse called Tempting Dash. The horse had become something of a legend already in the world of quarter-horse racing, having won two prestigious races in Texas over the winter. Graham had been working for months on the owner to recruit the champion to breed at their stud farm. He'd even agreed to bid on the owner's behalf at the January auction at Heritage Place. The owner's name, he'd told Hodge, was José Treviño.

It didn't take Hodge long to figure out that José was Miguel Treviño's older brother. The McAllen agent along with Hodge that day had been especially blunt with Graham about who the Zetas were and what they were capable of. Hodge could tell that Graham had no idea who he was dealing with. Their visit had shaken him and it had ended on a strained note. Now they would have to do some delicate footwork to convince him to help further their investigation. Graham had a choice: he could help them get José and his brothers, or risk going down with them. Everything would depend on whether Lawson could strike up a rapport with him and convince him to work with the FBI, Hodge said. *So, no pressure then*, thought Lawson, who was starting to sweat under his plaid shirt.

His jaw tensed as they pulled up to the farm's office in their unmarked car and Hodge called Graham's secretary on his cell. They didn't want the workers at the farm to know who they were and risk news about a visit from the FBI spreading. They got out of the car and went to look at a horse in a nearby stall. Lawson had worn his jeans and boots but not a cowboy hat – he didn't want Graham thinking he was trying too hard. He might sniff him out as something less than a real horseman. For any of the workers who might be watching, they pretended to be prospective buyers. Graham, in a baseball cap advertising the family farm, stepped out of his office and strode over to them, shaking their hands firmly. 'Let's go inside,' he said, gesturing with a tilt of his head towards the open door of his office.

Inside, Graham appeared unruffled by the two FBI agents standing in his entryway. The rustic wood-panelled walls of the office were crammed with glossy portraits of champion horses, including that of the legendary stallion Three Oh's, who had jumpstarted Doc's career as a horse breeder in 1970 and put Southwest Stallion Station on the map. Racing trophies lined the walls and framed newspaper articles highlighted the work of Graham and his grandfather at the farm and on the racetrack.

Graham gestured for Lawson and Hodge to take a seat on a worn leather couch. He plopped down on the couch opposite them. His callused hands and scuffed boots showed that he worked hard for everything he'd inherited but Lawson could tell by his nonchalant attitude that he'd grown up with privilege. He was used to things going his way, or bending them to his will, like his grandfather. Lawson and Graham were close to the same age. He tried to imagine what it would be like to have all of his responsibility running the farm plus a handful of other businesses.

They sized up one another as Hodge introduced Lawson, then began quizzing Graham again about Dashin Follies and the other three horses he'd purchased at the auction in Oklahoma City. They worried that this would be their last shot before Graham called in his lawyers. They needed him to understand he could be in real danger mixing with the Treviños and they wanted him to know the FBI could help. They didn't have enough on him to strong-arm him into co-operating. So Lawson needed to find common ground with him and draw him out.

'I hear Tempting Dash is a once-in-a-lifetime kind of horse,' he said. 'And I understand the farm needs him and you took that chance to build up the family business again. But now you're involved with the wrong people. To move forward, we need to know you're on board with us.'

At the mention of Tempting Dash, Graham stiffened. 'I haven't done anything wrong,' he said.

'I know,' Lawson said, 'but you're heading down that road.' He explained again who Miguel Treviño was – and his reputation for violence. He didn't want to scare Graham off but he wanted him scared enough that he would agree to help them in exchange for their protection.

Graham nodded, a dazed look coming over him. 'I'm going to show you something,' he said. He stood up and walked over to a framed photograph hanging on the wall. 'This is Tempting Dash,' he said. Lawson and Hodge also stood up and approached the photo to get a closer look. It was a winner's-circle photo taken at the Lone Star Park racetrack in Grand Prairie. 'That's José Treviño.' Graham pointed at a man in a tan baseball cap and brown Carhartt jacket standing next to a copper-coloured horse in front of the neon scoreboard. The man was looking at the horse and away from the camera, so his face could not be seen.

A month before the picture was taken, Graham explained, Tempting Dash's owner had been a Mexican horse agent named Ramiro Villarreal. Graham pointed to Villarreal in the photo, standing at the very edge of the crowd opposite José and the horse. Graham had known Villarreal for years, he said. He was well known as a top bidder who spent millions at Heritage Place and other horse auctions. He was also a mainstay at the racetracks. 'He sold Tempting Dash for next to nothing to José Treviño,' Graham said. Tempting Dash had qualified for the Texas Classic Futurity at Lone Star Park just weeks after he'd dominated the Dash for Cash and broken the track record in October. Why would Villarreal sell him just weeks before the November futurity? José had paid $25,000 for a horse that had just won $445,000. 'It's bullshit,' Graham said.

Lawson knew he was getting somewhere. Graham explained that his friend Eusevio 'Chevo' Huitron, Tempting Dash's trainer, had introduced him to José at Lone Star Park before the November Texas Classic Futurity. Chevo had described the horse's Mexican owners as having an endless cash flow. They loved to race but didn't know anything about breeding. They'd need help, he said, handling such a valuable asset.

By January, the horse had already won two prestigious races, set a new speed record and been awarded racehorse of the year at Heritage Place. Graham needed the champion to help revive his grandfather's stud farm. A horse like Tempting Dash would draw new clients to the Southwest Stallion Station along with profit and prestige. So Graham quickly got to work taking José and Chevo out for meals and drinks, trying to win José over before his competitors beat him to it. He'd even dropped $12,000 on a deer hunt in South Texas for José, his eldest son, and Chevo's son so that José would look more favourably upon the idea of sending his horse, Tempting Dash, to be bred at Graham's farm.

Lawson scrutinised the winner's-circle photo more closely. Two teenagers stood next to a giant white banner with black letters that read 'Texas Classic Futurity Winner 2009'. The girl had a beaming smile; she'd formed her fingers to make a 4 and a 0 for the picture. The boy standing next to her in a red plaid shirt was flashing a 4 and a 2 with his fingers. Behind them stood Tyler Graham in a pink button-down shirt, a faint smile on his face. Lawson was brand new to the FBI and the border; he didn't know much about the Zetas. But he knew that the nicknames for Miguel and Omar Treviño were '40' and '42'. It wasn't exactly subtle, he thought. Maybe they thought no one was paying attention.

Graham said he'd had a feeling something was off about José Treviño. But he hadn't known the full extent of it until the first visit from Hodge and the McAllen agent, which had rattled him even if he tried not to show it now. 'So how can I help?' he asked with an air of resignation.

Lawson was encouraged. Graham was opening a door for them. He offered him the deal: keep doing business with José Treviño and they would have his back. Graham would keep them apprised of José's movements, who he did business with and whether there was any contact with his brother Miguel. 'Just keep living life as normal,' Lawson assured him. 'But we'll talk regularly.'

Graham didn't say a word. He was mulling it over. He'd be sharing information with the FBI about one of the leaders of the most feared cartel in Mexico. It was a terrible deal. He was in over his head any way he looked at it. Go through with it and he could end up dead but, if he didn't, he'd risk getting crosswise with the FBI. He'd just spent months lobbying José for Tempting Dash, and José had finally agreed to send him the champion. He already had the other horses from the auction at his farm. One of them, Dashin Follies, was one of the highest-valued broodmares in the business. He didn't want to let go of Tempting Dash either. He nodded. 'Okay,' he said.

They shook hands. That dazed look had come over Graham's face again, as if he couldn't believe what had just happened. But he gave up little of whatever inner turmoil he was feeling as he ushered them outside.

'We'll talk again soon,' Lawson said. Graham stood in the doorway of his office. He nodded, then shut the door behind him. He'd be tough to beat at poker, thought Lawson.

ON THE DRIVE BACK to Laredo, Lawson remembered his first week at the FBI. His boss, David Villarreal, had told them that the best way to go after cartel leaders was through their relatives in the States. At the time, Lawson had barely listened. Stuck in a cubicle all day, he'd never have the chance, he thought. But suddenly, they had a real lead. From intel reports, Lawson knew Miguel had a large family on both sides of the border.

Over the decades, a lot of cops and federal agents had crossed paths with the Treviños but they'd never been able to touch Miguel or Omar. There was the Dallas drug bust in 1994 of Juan Francisco, known as Kiko. He was the oldest sibling and considered the family patriarch. He was put away for twenty years for running a marijuana-smuggling operation between Nuevo Laredo and Dallas. Both Miguel and José were in Dallas working as couriers for their brother, witnesses would later testify in court. But the two were never indicted. It was a close call, though. In court, Juan Francisco had blamed José for his downfall, saying he had been the real mastermind behind the smuggling operation.

Apparently, not enough evidence was ever found to put José in jail. Since then, he'd remained under the radar in Dallas, working as a brick mason and staying out of trouble. After Juan Francisco's arrest, Miguel had fled to Mexico. During the trial, Omar's name had never come up as part of the smuggling operation. He was already in Nuevo Laredo, where he'd soon join Miguel in his rapid rise through the criminal underworld.

Hodge was pleased with the way Lawson had handled Graham. As Lawson's training agent, he felt it was important he help him recruit his first source. Graham was a promising lead. He was already inside José Treviño's circle of trust. On paper, José had a clean record and appeared to be an average working-class guy. But he was also the elder brother of two drug lords. And he'd just dropped $1.2 million on four horses, with Graham serving as his front man at the Oklahoma auction. And now they had this other horse, Tempting Dash, a champion racer, which José had apparently bought for next to nothing. It had Miguel Treviño's fingerprints all over it but now they would have to prove it. That would be the tough part.

On the ride home, Hodge was even more nervous than usual. He was worried about the havoc they'd unleash if they went after José to get to Miguel. They were talking about trying to take down a man who considered murder his vocation. He also had his spies in Laredo. At one time, Miguel had even had his own cell of assassins carrying out hits for him on the US side of the river. Miguel's gunmen were just teenagers recruited from the poor *barrios* in Laredo and Nuevo Laredo who'd been enticed by the cash, kilos of cocaine and luxury cars. But the teen *sicarios* were merciless, though often reckless, sometimes killing the wrong people by mistake. They'd killed one man on his doorstep only to find out later that Miguel had wanted his brother dead. In the span of two years, they'd killed at least six people in Laredo.

They'd shot one man in front of his wife and kids in the parking lot of a Torta-Mex fast-food restaurant. The police had finally dismantled the cell in 2006 and put Miguel's teen hit men in jail. Hodge also reminded Lawson that Miguel's sisters lived in Laredo not far from his gated community. He was convinced that sooner or later he'd cross paths with one of the Treviño clan while he was out eating with his wife and kids.

Lawson knew it was a possibility. But he doubted they would run into Miguel or Omar. Most of the other agents thought the brothers wouldn't risk crossing the river now that they were on US law enforcement's most wanted list. North of the Rio Grande, the Zetas couldn't rely on the same impunity they'd bought in Mexico. But this also meant the agents would need help from Mexican law enforcement and the military if they ever hoped to arrest the Treviños on their home turf. Counting on co-operation in Mexico could be dicey since the cartels had infiltrated every level of the military and police. They never knew whom they could fully trust and who was taking orders from the Zetas or another cartel. The road forward would be a perilous one and even federal agents had to think twice before they took their next step. Hodge had a wife and kids. Lawson, who had grown up part of an extended tribe of half-siblings, had always been wary of marriage. Now he was glad of it. He had no one to worry about but himself.

FIVE

LAWSON WAS ANXIOUS TO MOVE FORWARD WITH THE INVESTIGATION. BUT AFTER their trip to Graham's farm, Hodge said he'd have little time to be chasing after horses. He was wrapped up in a drug-gang investigation involving a corrupt Laredo police sergeant. He'd been working on the investigation for two years but still didn't have an indictment. And he was desperate to solve the case by the end of the year so that he could leave Laredo without looking back.

So it was up to Lawson. He ran José Treviño's name through the bureau's deconfliction database, where federal and local law enforcement ran searches to see if another agency was investigating the same suspect. The DEA and Laredo PD were all over Miguel and Omar Treviño. But the database didn't come back with a single hit on José. Lawson opened up a case file under the FBI and added Jason Hodge as lead agent, and then typed in his own name.

He'd never worked a money-laundering case. He knew how to handle a drug investigation – he'd been doing nothing but that for the last five years in Tennessee, though he'd never worked anything on the scale of the Zetas. It was still too early to tell whether drugs would surface in their investigation. Both he and Hodge suspected that José was too careful. From the way he'd set up the bidding in Oklahoma, by using Tyler Graham as a straw buyer, he was laundering big money for his brothers and working hard to make the whole thing look legitimate. Bringing drugs into the mix would only draw the attention of law enforcement.

Not more than a week ago Lawson had toyed with the idea of quitting but now he'd stumbled upon what had the potential to be a career-making case. They had a direct line to two of the FBI's most wanted criminals through their elder brother, who wasn't on any other agency's radar as far as he could tell. And Lawson had the means through Tyler Graham to infiltrate José's operation without the Treviños ever suspecting he was watching. Now all he had to do was keep Graham from losing his nerve.

Graham had told him he'd call as soon as he had something to report. Before they'd left his farm in Elgin, he'd got him to sign an agreement to become a source and make it official. Lawson had held the paper down on a desk while Graham reluctantly scrawled his signature across the bottom as if he were signing his life away. As the days ticked past slowly in Laredo with no word from Graham, Lawson wondered whether he really had a case. All he had was a piece of paper and a promise.

AS WINTER TURNED TO SPRING in 2010, the collateral damage from the war on the other side of the river began to hit the FBI's Laredo office in waves. Kidnappings were reported daily but family members didn't notify the police in Nuevo Laredo because most of the police worked for the Zetas. So the calls rolled in about people who'd gone missing in Mexico. But the agents could only investigate kidnappings involving US citizens. Lawson didn't like seeing the families from Nuevo Laredo, just as desperate, be turned away. It didn't feel right but that was the bureau's policy.

Among those missing were the Garcia brothers, US citizens and successful businessmen from a large family that lived on both sides of the river. One afternoon, they'd gone to Nuevo Laredo to ride their motocross bikes and never returned. Lawson was assigned the case, his first as a lead agent. Within days, he'd gone from zero cases to two. He was finally starting to feel like a cop again.

But when it came to the FBI, he was still a rookie. He'd been a deputy so he knew how to work an investigation. But doing it the FBI way was different. For every hour of investigating it seemed like there were two hours of paperwork. He was still only halfway through the policy manual on his desk. He needed help from a streetwise and experienced agent. And there was only one agent on his squad he had in mind.

He knew that, at first glance, he and Alma Pérez seemed like an unlikely partnership. She was from the border and spoke fluent Spanish, and he was a gringo from Tennessee who was good at mangling it. But other than the home-cooked meals at Hodge's house, Alma Pérez was the only other reason he'd survived his first few weeks in Laredo. She'd arrived two weeks after he did, on a transfer from Miami.

Pérez had spent the last five years working narcotics investigations, wire-tapping Colombian traffickers and seizing multi-tonne bricks of cocaine. She was also the only agent on their squad who'd requested Laredo and was happy to be there and knew the area. Married and with two small children, Pérez wanted to be closer to her family. In her early thirties, with long, wavy black hair and dark-brown eyes, she also had an unflappable quality to her that he found appealing.

She didn't turn off her work phone at 6pm like some of the other agents. And she seemed just as anxious as he was to get back on the streets. One day, not long after she'd arrived, he'd invited her out to an early lunch and ended up telling her all of his doubts and frustrations about the new job. The FBI felt like a vast bureaucracy, with so many agents from different backgrounds and so many different divisions. He couldn't see where he'd fit in. Pérez admitted she'd felt the same way her first year in Miami. 'Just give it some time and you'll find your place,' she'd promised him. 'You won't be disappointed.'

In the weeks following, he'd relied on her to keep up his spirits. He'd also call his dad but it didn't help when his dad would remind him that real police work didn't happen from behind a computer. 'You need to get back on the street, son,' his dad would counsel him. 'Knock on some doors, start talking to some people.' *Yeah, try doing it in another language,* he felt like saying, but never did. He'd been using a computer program called Rosetta Stone to pick up more Spanish vocabulary but the voice-recognition software couldn't interpret his southern accent. After a couple of days, he'd given up. 'I don't think Rosetta Stone understands redneck,' he'd joked to Pérez.

Within a day of Lawson's being assigned the Garcia kidnapping case, Pérez jumped in to help. She got to work phoning FBI sources in Mexico, while Lawson began contacting the Garcias' relatives in Laredo. It didn't take long to realise that they had a problem: all of the evidence they needed was on the other side of the river. But he was learning that getting any help from the police chief in Nuevo Laredo was complicated. If the chief got a message from Miguel Treviño that it was Zeta business, he wouldn't touch it. The Zetas had their own code of justice. If someone committed a crime without authorisation from Miguel, the Zetas would take care of the offender themselves. If it was another organisation the FBI was investigating, like the Sinaloa Cartel – the Zetas' sworn enemies – then the police chief could be more than accommodating.

It was too bad, said one of the Laredo cops on his squad, that he hadn't been around in the old days. The Mexican cops would always make sure they got their fugitive. But in 2005, the Nuevo Laredo police chief had made the mistake his first day on the job of telling the media he wouldn't be intimidated by the Zetas. Within six hours, he was lying dead in the street surrounded by a halo of spent bullet casings. Several other policemen were also slaughtered. Miguel Treviño had made his message clear. After that, the Laredo cops were on their own.

Now Lawson didn't need to drive to the edge of the river to try and comprehend the tragedy that was unfolding a few hundred yards away. He only had to look into the grief-stricken faces of the Garcia brothers' wives and parents as they sat across from him at the FBI's conference table. He tried to understand what it was like for families like the Garcias, who saw the border as nothing more than an imaginary line. The elderly parents still crossed into Nuevo Laredo regularly, even though their sons had just been kidnapped there. The two cities, which the locals called 'Los Dos Laredos', had co-existed since the Treaty of Guadalupe Hidalgo was settled in 1848 after the Mexican-American War. They were inextricably linked by blood and by culture. Lawson asked the father, who was in his seventies, how he could risk travelling to Nuevo Laredo when he knew the city was controlled by the Zetas and there was a war going on. 'It's what we've always done,' he said. 'My sister lives there, most of my family is there.' To stop going would be unthinkable.

After the meeting with the Garcias, Alma Pérez couldn't help but think of her own family on the other side. Like most border families, they'd spent their lives with one foot in Mexico, the other in the United States. But since she'd come back from Miami, she hadn't crossed the river into Nuevo Laredo. Her relatives had told her not to risk it. The Zetas were targeting the military, politicians and the police in their campaign of domination and terror. Every day there were new and gruesome headlines about decapitations and mass graves.

Pérez knew these were mostly statistics and names for Lawson and the other agents on her new squad. But the massacres, the shootings were in Mexican border towns she'd known since she was a girl. She thought of her happy childhood memories of her *tías* and *tíos*, *quinceañeras* and *bodas*. She'd been born on the US side of the river but part of her was still rooted in Mexico. Everything she had known in her parents' homeland was slipping away and it would never be the same again. It was like living with a phantom limb that still ached. No matter how hard she tried, she could not reconcile the destruction she read about every day in the bureau's intel briefings with her own memories. So much had changed in five years. And she was still grappling with how to come to terms with it.

Pérez was an FBI agent but Mexico was not her assignment. Her new boss, David Villarreal, had made that clear to her already. Even before she'd arrived, she'd sensed that he was less than enthusiastic about her transfer to Laredo, even if she was an experienced agent. Of the more than 13,500 FBI agents, fewer than 20 per cent of them were women. So Pérez knew she was an outlier at the bureau. Most female agents with kids didn't want to work violent crimes because it was a reactive squad, meaning they could be called out to a crime scene at any moment. This made the days often long and unpredictable. But Pérez had liked working the drug squad in Miami and was pleased she'd been assigned to the violent-crimes squad in Laredo. And she was determined to make it work.

Maybe she'd partnered with Lawson because he was also an outlier in his own way. He'd never been to the border, could hardly speak Spanish. Some of the other agents and the task-force officers said they'd heard he'd come from somewhere out in the backwoods of Tennessee. They thought he'd be begging for a transfer by the end of the year.

SIX

WORKING HIS FIRST KIDNAPPING CASE, LAWSON WAS BEGINNING TO UNDER-stand just how small Los Dos Laredos could be. One evening, he stopped at a gas station to fill up his truck and, from across the station, he recognised one of the Garcia brothers' wives. He and Pérez had met with her a few days ago but she didn't acknowledge him now. He felt a rush of embarrassment. The woman was desperate to find her husband and here he was, sweaty and in his shorts, having just come from a nearby park. He'd been working on the case all day but she'd caught him when he'd gone to play softball after work with some of the local cops. Of course, it was nearly dark outside. Maybe she hadn't seen him? He got back into his truck and headed for home.

He had finally bought a home in the same gated community as Hodge and his family. His house was close to the Rio Grande, where there was nothing between him and Nuevo Laredo but mesquite brush and white-tailed deer, which he found ironic. The gate around their sub-division was more for show than anything else. He'd always lived out of duffel bags and in cheap apartments, and his new middle-class home made him feel like he'd made the right choice becoming a federal agent, even though it still held nothing more than a bed and a few plastic chairs in the kitchen.

As he turned onto Mines Road and headed north towards home, past the freight shipping companies and fast-food restaurants, he glanced in his rear-view mirror and noticed that the woman was right behind him now. Maybe it was just a coincidence, he thought. And maybe some of Hodge's paranoia was starting to rub off on him. He expected her to turn at any moment. But as he made a right and rolled up to the front gate of his sub-division, she was still there. He kept driving. As he turned into the cul-de-sac where he lived, she was still behind him. Maybe he should pull over, ask her what she wanted? He pulled into his driveway. He expected her to stop but, to his surprise, she kept driving, then parked in a driveway two doors down and got out, oblivious to his presence. He smiled at his own paranoia. They were neighbours. He wondered how many more of his neighbours had been touched by the evil on the other side of that placid green river.

LAWSON WAS LOSING ALL HOPE that Graham would call when he finally phoned on the third week. Tempting Dash had just arrived at the Southwest Stallion Station after months of Graham's lobbying. He and his grandfather had already spent hours with José going over everything from the finer points of horse shoeing to the best mix of feed before a race. José asked a lot of questions and wasn't afraid to admit he knew little about racing, even less about breeding. He appeared eager to learn, said Graham. And he seemed intent on entering the racing industry in a big way.

Lawson took notes at his desk as Graham talked. He still wasn't sure he could fully trust Graham. The first few weeks he knew would be a test, to see whether they could work together and whether Graham was feeding him useful information.

There was something else that Lawson needed to know, Graham said. Tomorrow a horse trailer would leave Graham's farm for Mexico. José was sending the two weanlings from the January auction.

Lawson imagined that Miguel wanted to see up close what he'd paid for in Oklahoma. Just like Tempting Dash, the horses would be trained and tested on the racetracks in Mexico. If they won, or seemed like they had promise, then they'd be sent north to compete in the big-money races.

If the horse trailer was headed to Nuevo Laredo, it would have to pass through Laredo first. Lawson could set up surveillance and start documenting the other players in José Treviño's horse-buying operation, as well as corroborate whether the information Graham was giving him was solid. Since Hodge was lead agent on the case, Lawson would need to run it past him first. He turned around in his office chair. Hodge was poring over some spreadsheet on his computer and messing with his shoe as usual.

'I finally heard from Graham,' Lawson said.

'Hey, that's excellent,' Hodge said, turning around in his chair to face Lawson. 'So what'd he say?'

'José's sending two horses this way in a trailer tomorrow.'

'We need to set up a surveillance,' Hodge said.

'That's what I was thinking too,' Lawson said, feeling slightly annoyed that he hadn't got the opportunity to show he was already on it.

'When's the trailer coming through?'

'Tomorrow afternoon,' Lawson said. 'Maybe we could put a tracker on the trailer?'

'Nah,' Hodge said, 'there wouldn't be enough time to get all the paperwork approved.'

'We can sit up on him and see where he goes, who he talks to,' Lawson said.

Hodge nodded. 'I'll tell the guys.'

The next day, Lawson and Hodge parked at a small rest area on Interstate 35 north of town. It was a barren spot with nothing but a single live oak for shade and a barrel trash can. But it was also on a rise above Interstate 35 and they'd be nearly invisible to anyone who was heading south. Lawson trained his binoculars on the interstate's southbound lanes.

Hodge had recruited a couple of the other agents and the Laredo task-force officers to help out on the surveillance. Lawson noticed that Pérez wasn't there. He wondered whether she'd been busy with another case, or whether Hodge had never thought to ask. He would ask her about it later, he thought. The task-force officers fanned out around the international bridge in their unmarked cars and trucks to get a spot on the trailer before it crossed into Mexico. Hodge and Lawson would follow the trailer south once it entered the city limits.

After they had waited nearly two hours, the trailer came around a bend on the interstate and Hodge radioed to the task-force officers that they were on the move. Lawson wrote the license-plate number down so they could run it through their databases and figure out whom the trailer belonged to. They hoped that whoever the driver was, he'd stop along the way so they'd have more leads to follow up on. The more new faces the better. But the horse trailer never stopped as it moved slowly through traffic south towards Mexico. As they got close to the international bridge, Hodge and Lawson pulled over and radioed to the task-force officers that the target was all theirs now as the trailer merged into the lanes heading south across the bridge into Nuevo Laredo.

'You think he's heading straight toward Miguel?' Lawson asked Hodge, who was in the passenger seat.

'He's probably right there, waiting for it,' Hodge said, his leg working up and down nervously as he stared again through the binoculars at the trailer, which was now nothing more than a glint of silver in the harsh sunlight as it disappeared into the heavy traffic on the bridge.

'It's gone,' one of the task-force officers' voices crackled over the radio a few minutes later.

Hodge put down the binoculars and picked up the radio. He seemed relieved it was over. 'All right, let's call it a day. Thanks, boys.'

As they drove back to the Laredo RA office, Lawson felt the crush of disappointment after the surge of adrenaline from tailing the trailer. One of the things that had convinced him to join the FBI was that he could cross any state line in pursuit of a criminal. He wasn't boxed in by jurisdiction like he'd been as a deputy in Tennessee. But he'd never taken into account being sent to the border, where he'd have an entire country next door that was off-limits.

BACK AT THE OFFICE, Hodge went back to brooding over his drug-gang case, while Lawson ran the license-plate number from the trailer. If their driver was a 'friendly' – someone tied in with the Zetas – they could try to flip him so he'd give them information. He ran a criminal check on the name that popped up from the plate search. The results were mixed. Their driver lived in Laredo, which was good. The bad news was that he was related to the Treviños, which meant it was too risky to approach him. Lawson walked over to Pérez's cubicle on the other side of the squad room, which the Laredo RA called its 'bullpen' – no one seemed to know why; it was just tradition. Lawson wanted to run his findings past Pérez first, before he took them to Hodge.

As he approached her cubicle in the corner of the office, he could see that she was busy typing something on her computer. There were photos of her son in his soccer uniform and her daughter wearing a purple bow tacked up above her desk and neat stacks of paper. It was the picture of organisation compared to his workspace, littered with the bags of sunflower seeds that he was using to try to replace the craving for the can of tobacco he usually kept in his back pocket.

'Missed you on the surveillance the other day,' Lawson said, standing near her desk.

'I guess I didn't get the email,' she said, looking up from her computer with a half-smile to show it hadn't really fazed her. 'I'm slammed with another AFO case anyway, and there's the Garcia kidnapping.'

Their office got a lot of AFO cases, which meant 'assault on a federal officer'. These were mostly charges filed by Border Patrol agents against immigrants who had resisted arrest and fought back. Or sometimes, rocks were thrown at the agents from the Mexican side of the river so they'd be distracted while the smugglers brought across their drug loads. Most of these cases were more of a paperwork exercise than anything else, since the rock throwers were in Mexico and usually long gone by the time the case would arrive on their desks.

With five years already on an investigative squad, Pérez should have been working on something more ambitious. During their frequent lunches together, he'd told her about his meetings with Graham and could tell she was intrigued by the case. Her squad in Miami had specialised in four- to five-month surveillances and big-scale coke busts. But they'd rarely followed the money.

'Can I run something by you?' he said.

'Sure,' she said, turning towards him in her chair, giving him her full attention now.

Lawson went through what he'd found: the suspect's background and the fact that he was a relative of the Treviños and lived not far from Lawson's neighbourhood. It was Hodge's nightmare come true.

'I'm not surprised,' she said. 'Laredo's a small town and they're a big family.'

'It'd be too risky to approach him,' Lawson said.

'Yeah.' Pérez nodded in agreement. 'In Miami we'd stake out the place for a couple of days, see if anybody else comes around.'

Lawson had been thinking the same thing. He wasn't ready to cut the driver loose just yet. And it felt good to hear Pérez come to a similar conclusion.

'Have you talked to the source in Zapata yet?' Lawson asked, changing gears now to the Garcia case. He'd done a phone analysis on the Garcia brothers' mobile phones and found that several calls had been made in Mexico from one of the phones to a number in Zapata County, a rural border county to the south of them. Since every mobile phone left a digital trail through its constant connection to the cell towers, they could track the Garcias' kidnapper if he ever crossed the river.

Lawson had already driven out to Zapata and located the woman who was receiving the calls. It turned out she was a relative of their suspect. But she'd readily agreed to co-operate – she knew he was no good, she said – and was willing to help as long as she could do it in Spanish. So Pérez had been speaking with her and gathering information.

'She says he can't cross legally because he's got a warrant on him,' Pérez said. 'But he still comes across anyway. Next time she'll let us know.'

Lawson sat up most of the night watching the trailer driver's apartment, which was in a run-down complex a few blocks from the interstate. He pushed the driver's side seat back and dipped into his can of tobacco. He'd given up on the sunflower seeds already. His thoughts strayed to his dad, as they often did during a long surveillance. His dad loved being a cop but the job had taken its toll. He was a chain-smoker and a drinker who'd been married five times. Lawson knew his dad was proud of him, even if he'd never said as much. He knew because his older half-brother had told him that their dad often bragged about his son in the FBI to his friends back home. But his dad still seemed wary of his choice to follow him into law enforcement. He'd told Lawson a story over the phone one night, not long after he'd arrived in Laredo, and he still wasn't sure what to make of it.

His dad said that he'd been on the force for only a few years like Lawson and was working the night shift at the sheriff's department, when he was called to the scene of an accident. It was late at night and snowing, and the car had flipped over on the highway. When he looked inside, he saw a young boy and his parents. They were dead but the boy was still alive. He pulled him from the car. He remembered as the paramedics loaded the boy into an ambulance that all he could think about was clocking out and going home. He felt nothing, really. It was late and he was exhausted.

The family's clothes were spread out all across the highway, and he and another deputy kicked their belongings into a ditch so other cars could get through. Then he got in his patrol car and headed to the office. But when he pulled into the parking lot, it suddenly hit him hard – what a cold-hearted bastard he'd become. That six-year-old boy had lost everything and it hadn't even registered. He'd just kicked everything he had left into a ditch. So he turned around and went back. It was nearly dawn and still snowing but he collected all of the clothes, everything from the ditch, and drove to the hospital.

'The job will harden you,' his dad warned. 'Don't let it. Don't ever lose your heart.'

In his short career, Lawson had already seen how some of the older deputies back in Tennessee had stopped caring about the victims in their cases and were just counting down the days to retirement. He thought about the Garcia family and made a promise to himself that, if he ever started phoning it in on the job, he'd find a new line of work.

AFTER A COUPLE OF DAYS of watching the apartment with no new leads, Hodge called off their surveillance. It wasn't the bold start Lawson had hoped for. Not wanting to lose any more time, he called Graham to see if he had anything else that could be useful. He was still wary of Graham's motivations and whether he was sharing everything he knew or giving him half-truths. He needed to know whether he could trust him. He asked whether he'd seen anyone else associating with José and whether he knew of other horses besides the ones from the January auction that might have been bought by Miguel.

He was encouraged by Graham's response. José had just sent ten more horses to his farm, he said. And along with the horses had come a new player: Carlos Nayen, or 'Carlitos', as José called him. Nayen, who didn't look much older than Graham, explained that he would be in charge of making sure boarding and breeding expenses were paid. Through a smattering of English and Spanish that passed between them, Graham understood that Nayen would be coming to the farm regularly.

Not long after their meeting, Graham said, Nayen introduced him to Fernando Garcia, also in his mid-twenties. In his faded Levi's and work boots, Garcia looked more like a regular horseman than Nayen, who always wore a flashy gold Rolex and designer shirts to the stables. Garcia also spoke English, which made doing business with him easier, since Nayen struggled with the language. It seemed like Nayen was replacing Ramiro Villarreal, the former owner of Tempting Dash. Graham had also noticed that Villarreal wasn't spending large sums of money at the auctions like he used to. Lawson wanted to know more about the two men who'd replaced Villarreal. He asked Graham to keep him updated with anything he heard.

To build a prosecutable case, Lawson was working off what he knew from his days as a narcotics investigator. But his knowledge had its limits, especially when it came to money laundering. Financial documents and accounting was Hodge's wheelhouse so, after conferring with him, Lawson knew he'd have to push Graham for more on José's purchases. With his access to his grandfather's auction house, Heritage Place, he could pull documents without anyone knowing the FBI was involved. Lawson had already gathered that the world of quarter-horse racing was a small and insular one, with Heritage Place at its centre. The last thing he wanted was news of their investigation leaking, which could tip off José and his brothers. But he thought he'd seen enough of Graham's character already to know that he had the nerve to pull it off.

Lawson made his pitch to Graham and, much to his relief, Graham agreed. He would do some digging for the purchase records, saying he needed the information on behalf of José since he was boarding many of his horses at his farm.

A few days later, Graham called to say he had the documents. Since he was a board member of Heritage Place and the grandson of the owner, his enquiries had hardly been questioned, which put Lawson at ease. The results of his search had yielded useful evidence. In the documents from the January auction, Lawson could see that ownership of the expensive broodmare Dashin

Follies was listed not under José's name but under another man named Luis Aguirre. To make it even more complicated, Heritage Place had received wire transfers from an Alejandro Barradas, who owned a customs agency in Veracruz, Mexico, called Grupo Aduanero Integral, to pay for Dashin Follies and the other three horses. Only these payments had fallen short. There was still a $100,000 balance owed at Heritage Place.

Graham said he'd already reminded José and Nayen about the money several times. Behind the venerable auction house, whose motto was 'where champions are sold', was his family's reputation, and the former owners of the horses were still waiting to be paid.

Not long after Lawson got the documents from Graham, he called with a new development. Graham said that, that morning, Nayen and Garcia had pulled up to his farm and Nayen had handed him a heavy, bulging backpack. When he unzipped the top, he could see it was filled with bundles of hundreds and twenties. Nayen told him it was the $100,000 they owed to Heritage Place. When Nayen opened the car door, Graham had noticed five or six more backpacks like the one Nayen had just handed him. After some small talk about the horses and the weather, the two men drove away. Their car probably held half a million or more inside it.

SEVEN

BEFORE ARRIVING IN LAREDO, LAWSON HAD ALWAYS THOUGHT OF LAW enforcement as a collaborative exercise. Working on narcotics, he'd never had a problem sharing an investigation with other cops or federal agencies in Tennessee.

Laredo showed him how naïve he'd been. There was no more competitive environment than the border, where state, local and federal law-enforcement agencies were all vying for the same targets. There was only so much government money to go around and arresting a high-level cartel operative would mean a promotion and more funding from Washington. So the stakes were high.

Every agency had its sights on Miguel and Omar. But no one was looking at José. Lawson knew it was only a matter of time. He'd been working the investigation for three months and, sooner or later, they'd need to pull in another agency to get a federal prosecutor to sign on to the case. The logical choice was the DEA, which had the largest presence in Mexico and could help them make the connection between Miguel's cocaine business and the horses in the States.

Lawson had got to know a DEA special agent upstairs. Over beers, Jeff Hathaway was aggressive in his attitude and his opinions about how cases should be handled. He'd been at the border a couple of years already and, to Lawson, he sounded like an experienced veteran from the front line of the drug war. But Hodge had warned him to be careful. Any investigation that had a nexus with drug trafficking, the DEA wouldn't hesitate to claim for itself. There were only two things that could persuade the DEA to share an investigation, especially with the FBI, which it would view as treading on its territory, and those were wiretaps and an iron-clad source, Hodge said. Lawson didn't have the wires, which would make him dispensable in their eyes, but he did have Tyler Graham. As long as the agreement between Graham and the FBI held, he had something the DEA wanted.

With this in mind, he took the elevator upstairs. He considered Hathaway a friend but he knew he had to be wary. Right off, he made a point of letting Hathaway know that he had a well-placed source inside José Treviño's inner circle, but the source would only work with the FBI. So if the DEA was interested, it would be a package deal. What Lawson had so far was a money-laundering case but they would have to prove that the money used to buy the horses in the States had come from the Zetas' cocaine proceeds. And most of that evidence would be in Mexico, where the DEA had a much larger presence than the FBI.

Hathaway nodded and wrote a few things down in a notebook. He seemed open to the idea of a partnership. Lawson left the meeting feeling encouraged. But the good feeling didn't last for long. A few days later, his boss, David Villarreal, summoned him and Hodge into his office and, by the look on his face, they knew it wasn't going to be good. 'The DEA wants us to back off the case,' Villarreal said. 'They're working a case out of their

Houston office and they've got their own source inside the horse operation already. So they want us to take a hike.'

Lawson let it settle in. He knew it couldn't be Tyler Graham – there was no way. 'Did they say who it was?'

'Are you kidding?' Villarreal said, running his hand through his hair as he sat back in his chair, contemplating their options.

'No way they've got a source like Tyler . . . You know it, Boss,' Hodge said, shaking his head. 'They're just pulling our strings.'

'I've already called Houston and set up a meeting,' Villarreal said. 'They're going to have to tell us to our faces if they want us to roll over on this case. I want to hear what they've got first.'

EIGHT

WITH TEMPTING DASH NOW A CHAMPION AND UNDER HIS BROTHER'S CONTROL, Miguel's plan was flourishing. He called a meeting at one of his ranches in the city of Piedras Negras in Coahuila, another border state not far from Nuevo Laredo, to discuss his plan's next phase. Some of the most lucrative purses in quarter-horse racing, including the All American Futurity, were just a few months away.

In Mexico, the war was intensifying. The Gulf Cartel had joined forces with the Sinaloa Cartel, their former competitor, to wipe out their greater enemy, escalating the war with a ferocious intensity. For Mexico's drug bosses, the Zetas' rapid rise to dominance had been as unexpected as their increasingly bold ambushes deep inside El Chapo's territory.

In Nuevo Laredo, convoys of SUVs bristling with heavily armed men in tactical gear, their back windows emblazoned with the logo CDG, for Cártel del Golfo, or Gulf Cartel, snaked through the narrow boulevards searching for Zetas to kill.

But Treviño and Lazcano had already secured the neighbouring border state of Coahuila as a safe haven where they could operate freely with the protection of the police. This would be Miguel's new home base, where he could conduct his business. He summoned to his ranch the handful of men who would be crucial in building his American racing dynasty. Francisco Colorado Cessa, whom everyone called 'Pancho', flew in from Veracruz on his private plane along with Alejandro Barradas. Colorado owned ADT Petroservicios, an oil services company, in Tuxpan and had become wealthy off its lucrative contracts with Pemex, the national oil company. He was also a long-time gambler and horse-racing aficionado. Barradas, the owner of Grupo Aduanero Integral in the city of Veracruz, had been, like Colorado, involved in horse racing for years, often mixing with the Zetas and other cartels that would organise the races.

Besides Miguel and Omar waiting for them at the ranch, there was also Enrique Rejón Aguilar, or Z-7 – whom everyone called 'Mamito'. His relationship with the Treviños had been a complicated one ever since Lazcano had made Miguel his second in command. Mamito was a former soldier and an original founding member of the Zetas. But the Treviños had valuable smuggling contacts on the border and Miguel had made the Zetas a significant amount of money. He was also just as willing to kill a friend as an enemy, which was why many believed Lazcano kept him close. Miguel's rapid rise also rankled Mamito because he was from the streets, not military-trained.

And even worse, Miguel had taken Tempting Dash from him. Mamito was obsessed with racing and it was nearly all he talked about to the others. Owning the best bloodlines was a sign of status. And it was Mamito who had originally requested that Ramiro Villarreal buy him Tempting Dash in California. The colt was the progeny of First Down Dash, one of the most coveted racing sires in the United States. The asking price of

$21,500 was a bargain for such a prized bloodline. But shortly before the auction, Miguel had demanded that Villarreal buy the horse for him. And Mamito had had no choice but to comply since Miguel was now his superior.

Rounding out the meeting was one more key figure who would be important to the success of Miguel's plan. Mario Alfonso Cuellar, also called 'Poncho', was one of Miguel's key money men, responsible for shipping tons of cocaine across the border every year. From Piedras Negras, Cuellar made sure the cocaine got to the Zetas' wholesale dealers in the United States. Then he collected the US dollars sent back in false compartments in trucks or smuggled by couriers across the river. Altogether, he collected about $20 million a month.

The meeting would be an all-day affair. Colorado, a *bon vivant*, cooked up some shrimp he'd brought from Veracruz.

'Don't tell me you know how to cook too?' joked Omar.

'Of course,' Colorado said.

Cuellar and Barradas shot games of pool while Miguel, Omar, Mamito and Nayen watched a live simulcast on Miguel's computer of one of his horses racing in California.

After the race, Miguel laid out his reasons for the meeting. He had a plan for expanding his empire north of the border. What he needed were successful businessmen who could spend millions in the United States without raising suspicion with authorities. Colorado had sizeable bank accounts in the United States and often did business there. Barradas, with his customs agency, also frequently wired cash to the States. It wouldn't be unusual for two wealthy men, who were passionate about racing, to spend a significant amount of money on horses in the United States.

Colorado and Barradas were so intertwined with the Zetas already, it would be difficult to say no. Like Coahuila, their state of Veracruz was under the control of Miguel Treviño and the cartel.

The former leader in Veracruz, Efraín Torres, or Z–14, had given Colorado at least $18 million to start his oil services business, ADT Petroservicios. Colorado had also served as a go–between during the 2004 gubernatorial election in Veracruz, passing on several million to the PRI candidate, Fidel Herrera, from Z–14 and the Zetas. Herrera had won the election. Afterwards, the new governor had made sure that ADT Petroservicios received prime contracts from the government-run Pemex, which had made Colorado a wealthy man (Herrera has denied allegations he collaborated with the Zetas). But Colorado also had expensive tastes and Pemex was notorious for being slow to pay its vendors. Desperate to keep his business afloat during dry times, Colorado had borrowed from Miguel, who always had several million in cash on hand and seldom charged him interest. But Colorado had been around long enough to know that any loan from Miguel wouldn't come without its price. Currently he owed Miguel $2 million. And it was never good to be in the drug boss's debt for very long.

So Colorado was quickly amenable to the plan. '*¿Somos o no somos amigos?*' he said to Miguel. 'Are we or are we not friends?' Barradas didn't hesitate either. Since Cuellar handled the drug proceeds coming through Piedras Negras, he would ensure they got the money to purchase the racehorses. It would be up to Barradas and Colorado to absorb the drug profits into their business accounts, then use the cleaned–up money to pay for the horses and their expenses in the States. In this way, they would help Miguel's brother José expand his newly formed racing company, Tremor Enterprises.

But first Colorado knew he needed to pay the debt he already owed. After he returned to Veracruz, he called Nayen. The twenty-five-year-old Nayen considered Colorado a father figure, often referring to him affectionately as *padrino*. He had been buying valuable racehorses for the wealthy rancher and arranging races for him since he was a teenager. But now he had moved on to managing Miguel's horses. 'I'm ready . . . I have the money to pay my debt,' Colorado told him. Nayen said he would speak to Miguel, then let Colorado know his answer.

A few minutes later, Nayen phoned with Miguel's somewhat cryptic response. 'He says to be ready. He'll tell you when and how he wants you to pay your debt.'

NINE

LAWSON SAT AT THE CONFERENCE TABLE PACKED WITH DEA AGENTS. HE WAS starting to sweat in his suit and tie despite the air conditioning, which was on full blast in late May. He didn't know any of the faces other than Jeff Hathaway, who sat across from him, and René Dieguez, a veteran agent who ran the DEA's Nuevo Laredo office. Lawson counted nine DEA agents in total in the room to the FBI's three.

The DEA's Houston headquarters were in the River Oaks district, one of the most affluent areas in the city. The offices were massive and teeming with agents, and it seemed the whole meeting had been calculated to show the FBI agents from their small, backwater agency on the border that they were completely out of their league. Not surprisingly, the meeting didn't get much better from there. The group supervisor from the DEA's Houston office did most of the talking and Lawson, Hodge and Villarreal listened.

He explained that the DEA had been surveilling an insider who was close to Miguel Treviño and his brother Omar. His name was Ramiro Villarreal, he said. Lawson kept his expression flat at the mention of Villarreal's name. He nodded and listened, playing the role of the ignorant rookie, as the DEA supervisor explained who Villarreal was and how he had no idea the DEA was monitoring him. The FBI's investigation would only risk tipping him off.

They didn't care about José Treviño, the money laundering or the horses. The horses would be an expensive logistical headache for any federal agency to undertake. Besides, they had drug indictments already in the United States with Miguel's name on them. And they were going to use Villarreal to get to him in Mexico, where he was still out of their reach. What they wanted was Miguel's current location so they could send in a vetted team to arrest the drug kingpin, who so far had eluded them. With his money, Miguel had been able to ensure that his contacts in the Mexican military and police would always tip him off hours before a raid.

But Lawson doubted they were really working the Villarreal angle as hard as they claimed. If they were, then they'd know that Villarreal was no longer part of Miguel's inner circle and had been replaced by Carlos Nayen. Lawson understood that arresting Miguel and Omar Treviño would be a career-making coup for any agent, and that taking down the two kingpins was at the top of their list. But the DEA had just told the FBI to get lost so, if they didn't know about Nayen, he wasn't going to do their job for them.

Finally, their boss, David Villarreal, interrupted the DEA's monologue. Surely there was some kind of middle ground, he argued. His agents could work with the Laredo DEA agents and keep them updated on the progress of the money-laundering case, while the DEA in Houston kept working its lead on Ramiro Villarreal. Either way, the DEA would have a stake in it.

Lawson and Hodge quickly assured the Houston DEA agents

that they wouldn't go anywhere near Ramiro Villarreal. And they'd keep Hathaway and Rene Dieguez advised on their every move. Hathaway already knew that Lawson had Tyler Graham as a source, so he was quick to agree. The Laredo DEA would work with the FBI, he assured the Houston agents.

The meeting ended better than he'd imagined. He could keep working with Tyler Graham while the DEA went after Ramiro Villarreal. He knew the FBI's goal was to send a message to Miguel that he couldn't set up businesses in the United States with his blood money. Thousands of people were dying in Mexico just so the Zetas could control a bigger share of the international drug trade, and Americans were lining up to buy whatever Miguel had to sell. And with those profits, he was building his horse-racing dynasty in America. His ego let him believe he could pull it off without the FBI or anyone else noticing. As they flew back to Laredo, all Lawson could think about was how he could use José to get to Miguel. Not only would they dismantle Tremor Enterprises, but they'd also send in their own vetted team to arrest Miguel and Omar in Mexico. That was *his* goal. And Tyler Graham would help him get there.

TEN

LAWSON WATCHED TYLER GRAHAM'S WHITE PICK-UP TRUCK PULL INTO THE half-empty lot of the grocery store. Since Graham was constantly busy running his grandfather's empire, Lawson had made it easier on him this time and arranged for a meeting in Elgin, closer to his farm.

Last time, they'd met at the Omni Hotel in downtown Austin. After the debriefing, they'd walked a few blocks to a pub and ordered burgers and a beer. When an old-school rap song came blaring out over the speakers, they'd both started singing the lyrics, each surprised that the other one knew the song. They weren't on the clock anymore but just hanging out over beers. Lawson realised they had a lot in common. He'd chosen to follow his father into law enforcement and Graham had chosen to run his grandfather's businesses. They'd both grown up around horses but, for Graham, the horses were a money-making enterprise while, in his family, the horses had only fuelled tensions at home over money. It was hard not to fantasise about a life like Graham's – inheriting a ranch and making money off racehorses.

Lawson had driven Hodge's Pathfinder because he didn't

trust the beat-up gold Chevy Impala the FBI had given him for undercover work to make it all the way from Laredo. The Chevy, its front bumper cratered in because the last agent had hit a deer, was standard rookie issue. So they took Hodge's SUV but Lawson had insisted on driving since Hodge tended to hit the gas then let up all of sudden whenever he got worked up about something, which was often. From the passenger seat, Lawson would feel like he was adrift in a roiling sea.

By now, he'd grown to trust Graham. The young horse breeder never balked at anything that Lawson had asked him to do. And his information had been invaluable. Graham pulled up alongside their SUV and rolled down his window. 'How's it going?' he said casually.

'It's going,' said Lawson. 'Thanks for coming.'

'Why don't you get in the back seat,' said Hodge, reaching around to unlock the door.

Graham climbed out of his pick-up and got into the back of the SUV. He was wearing a maroon Texas A&M baseball cap, his alma mater.

Lawson got to the point. He knew that, if Graham was gone for too long, it would be noticed. There was also always the danger of being spotted by Nayen, or someone else who worked for José, since they were close to Graham's farm.

'Tell us more about how José's organisation works,' said Lawson. Graham said he'd just been out at the trials for the Rainbow Futurity in Ruidoso, New Mexico, where he'd noticed that José, Nayen and Garcia had run several horses under different owners' names. And there was another unusual thing: all the horses had been renamed after expensive sports cars like Bugatti and Porsche Turbo, which was peculiar because most owners wanted to keep a horse's original name, especially if it was an expensive one, because it showed its pedigree.

Lawson listened closely. This was the first time he was hearing about Ruidoso, and it was frustrating to learn he'd already missed an opportunity to see José and his crew in action.

'So what were some of the names of these owners?' he asked. Graham didn't respond right away. Lawson could see he was searching back into this memory.

'Most of them were LLCs: Santa Fe Roldan, Fast and Furious . . .' Graham said.

Lawson wrote down the names in a notebook. He was starting to feel that rush of adrenaline he got when he knew he was on to something.

'When's the next big race?' he asked.

'The All American Futurity,' Graham said. This year there would be a $2 million purse – the largest in its history. Anyone serious about racing would be there. The All American was considered the Kentucky Derby of quarter-horse racing. It was held every Labor Day, following one of the biggest auctions of the year for yearlings that would be trained to race for the following season. Graham said José would be running several horses in the trials, which were notoriously gruelling. Only ten horses would qualify for what was billed as the 'world's richest quarter-horse race.'

Lawson wrote down the date of the race in his notebook. If José was going to be in Ruidoso, then he'd be there too.

ELEVEN

WHEN THEY GOT BACK TO LAREDO, HODGE SAID HE WAS TOO BUSY TO GO TO New Mexico. He already hated the long drives to Elgin to meet with Graham. And now he acted like he was doing Lawson a favour by letting him go alone to Ruidoso. But Lawson couldn't do the surveillance without another agent. It was standard policy. He wanted to ask Alma Pérez but didn't feel comfortable enough yet asking her to go on a three-day trip over a holiday weekend. There was also the hitch that she was six months pregnant, which had come as a surprise when she'd told him about it several weeks earlier, though he knew she'd always wanted a big family. Now he felt an extra responsibility towards her when they went on callouts or were working the Garcia kidnapping. But if he ever let her know his feelings, she'd be furious. There wasn't anything worse he could do to Pérez than treat her differently from the male agents on the squad.

By the time he'd found out about the All American from Graham, almost every room in Ruidoso had already been booked. The race was a big deal for the small mountain town. The only room he could find was at a run-down Best Western for $280 a night. This hadn't pleased Villarreal but he knew what was at stake, especially after their meeting with the DEA in Houston. For the first time, Lawson would be entering José's world and could document who the players were, the front companies and the horses. He decided to ask Raúl Perdomo, one of the Cuban agents who'd come from Miami, to help him out. To save money on the travel budget and to make Villarreal happy, they could also share the hotel room.

Lawson had already devised a cover story for them: if anyone asked, they'd say they had a rich friend back in Texas and they were speculating at the auction on his behalf.

Before they'd left Laredo, Lawson had asked Perdomo to do his best at playing the part of a rancher while they were in New Mexico. But Perdomo had a hard time denying his Caribbean roots. 'Don't worry, I'll look redneck enough,' he joked, which didn't exactly put Lawson at ease.

After they checked into their room at the Best Western, Perdomo pulled out of his suitcase a pair of pointy white boots and a purple shirt with a dragon emblazoned across the chest.

'Jesus,' Lawson said, surveying the colourful get-up. 'You can't wear that *Miami Vice* shit to the track.'

'What's wrong with it?' Perdomo said, looking wounded.

'Ah, forget it,' Lawson said.

Early the next morning, they drove over to the Lodge at Sierra Blanca, a resort and golf course where Tyler Graham stayed whenever he was in Ruidoso. Lawson felt a twinge of envy driving up to the front of the gleaming white resort, which made their room at the Best Western seem even shabbier. The parking lot was filled with expensive diesel trucks and fancy horse trailers.

Graham answered the door in jeans and a polo shirt. He was going golfing after their meeting, he said casually. Lawson was impressed, once again, by his ability to take a moment most would find stressful and compartmentalise it so that he scarcely broke a sweat. Two FBI agents in his hotel room was no big deal. Lawson and Perdomo each pulled up a chair and sat down, while Graham turned down the television.

Lawson wanted to know what they should expect and what to look out for in the coming days. Graham explained that the weekend would be devoted to the auctions where buyers would be bidding on some of the most valuable racing bloodlines the industry had to offer. All of the big players would be there evaluating the upcoming crop of yearlings. The three-day weekend would culminate in the All American Futurity on Monday, which was Labor Day.

Graham showed them a dog-eared sales catalogue for the upcoming auction and explained what hip numbers were. Each horse up for sale would have a hip number that corresponded to its entry in the catalogue, along with a description of the year it was foaled, its pedigree and other traits. There were certain bloodlines that Graham knew José would be drawn to. This was because they were the most valuable, most expensive horses up for sale.

'Keep an eye out for these horses.' Graham flipped through the thick catalogue and pointed out a handful of horses that José had told him he already planned to buy. Lawson wrote the names and hip numbers down in a small notebook he'd pulled from his back pocket.

'Here's some others they will probably buy because they're expensive,' Graham said, pointing to a few more entries in the catalogue. Lawson and Perdomo leaned in closer to scrutinise the names of the yearlings, all descended from top sires, including First Down Dash, Corona Cartel and Mr. Jess Perry – all of them would probably go for tens of thousands of dollars at the auction. Lawson wrote down the hip numbers.

'Thanks for this,' Lawson said, closing the small spiral notebook and shoving it into the back pocket of his jeans.

Graham nodded. 'Sure,' he said.

'Once things get rolling, it will be too risky for us to meet up again,' Lawson said. 'Better we text or phone.' He couldn't bury the fear that they'd be spotted by José. It had started as a small nagging thought when they'd landed in El Paso the day before and grown exponentially the closer their rental car got to Ruidoso. Maybe it would be Perdomo's purple dragon shirt, or Lawson and his camera, that would suddenly draw his suspicion. He'd heard from other agents that José was a paranoid guy – someone who'd spent decades staying off law enforcement's radar. And he suspected he'd be hyper-vigilant, especially while he was spending his brother's money in New Mexico.

THE RUIDOSO DOWNS RACETRACK sat in a green valley dotted with juniper scrub, surrounded by pine-tree-covered mountains. The sky was a vibrant blue but the heat wasn't humid and suffocating like it was back in Laredo. Much to his surprise, when they got to the track, Perdomo blended in better than Lawson. He didn't have to say, 'I told you so.' The grin on his face said it all. Some of the Mexican men were decked out in the latest in narco bling: massive diamond watches, Ed Hardy jeans with rhinestone-studded pockets, and brightly coloured cowboy boots that curled up at the tip. Lawson wondered whether they worked for Miguel or another cartel. They were outshone only by the wealthy women from Texas in their long leather-fringed jackets with matching custom cowboy boots and piles of silver southwestern jewellery.

The agents spent the first day milling around the sales pavilion just east of the racetrack. The pavilion looked like an oversized barn made of corrugated steel surrounded by long rows of stalls where the horses were kept. Inside was an indoor amphitheatre where ranchers sat in clusters bidding on the horses led before them in the sales ring. A portly auctioneer in a black cowboy hat sat on an elevated stage behind a console at the rear of the ring, calling out each horse's name and hip number in a droning baritone punctuated by the sharp crack of his gavel when a horse was sold. The bidding was a subtle dance and it was difficult for Lawson to decipher who was doing what. It was up to three older men in western shirts who paced up and down the aisles scrutinising the crowd to determine whether a blink of an eye was a bid or an involuntary muscle spasm. When one of the men had a bidder locked in, he'd whoop out a loud 'Hep!' and the auctioneer would register the bid: 'I've got one-fifty, one-fifty, how about two hundred?"

Nayen was easy to spot near the edge of the sales ring: he wore a pink shirt unbuttoned nearly to the navel and topped with a gold chain. José, in a white cowboy hat, sat nearby sizing up each horse. But Lawson noticed he never bid.

No one would ever guess, in his jeans and beat-up cowboy boots, that he was the elder brother of two wealthy cartel leaders. He didn't gravitate towards flashy jewellery or clothes like Nayen. He'd been good at being invisible. But Lawson knew that, as his brothers had become more notorious, José had increasingly come under scrutiny. Every time he crossed the bridge from Nuevo Laredo into Laredo, he was held for hours by Customs and Border Protection agents and questioned about his brothers.

Lawson took a seat on the other side of the ring so he could get a good angle with his camera, while Perdomo went outside to find the stables where Fernando Garcia was keeping some of the cartel's horses. In his grey cowboy hat and boots, he hoped he looked like just another horseman looking to buy. He aimed his camera towards the ring as if he were taking pictures of the horses. Whenever José and Nayen looked away or were distracted he'd take a picture. As the camera clicked, he could feel his heart beating in his chest like a kick drum. Graham stood near Nayen with the open sale catalogue in his hands. Lawson knew he could count on Graham's poker face if he spotted him in the crowd.

Each time he bid, Nayen would take a photo with his mobile phone of the neon board flashing the sales price, then start furiously texting. He scarcely looked up from his BlackBerry phone. Lawson imagined he was texting Miguel the sales prices. He snapped more photos . . . *click, click, click*. Suddenly, José turned and seemed to be staring straight at him. Lawson involuntarily sucked in his breath. The worst he could do was panic and bolt from the amphitheatre. Quickly, he feigned interest in the catalogue he'd grabbed at the entrance. He was already beating himself up for blowing the surveillance. He imagined Villarreal regretting he'd sent a rookie instead of a seasoned agent. He thumbed through the pages for a few minutes, then looked up again. Graham was consulting with José over something in the auction catalogue and he appeared entirely engrossed in whatever they were discussing. Lawson hoped he hadn't been made. He'd phone Graham as soon as he got the chance. Having had enough excitement for the afternoon, he quickly packed up his camera, a feeling of dread in the pit of his stomach, and headed for the exit.

His anxiety didn't ease until Graham finally returned his call a couple of hours later. Much to his relief, Graham told him that José had never spotted Lawson across the ring. Graham was sure of it, he said. So their surveillance hadn't been compromised after all. And he'd been so quick to assume the worst.

When Labor Day came around, the stands overflowed with

spectators for the race everyone had been waiting for. Lawson and Perdomo pushed their way up to the railing to watch the slender jockeys on their mounts warming up on the backstretch for the All American Futurity. The jockeys clung to their horses as they sprinted down the track in perfect aerodynamic union. To Lawson, they seemed to almost glide over the backstretch. Before the race began, they made a quick pass through the indoor betting area crowded with betters and people lined up for drinks at the kiosks. They made some three-dollar and five-dollar bets to look busy. Lawson had learned just enough from Graham about the top racing bloodlines that he felt he could make an educated gamble on the All American. He figured, if he put his money on a few win, place and show bets on the horses with the best pedigrees, he would at least come out even. He put three dollars down on Mr. Piloto, the biggest long shot in the race. The large sorrel stallion had a first-rate pedigree but hadn't exactly lit up the track, scoring one of the slowest qualifying times in the history of the All American and ranking last among the ten horses that had qualified.

Graham had told him that qualifying for the 440-yard race was notoriously gruelling. More than four hundred horses had competed over three days in August for one of the race's ten slots. Horses that won a coveted place in the All American could claim to be some of the world's fastest. A world speed record had been set during the 2006 race when a horse called No Secrets Here had demolished the 440 yards in less than 21 seconds, clocking a speed of 43 miles per hour.

Half of the $2 million purse would go to the winner and the rest would be divvied up among the other nine horses according to how they placed. Winning the Futurity was a dream lusted after by every jockey, horse owner and trainer in the industry. There were racing veterans who'd worked for decades to qualify for the All American but still hadn't succeeded. For José's Tremor Enterprises, which had only existed little more than a year, to have a horse in the race was viewed by most as an incredible stroke of good fortune. They had no idea, of course, that luck had nothing to do with it. José had simply run several high-dollar horses in the trials under various straw owners and companies, until one of them had qualified. It was the law of averages, no more and no less. 'José's no great horseman,' Graham had told Lawson. 'He just buys the best.'

He'd already texted Lawson to let him know where he'd be during the race – standing with José and the others on the inside of the track near the scoreboard and the finish line. Lawson had made sure he was sitting in the bleachers directly across from them so he'd have a clear view. He pointed the camera's telephoto lens towards the finish line. He could see Graham in dark sunglasses standing next to José in his white cowboy hat and Nayen, who wore a black suit, probably Italian and expensive. It was five in the afternoon and race fans had been drinking cheap beer and tequila all day under the sun. Everyone, including Lawson, was sunburned and ready for the race to finally begin.

By studying the rise of Mr. Piloto, he was starting to piece together how the organisation worked. In the August qualifying trials for the All American, José had run at least ten horses under various limited-liability companies. Mr. Piloto had been owned by Garcia Bloodstock and Racing, which belonged to Fernando Garcia, who had started the LLC just a few months before the race. The twenty-nine-year-old had several expensive horses under his name, including Mr. Piloto. It had been Ramiro Villarreal who bought the racehorse for $81,000 at a Heritage Place auction back in September 2009. The horse's name had been Maverick Perry before Nayen had changed it.

After Mr. Piloto qualified at the trials for the All American, the ownership was transferred to José's Tremor Enterprises, an LLC he'd formed after he acquired Tempting Dash. The LLCs were easy to incorporate – all it took was $300 and filling out a few forms with the Texas secretary of state. José was shuffling the horses from one LLC to another and, once a horse won a race and became more valuable, it became property of Tremor Enterprises LLC.

As Lawson and Perdomo waited for the All American to start, Lawson tried to reposition himself more comfortably on the hard aluminium bench – no easy task with a Glock pressing up against the inside of his boot. He noticed that most of the spectators sitting around him in the crowded bleacher seats were Mexican or Mexican American. The Mexicans had brought their love for racing with them from the rural countryside and the dirt tracks in northern Mexico and the Gulf coast. Up above the bleachers, in the air-conditioned Turf Club and VIP boxes with the premium views, many of the faces were still white. But they were getting older; their children didn't have the same fire for horse racing: too much risk, too little gain. It was no secret the future of US quarter-horse racing was Latino. Lawson noticed that even Tyler Graham spoke fairly decent Spanish. Graham had even picked up some Portuguese after a recent trip to Brazil, where the quarter-horse industry was growing. Horse racing, like almost everything else, had to become a global enterprise to survive.

The bugler played the Call to Post and the horses filed down the red dirt track towards the starting gate. Excitement rippled through the crowd and people cheered as the horses passed by. Mr. Piloto wore a red, white and green nylon blinker hood to keep his eyes focused on the track. In the middle of the hood, an eagle grasped a snake in its beak, the symbol of the Mexican flag. 'Hecho en México' was written above it. Lawson had heard that Miguel resented how the rich white people in Dallas had treated him and his family. No doubt it would give him satisfaction if Mr. Piloto won and the *gabachos* up in the VIP boxes would know the champion's owner was Mexican.

Lawson could barely see the horses at the starting gate from where he sat near the finish line. Quarter horses sprinted so fast, if he looked away for a few seconds, he'd miss the whole thing. A 440-yard race, which was quarter of a mile – the distance for which the horses were famously named – could be over in less than half a minute. The crowd hooted and yelled for the race to begin. Lawson heard the clap of the metal starting gates fly open and the distant rumble of hooves thundering down the track. He could see the other horses bunch together towards the inside rail as Mr. Piloto veered hard to the outer edge. The horse was so close to the railing, Lawson could hear the crack of the jockey's whip and see clumps of dirt flying up from the stallion's hooves as Mr. Piloto tore down the track. Towards the finish, the horses clustered together in a blur of bright jockey silks and horseflesh. When they crossed the finish line, it was impossible to tell which horse had won. Confusion mounted as the racing stewards waited for the photo finish to be analysed. After a handful of awkward minutes, they finally made their call – Mr. Piloto by a nose.

José, Nayen and several others around them vaulted over the railing and onto the track, rushing towards Mr. Piloto and his jockey, Esgar Ramirez, as they took a celebratory turn in front of the spectators. Lawson snapped a photo as José took off his cowboy hat, looked up at the sky and made the sign of the cross. Then he dialled his mobile phone, no doubt calling his brother in Mexico. Lawson snapped more photos as José, who was still on the phone, took the reins of Mr. Piloto and led him towards the winner's circle. There, Garcia hugged José. Here were the seller and buyer of Mr. Piloto hugging one another in the winner's circle. Lawson wondered what Garcia had to celebrate. He'd just sold Mr. Piloto for next to nothing and the horse had won a million dollars.

Lawson noticed Nayen off to the side texting with the same intensity as the day before. It was clear to Lawson by the chatter around him that Mr. Piloto's win had taken everyone by surprise. The odds of the horse winning had been 22-to-1. Even track veterans who accepted that racing was a fickle business, full of unpredictable twists and turns, couldn't quite believe it. Mr. Piloto's win had not only been the most lucrative, but also accomplished against the longest odds in All American history. Lawson made his way over to the betting window and collected his money.

BACK AT THE BEST WESTERN, Lawson received another text from Graham. José and his crew were going to continue their celebration at a casino called the Inn of the Mountain Gods. Graham would be there too. Lawson and Perdomo got ready for a night out on the town.

The Inn of the Mountain Gods casino and hotel was spread out across a small valley with an artificial lake and a triple-tiered parking garage almost as tall as the casino. To reach the valley on the outskirts of town, the Mescalero Apaches, who owned the casino, had blasted a tunnel through the forested mountain. In the pitch-dark night, the tunnel's entryway glittered with small twinkling white lights inviting gamblers to come and try their luck.

Lawson and Perdomo walked through the banks of whirring and blinking slot machines to a sports bar in the back of the casino called Big Game. Its walls were lined with mounted deer heads, and the place smelled of beer and stale cigarette smoke. The bar was half-full and Lawson made a point of not looking towards the back corner where Graham, José, Nayen, Garcia and a couple of other men sat around a table drinking bottles of beer. The agents took a seat at a table that had opened up nearby. A mounted deer head peered down at Lawson with sad eyes. He glanced towards José's table and noticed a dark-skinned Mexican man sitting beside José with a dour expression, nursing a beer. From his body language and the way his eyes scanned the bar, it looked like he was José's bodyguard for the evening.

Lawson tried to overhear what was being said at the table, while pretending that he and Perdomo were deep in their own conversation. He'd made out enough to know that Graham was trying to convince José to race Mr. Piloto again. The horse had won the All American Futurity but it had been the slowest time in the race's history. Mr. Piloto needed another shot at burnishing his title as champion before José retired him for breeding. José seemed unconvinced.

Lawson watched him down several more beers and get successively drunker. Suddenly, he stood up from the table, unsteady on his legs. Lawson guessed he was headed for the bathroom. As he passed the bar, José swayed, then his legs buckled underneath him. The crowd parted as if for a falling tree. An elderly Apache man reached out to help him to his feet. José swore at him in Spanish, then took a wild swing at the man, who was surprisingly agile and quickly ducked out of the way. The whole humble, nice-guy routine José had been playing for his new racing friends was nothing more than an act, Lawson thought, noting the look of rage that had transformed his face. When it came down to it, he was more like his brothers than he let on.

A bouncer moved quickly towards José, ready to kick him out of the bar, but Nayen, Graham and the others were able to persuade the man to return to his post near the entrance. They ushered José out of the bar. Lawson and Perdomo put down some cash for their beers and followed, giving them some distance as José, his bodyguard and Graham moved through the casino and out the automatic doors to the parking lot.

After they were gone, Lawson and Perdomo made their way to the rental car. Lightning flashed in distant thunderclouds up above the mountains, threatening a downpour as Lawson got behind the wheel. Their time in Ruidoso had been well spent. He'd been able to document how the organisation operated behind a façade of sham owners and LLCs. The fact that Mr. Piloto had won only made it better. A year ago, José had been clearing $50,000 a year at most and now he was a millionaire. Lawson knew that today's win would embolden him and his brothers to spend even more money, which could only help their investigation. As they drove back down the dark mountain road towards town, the clouds parted and a full moon illuminated the way.

WHEN LAWSON RETURNED to his office in Laredo, there was a message to call the FBI office in Las Cruces, New Mexico. He dialled them immediately. The agent who answered said they'd received two separate complaints from long-time auctiongoers at a horse sale in Ruidoso and he thought it might be something Lawson could use on his horse case. Lawson imagined him smirking on the other end. The guys on his squad teased him mercilessly about the horses. More than once he'd heard neighing from the other side of his cubicle followed by muffled laughter. Most of them thought the horses were a dead end. Even Hodge was often lacklustre about the case and hated the travel because it took him away from his family. The other day, an agent in the white-collar squad had asked whether he'd put the cuffs on Mr. Ed yet.

Lawson asked the Las Cruces agent for the details. He told

him that the complaints were about two teenagers who'd bid
on horses worth a quarter of a million dollars. The manager of
the auction house had even gone down to speak with the boys
once he'd noticed they were signing the bidding tickets; he had
wanted to make sure they were good for the money. Lawson
remembered seeing two young guys in T-shirts in Nayen's group
but he hadn't realised they were signing bidding tickets too. He
thanked the agent for the information, then phoned Graham.
He'd been tempted to visit the sales office after the auction but
had decided he still needed to be careful and not yet expand
the parameters of the investigation too wide. He knew that any
hint that the FBI was looking into the auctions and races would
quickly become fodder for gossip. So he'd asked Graham to
check out the records for him.

Graham had known the sales manager at Ruidoso for years,
so the manager didn't ask him too many questions. Graham said
he was helping out José, which was true, since he'd be hauling
many of the horses he'd bought at the auction back to his farm
in Elgin. The sales manager told Graham the horses were good
to go. The morning after the All American Futurity, a heavy-set
middle-aged man in an expensive suit had arrived in his office
to pay for them. Flanked by two younger men who sounded
from the description like Fernando Garcia and Carlos Nayen, the
man had asked the bookkeeper in Spanish how much he owed
and Garcia had translated his request into English. The bill, she
replied, would be $2.2 million.

The man didn't flinch, even though it was the highest sum
of money they'd ever seen anyone spend at once in the history
of the auction. He pulled out his chequebook and wrote the
cheque. José and his crew had bought twenty-three horses – and
not just any horses, but the finest, most expensive pedigrees. The
manager was so thrilled with the sale that he'd presented the man

with a bronze statue of a horse and jockey. With some further prodding, Graham was able to find out his name – Francisco Colorado Cessa – and that he'd written the cheque from a BBVA Compass bank account in California. Lawson wrote the name down on a pad of paper on his desk. He would subpoena BBVA Compass for Colorado's bank statements. Then he'd check the criminal and intel databases to see if he got any hits on the wealthy cheque writer's name.

Now it wasn't just wire transfers from Mexico, but a businessman from Mexico personally writing a cheque. Ramiro Villarreal, he'd noticed, had never materialised at the All American or at the auction either, so he was definitely out of the group. And now there was this new player showing up to write a $2.2 million cheque.

TWELVE

RAMIRO VILLARREAL MOPPED THE SWEAT FROM HIS FOREHEAD. THE HOUSTON airport was teeming with screaming children and people racing back and forth with their carry-ons. His feet were killing him. And he needed to make the connecting flight to Oklahoma City, where the next big auction was held every year after the All American.

Technically, he still worked for Miguel. But he hadn't been asked to go to the auction in Ruidoso. He'd be lucky if Miguel let him bid on one or two yearlings at Heritage Place. In the past three years, Villarreal had funnelled more than $3.5 million into US racetracks and auction houses for the cartel boss. With the help of a man who owned a peso exchange business in Monterrey, he'd created a front company called Basic Enterprises. Every month he'd arrived at the peso exchange house with briefcases full of American cash to wire to the United States. Initially, he was told that it would be cheaper if he used Mexican pesos. Villarreal was paying twice as much in fees, the man at the peso exchange explained, because he would have to turn the dollars into pesos then back into dollars again to pump it legally through the international banking system. Villarreal said he'd pay whatever it cost. 'My clients pay me in dollars. So that's what we have to do.'

Now, as he approached his gate, lugging his laptop, he noticed two official-looking men approaching him. 'Could we speak with you for a moment?' one of them asked, though it wasn't really a question. They were already steering him towards a back room. They closed the door behind them. One of the men explained to Villarreal that they were with a DEA task force in Houston.

Much to his shock, they told Villarreal that his phone had been tapped by the DEA. They had his calls with Omar, Mamito and others on tape. Once Miguel had employed Villarreal, he'd become an easy target, since Miguel's passion for horse racing was well known. For several hours, the two agents questioned Villarreal about his meetings with Miguel and other cartel members. One of them took Villarreal's mobile phone and downloaded all of his contact information. Finally, the dishevelled horse agent was allowed to catch the last flight to Oklahoma City but only on the provision that he report back to them in Houston after the auction. They confiscated his laptop, which held all of his important accounts and other information about his horse business, to make sure he followed through.

The day after the auction, Villarreal returned to Houston – as he had agreed – and this time, he met with a DEA special agent named Rene Amarillas, who had flown in from the Monterrey, Mexico office. Amarillas had been tasked with tracking Miguel Treviño in Mexico – no easy assignment since the drug lord constantly changed his phones and safe houses. Miguel had been on the DEA's radar since 2007, when they'd seized eight tonnes of Colombian cocaine in the northern Mexican port city of Altamira. The shipping container of coke, it turned out, had belonged to Miguel Treviño and, from the sheer size of the bust, they knew he'd become a major player in the cartel. Amarillas explained to Villarreal that he already had hours of wiretaps of Villarreal discussing Tempting Dash, the futurities in Grand Prairie and auctions with Miguel and Omar. There was plenty there to put him in jail. But Amarillas wasn't really interested in Villarreal's horse scam. What he wanted was Miguel.

And Villarreal was going to help him. Villarreal begged to be let go. He knew what Miguel did to informants. But Amarillas insisted. Villarreal could go to jail or lead him to Miguel. Those were his choices. Just like the Zetas, the DEA wouldn't take no for an answer.

THIRTEEN

LAWSON WAS HUNCHED OVER HIS COMPUTER CHECKING ON THE PROGRESS OF HIS subpoena for Francisco Colorado's bank statements when Pérez stepped into his cubicle.

'*¿Cómo estás?*' she said.

Lawson looked up from his computer. He knew she was referring to the Treviño case, which they often discussed. '*Así, así,*' he said. 'That means "so-so", right?'

'*Sí.*' She nodded. '*Muy bien, güero.*'

'*Gracias, morena,*' he said.

Pérez gave him a knowing look. 'Someone's been giving you lessons.' One of her favourite pastimes was teasing him about how he'd fall in love in Laredo, get married. His plans to make a clean break for Tennessee would be dashed. Pérez was wearing khaki cargo pants and a loose-fitting blue polo shirt to accommodate her swelling waistline. He knew she was due next month around Thanksgiving.

By now, they were working a handful of cases together and the rest of the squad expected that, if there were a callout or a reactive case, Pérez and Lawson would go together. The other guys were relieved because they didn't know how to deal with Pérez's pregnancy.

'Watch out you don't end up delivering the baby yourself,' one agent had cracked to Lawson, who'd given him a withering look.

He had a younger half-sister and he'd spent much of his childhood with his mum after his parents' divorce. He liked to think he could get beyond the macho attitude of some of the other guys on the squad.

Hodge had finally got his indictment in the drug-gang case with the help of an IRS criminal investigator from Waco. Lawson was impressed with Steve Pennington, who knew his stuff but didn't feel the need to advertise it. Hodge had been unusually upbeat since the indictment. With the case finally coming to an end, he was one step closer to leaving Laredo.

Lawson had learned a lot from Hodge about how to keep up with the paperwork the FBI required for every step in an investigation but, when it came to a true partnership, he looked to Pérez.

'Any word yet from our source on the Garcia case?' he asked.

'*Nada, todavía,*' she said. A few weeks earlier, they'd finally been able to piece together what had happened to the brothers through sources from Nuevo Laredo. Some Zetas had intercepted the brothers outside the ranch where they were going to ride and demanded their motorbikes and pick-up truck. When they'd refused, the gunmen had killed them.

It turned out the guy using the Garcia brothers' mobile phone had given the order to shoot. They'd already given the information to the police in Nuevo Laredo but, predictably, they'd done nothing with it.

'What about our pilot? Has the helicopter taken off yet?'

Pérez was pivoting to another case they'd recently taken on:

a murder in neighbouring Zapata County. A man had gone jet skiing with his wife on Falcon Lake, a reservoir on the Rio Grande. And they had made the mistake of straying into Zeta territory on the Mexican side of the lake, where they'd been shot at with AK-47s. The man had been killed but his wife had escaped on her jet ski. Weeks had already passed since the shooting and they'd yet to recover his body. And neither Lawson nor Pérez could cross the border into Mexico. A Mexican police commander had volunteered to help but a week later his head was delivered in a suitcase to a Mexican army barracks near the lake.

After the death of the police commander, they'd scrambled to find anyone who could stage a search for them in Mexico. Lawson had finally found a seasoned Texan pilot to fly a helicopter used by Mexican volunteer firefighters over the area where the man had disappeared. A couple of the firefighters had agreed to go along with him in case they located the body.

Lawson checked the time on his mobile phone. 'The helicopter should be out there by now. We should hear something soon.'

'Let me know when you hear from them,' Pérez said, heading back towards her cubicle in the corner of the office.

About thirty minutes later, he appeared at her desk, his face flushed. Pérez could tell it was bad news.

'I just got a call from the pilot. They flew over the area but were shot at from below, and now they're running out of fuel. He says it's too dangerous for them to land.'

'Oh shit,' Pérez said, getting up out of her chair with some difficulty. They already harboured enough guilt about the police commander. He could have refused to help them, like the others, but he hadn't and now he was dead.

'I'll work on getting them permission to land in Texas,' Pérez said with urgency, reaching for her mobile phone.

'They need fuel,' Lawson said. 'I've got to figure out how to get it to them.'

'I'm going with you,' Pérez said, sitting back in her chair and strapping on her ankle holster.

'Why don't you stay here,' Lawson suggested.

'Hell no,' Pérez said and grabbed her jacket from the back of her chair.

She'd made a point of telling Lawson about her last pregnancy in Miami, where she'd worked up to delivery day. She was proud that she'd helped take down a Colombian coke dealer when she was eight months pregnant. She'd stuck out the surveillance for seven hours, taking bathroom breaks in the bushes. Later she found out that her squad leader had forgotten all about her, which was why he'd never relieved her from her shift. A rookie at the time, she was determined to make a good impression on the all-male squad, so she'd rolled with it without complaint. When they finally hit the house, she was right there with them. Afterwards, the agents took photos with the seized merchandise. Pérez posed for a sassy side profile with her pregnant belly and the bricks of cocaine.

'I'm co-agent on this case,' she said. 'I'm going with you.' Lawson could see the determination in her face. There was no way he was going to talk her out of it. He slipped his Glock 27 into the concealed holster on his waist.

'All right, let's go, pregnant lady,' he said.

On the way out, he asked Perdomo if they could borrow his squad vehicle, because it was a pick-up truck. From their office they sped north to the outskirts of Laredo where the airport was located. There they bought two fifty-five-gallon drums of jet fuel. While a man filled the barrels, Pérez worked her mobile phone trying to get the Mexican helicopter permission to land on the US side of the border. It would take them at least an hour on a patchy road to get to Zapata and the helicopter.

Their drive south on the highway with two highly volatile barrels of jet fuel sloshing around in the bed of the pick-up felt like an eternity to Lawson. 'I can't believe I'm doing this,' he said, glancing at Pérez and her very pregnant stomach.

'Just forget about it,' she said, in a tone that told him not to bring it up again.

He changed the subject. 'Do you sometimes feel guilty about the police commander?'

'Sometimes,' she said. 'We can't let these guys down.' Pérez had finally secured permission for the helicopter pilot to land on the US side of Falcon Lake.

When they arrived, the exhausted helicopter crew was waiting. The pilot quickly fuelled up the helicopter's tank, then they watched it head south again for home. The crew had decided not to risk another dangerous foray over the lake. Once again, they'd come up with nothing. As the Zetas' power was becoming more absolute on the other side of the border, Lawson was constantly being reminded of his limitations. The sense of powerlessness it gave him only strengthened his resolve to take down Tremor Enterprises and Miguel.

FOURTEEN

LAMIRO VILLARREAL HAD KEPT HIS END OF THE DEAL WITH THE DE A AND TOLD THEM where they could find Miguel. The Zeta leader, surrounded by his bodyguards, sat calmly near the finish line watching his horses win at the racetrack on the outskirts of Nuevo Laredo.

It couldn't have been too much of a surprise since Miguel had reopened the racetrack after it had fallen into disrepair when the government ran it. Nearly a year had passed since the Zetas' rupture with the Gulf Cartel, and Nuevo Laredo was still in a state of siege. La Familia Michoacana, a religious-cult-like cartel from western Mexico, had joined the Sinaloa and Gulf cartels in a federation to wipe out the Zetas. And the Zetas had responded in kind by allying themselves with the Juarez and Tijuana cartels and the Beltrán-Leyva organisation, a former arm of the Sinaloa Cartel. A full-blown civil war was erupting among Mexico's most powerful drug syndicates.

In Nuevo Laredo, the Zetas blocked city streets with hijacked semis and buses, ambushing government soldiers or enemy gunmen. Day and night, a cacophony of high-calibre weapons echoed in the streets. The government, after Calderón's failed military offense, was battling to regain some semblance of control as territories were invaded and lost and then reinvaded by the two warring alliances. Innocent civilians could only watch in dismay and horror as their neighbourhoods were turned into battle zones.

The Zetas had been preparing for independence for years. School buses with blackened windows shuttled new recruits to training camps in the states of Veracruz, Coahuila and Tamaulipas. They'd even hung giant banners over highways advertising for military or ex-military to join their ranks, with a phone number to call. 'We offer a good salary . . . You won't suffer from hunger and we won't give you sopa Maruchan [instant noodle soup],' promised one banner in Nuevo Laredo – a dig against the Mexican army and its low wages. The cartel also stockpiled weapons from US gun shows and the Guatemalan military. They had M–16s, rocket launchers, grenades, bazookas and belt–fed machine guns. And Lazcano had bought a helicopter and a Cessna to monitor their expanding territories.

With the constant skirmishes, Miguel never stayed anywhere for too long. But he still found time to watch his horses at the track, which sat in the arid ranch land south of the city. Usually it was only half-full because no one wanted to be near the kingpin or his bodyguards if there was a confrontation. But at the DEA's insistence, a handful of undercover Mexican federal police, who had been vetted and trained in Quantico, were sent to the racetrack to arrest Miguel.

Special Agent Amarillas and the other DEA agents waited for news of their progress, then waited some more. Nothing happened. When they enquired with the federal police, they were told that it had been too risky. There were not enough of them and too many people might have been killed if they had moved in to arrest Miguel. It was yet another frustrating setback for the DEA. Miguel had been less than five miles from the United States but in Mexico he was still untouchable. When Villarreal got news of the failed arrest, he begged to be let out of their agreement. But the DEA wasn't about to let a good informant walk away.

A FEW DAYS AFTER the failed operation at the Nuevo Laredo racetrack, Villarreal received a call from Omar. Miguel wanted him to come to his ranch in Coahuila. José and Nayen would also be there. Omar told Villarreal that Miguel wanted to know where everyone stood with his horse expenses. Villarreal had no idea whether the brothers knew of his betrayal yet but he knew that not showing up for the meeting would make Miguel immediately suspicious, which he couldn't risk. Omar had already made a point several months ago of letting Villarreal know they knew where his parents lived in Monterrey, and how to find them.

Much to his relief, when he arrived at Miguel's ranch, the brothers acted as they normally did, calling him 'Gordo' and slapping him on the back. At the meeting, José presented Miguel with a spreadsheet that listed more than $1.8 million in expenses. People in the States were clamouring to be paid. Villarreal had become adept at laundering and moving money across the border to handle expenses just like these. But when Miguel directed that the $1.8 million be sent to Nayen's accountant in Nuevo Laredo, a tall, chubby thirty-year-old named Ricardo Carabajal, known as 'Yo', it became even more clear that his services were no longer needed.

Nayen was still basking in the glory of Mr. Piloto's win at the All American Futurity, the horse that Villarreal had first purchased for Treviño. Villarreal watched as José presented his younger brother, Miguel, with the trophy from the race. He was sure

Nayen had something to do with his misfortunes. Ambitious and manipulative, Nayen had always been jealous of Villarreal's success and now he was making himself indispensable to Miguel. Villarreal had already been pushed out of the deal on Tempting Dash and Mr. Piloto. He'd not only bought them, but he'd even risked his life taking Tempting Dash away from Mamito. Still, he remained quiet for most of the meeting. He didn't want to anger Miguel or his brothers. When the meeting was finally over, he was relieved when Miguel let him leave. For the moment, he was safe.

Back home in Monterrey, he tried to find new clients. But it felt like a noose was tightening around his neck. Miguel was no longer asking him to buy horses and he already knew too much about Miguel's plans with his brother in Texas. This made him a liability. He knew his time was running out.

A COUPLE OF WEEKS passed before Miguel summoned Villarreal to another meeting, this time in Nuevo Laredo. If he didn't show, he knew there would be consequences for his family.

In Nuevo Laredo, he waited where he had been told at a convenience store. A truck arrived full of *sicarios*, brandishing their weapons, who forced him into the truck's bed next to two fifty-five-gallon drums: the kind he knew that the Zetas used to burn bodies. A gunman sat next to him and didn't take his eyes off of Villarreal until they were at the outskirts of the city. In the twilight, they waited in a barren expanse near a deserted ranch house. The minutes felt like hours. Finally, Miguel's convoy arrived.

Miguel greeted Villarreal and hugged him. 'You're not screwing me, are you, Gordo?' he asked.

'No, of course not, Papi,' Villarreal stammered.

Miguel's gunmen unloaded a blindfolded man from one of the trucks in his convoy. Miguel excused himself for a moment, then walked over to the trembling man, ripped off the blindfold and shot him in the head.

Villarreal's knees buckled and everything went black. When he regained consciousness, Miguel was slapping his face and laughing. 'What's wrong, Gordo?' he said. 'You can't handle seeing me kill someone? Next time, I'm going to have you do it.'

Miguel strode back to his convoy and left the terrified Villarreal standing in the field with the two fifty-five-gallon drums – one of them for the blindfolded man, the other one still empty.

FIFTEEN

WHENEVER LAWSON PUNCHED THE SIXTH-FLOOR BUTTON ON THE LIFT TO GO TO the DEA's office, he felt himself making excuses not to go. But in a good-faith effort, he'd been meeting with Jeff Hathaway every three weeks and sharing what he'd learned. He told him about the All American Futurity, the LLCs and the straw buyers, and the DEA agent listened closely and wrote it all down.

In his typical hard-charging style, Hathaway was putting pressure on Lawson to be more aggressive with Graham as a source. He told Lawson they'd set up a bank account for Graham and they wanted him to have José and the others make deposits into it to bolster their money-laundering evidence. But there would be one condition to Graham's using the account – he had to report to Hathaway.

His dad had an old saying about friends like Hathaway: 'They'd knife you in the chest instead of the back.' Lawson wasn't about to give up his source to Hathaway. He explained that Graham had already had an IBC bank account flagged, then closed, after José had had someone funnel deposits into it from Laredo. The deposits, each $9,000 or less, had made the bank suspect that they were trying to skirt federal reporting requirements, a red flag for money laundering. José had panicked when he found out about it and Lawson had worried he'd put distance between himself and Graham.

Luckily, the whole thing had blown over. And he didn't want to risk José and the others becoming suspicious again. He also knew that Graham was stubborn and didn't like being told what to do. If they pushed him too far beyond his comfort level, he'd be out. And they didn't have enough on him to make him stay. The DEA were used to flipping dope dealers. They'd seize ten kilos then force the guy to become an informant or go to jail. Graham was a businessman from a wealthy family and they didn't have that kind of leverage on him. He'd just disappear behind a wall of high-priced lawyers, which would torpedo their entire investigation.

The look on Hathaway's face told him that he wasn't persuaded by Lawson's argument. So to buy himself more time, Lawson promised to bring it up with Graham and get back to Hathaway later with an answer.

LAWSON KNEW HE WAS in a tough position. He needed to work the wiretap angle harder, which in FBI parlance was called a Title 3. This involved writing an affidavit several pages long with a convincing legal argument for probable cause, then running it through an assistant US attorney and a federal judge for approval. It was a skill that needed to be learned and practised, and neither he nor Hodge had done one before. But he knew Pérez had in Miami. Her Colombian drug squad had turned out Title 3s like hot bread. But Hodge and Lawson were still the assigned case agents. She'd have less time to work on her own cases, and any work she did on the Treviño investigation couldn't be used towards a promotion. He knew more than anything that she wanted the border-liaison job if it ever opened up in Laredo. The FBI would give her an armoured squad car and she'd be able to cross the river and work with their Mexican counterparts. Lawson didn't trust anyone south of the river and thought she was crazy to want the job. But Pérez said he'd never understand. Part of her was still Mexican and that would never change.

So if she agreed to help him, she would have his eternal gratitude, which he knew wasn't much of an incentive. He would make his pitch to her over lunch.

Pérez was on her computer and she looked up as he approached. 'Do you want to go get some lunch? We can go to Don Martin's. I'll buy,' he offered. La Fonda de Don Martin was one of her favourites.

'Really?' Pérez said, feigning surprise. 'It must be important if you're willing to give up the fried chicken and gravy.' She was making fun of the fact that Lawson had discovered a cafeteria at the mall that served southern-style gravy and fried chicken. It was a poor substitute for the southern food he craved from home but it was always his first choice.

Pérez looked at her watch. 'Sure,' she said. 'Just let me finish this up and I'll be right over.' She turned back to her computer.

They drove to the restaurant in Lawson's pick-up. Don Martin's was an old Laredo favourite. Increasingly, it faced heavy competition from a recent influx of newer Mexican restaurants, almost exact copies of well-known restaurants from Nuevo Laredo, with the same owners, even some of the same employees. In Nuevo Laredo, restaurant owners were now charged a monthly tax by the Zetas, called a *cuota*. The money went towards the cartel's war effort. If the owners refused to pay, their family members were kidnapped and killed. Many had finally had enough; they'd shuttered their businesses and fled to Texas to wait for the chaos to subside back home.

At Don Martin's, the waiting staff shouted their orders to the cooks in Spanish as they hustled steaming plates of enchiladas and *chiles rellenos* to the tables for the lunchtime rush. The smell of meat grilling reminded Lawson that he was hungry. He ordered steak fajitas and Pérez ordered the *sopa de fideo*. Lawson told Pérez about his predicament. 'I feel like I'm on to something big,' he said. But he risked losing it if he didn't step up the pace of the investigation. He told her about Hathaway, who was pressuring him over Graham. He could tell by the look of amusement on Pérez's face that she knew where he was headed.

'You're the only one I trust on this,' he said. 'I know you've done a Title 3 before.'

Pérez didn't say anything. She ate a spoonful of soup. She seemed to be mulling it over, even though Lawson knew she had been interested in the case since the beginning. He sipped his iced tea and waited. She was killing him slowly.

'So, where are you at with the investigation?' she asked finally. Lawson brought her up to speed with everything he had so far.

It took nearly thirty minutes to fill her in on his numerous meetings with Graham, the All American, Francisco Colorado, and the rest. 'So, what do you think?' he said finally.

He knew Pérez was used to fast-paced Miami and was still struggling to adjust to the slower rhythm of Laredo, which could work to his advantage.

'Yeah, I'll do it,' she said finally, with a smile. 'Let me see what I can get done before I take maternity leave.'

'Thanks, Alma. I owe you one,' Lawson said, feeling his shoulders relax. He dug into his plate of fajitas with renewed gusto. He'd forgotten that he was starving.

SIXTEEN

BY THE END OF 2010, THE ZETAS WERE FIRMLY IN CONTROL OF THE STRATEGIC state of Veracruz, a former jewel in the Gulf Cartel's empire. For months, murders and kidnappings had engulfed the state as the former allies fought to the death for the territory. The city of Veracruz was the home of the biggest, most valuable heavy-cargo port on the Gulf coast and the largest in the country. And it was as vital to Mexico's drug trade as Nuevo Laredo.

As gun battles, kidnappings and killings intensified in the city, the violence began to touch even the most privileged Veracruzanos, like Alfonso del Rayo Mora, a young and wealthy real-estate developer. A member of the PRI, del Rayo had dipped his toe into politics in Veracruz as a member of the city council but he'd never dived in so deep that he'd become acquainted with men like Miguel Treviño. But that would soon change.

In early December, del Rayo was on his way home from a nightclub in the early morning hours when, at a stoplight, a small four-door Nissan pulled up alongside his Porsche SUV. Two men in black tactical gear sitting in the back of the Nissan pointed their AK-47s at his driver's side window and the Nissan's driver gestured for him to pull to the curb. Del Rayo put his foot on the gas.

He pushed the accelerator past a hundred miles per hour as he took a traffic circle and, for a moment, he felt the SUV go airborne. In his rear-view mirror, he could see the Nissan labouring to keep up.

But behind it were two more cars filled with heavily armed men. The whole thing had to be a case of mistaken identity, he thought. He decided to circle back to the nightclub, El Candelabro, that he'd just left.

He pulled into the valet parking and ran towards the front door. He could hear music and laughter inside. Some of his friends were still there. But the doors were locked. Desperate, he banged on the front doors wildly with his fists. 'Help me!' he screamed. 'Let me in. It's me, Alfonso.'

The convoy of armed men pulled into the parking lot. At least twelve of them surrounded del Rayo. The men wore uniforms of the Agencia Federal de Investigación, or AFI, a federal police agency tasked with fighting narcotrafficking. But del Rayo knew they couldn't be police. Some of them were barely out of their teens. He'd heard of other wealthy businessmen who'd been kidnapped. They even had a verb for it now – *levantar* – to be 'picked up', as if they were being lifted to the heavens rather than bundled into SUVs by hooded commandos. Maybe they were, in a certain sense. Because most never returned, which meant they were surely dead. Because of fear and the stigma, the wealthy never talked about it openly. They would assume the kidnapped person was somehow mixed up in some dirty business with the cartel. No one knew for sure, and chances were they never would. It would never be reported to the police, never investigated, because the police often worked in tandem with the Zetas. This reality haunted their daily lives, yet they all felt that the rash of kidnappings would never touch them or their families. That had been del Rayo's feeling too, until now.

'I've done nothing!' del Rayo yelled. 'You've got the wrong person!' Two of the men grabbed him and tried to throw him head first into the backseat of the Nissan. Del Rayo kicked wildly as the two piled on top of him and bashed his head with the muzzles of their AK-47s. Blood poured down his face. Del Rayo thought they'd kill him right there. One of the men forced him into the back seat, face down. He imagined his friends watching from behind the tinted windows of the nightclub. Where was the club's security team? The other handcuffed his wrists behind his back and shackled his feet. Then another gunman lay on top of him so he couldn't struggle anymore. Del Rayo tasted the salt of his own blood.

A few miles down the road, the *sicario* lying on top of him realised he'd left his AK-47 in the parking lot. The other men cursed at him – *pendejo,* they yelled. The wheels of the car squealed as they did a U-turn on the boulevard. They pulled into the parking lot again. Del Rayo heard one of the gunmen thanking someone from the club. *Joder,* he thought. The security guys were taking care of the AK-47 in case the men came back for it. Now he knew he was truly alone. The world went dark.

When del Rayo regained consciousness, they were pulling him up a flight of stairs. The sun was beginning to rise. He was handcuffed and his ankles shackled. He groped for the wall or a railing; the blood from his head wounds stained everything he touched. His shirt was soaked. From the outside, the house looked ordinary, like any other in a working-class neighbourhood. But inside, the barred windows were covered with sheets. It was the smell that assaulted him first – a stench like an overflowing toilet. There was no furniture, just a few chairs and a folding table in the front room.

The gunmen stripped him of his clothes and shoes. The *sicario* who had shoved him into the Nissan slipped on del Rayo's Gucci loafers and looked at them admiringly, while another put on his designer jeans and paraded around for the other men, who wolf-whistled. A third complained that he'd only been left with the shirt and it was soaked in blood. 'It's ruined,' he said, pouting.

After a few minutes of this, they faced del Rayo, who was left only in his underwear, towards the living-room wall and began beating him with long wooden sticks. 'This is what you get for fighting back,' said the *sicario* wearing his Gucci loafers. He was the one who had been lying on top of del Rayo in the back of the Nissan and who had forgotten his AK-47 at the nightclub, which had made him the object of ridicule. 'This is what you get for messing up our car,' said the *sicario* in del Rayo's designer jeans, who whacked him violently in the kidneys.

It felt like the beating would never end, that he would die right there. But, finally, they seemed to grow tired of it. A man who called himself Capitán Muñeco, 'Captain Doll', addressed del Rayo, who lay in a crumpled heap on the floor. 'We are the Zetas,' he said. 'We are the law, and what we do for a living is kill people. We want four and a half million dollars. You have three days to pay us.'

'I don't have that kind of cash,' del Rayo said. 'I need to sell properties, land, to get you the money. You'll have to release me. I need more time.'

'Three days or consider yourself dead,' said Capitán Muñeco. He assured del Rayo that the Zetas knew he could pay. 'We've been to your house, we know where your children go to school, what cars you drive; that you have a pretty wife.' He leered. 'We've even watched you in El Candelabro.'

The *sicario* wearing del Rayo's Gucci loafers took him to the back of the small house. In the service room, where there would normally be a washer and dryer, there was a family being held hostage. The Zetas were trying to find a relative, anyone who might pay up for their release. But they were so poor just to look at them that del Rayo could only feel pity. The old man, with his gnarled hands, and his ancient wife sat tied up next to their two middle-aged sons and their wives and children. *Campesinos* from Central America, they had nothing but threadbare clothes and worn shoes. They had been on their way to the United States. It seemed they had been in the room for several days without access to a toilet. The smell made his eyes water. But next door it was even worse. Several blindfolded teenagers were on their knees, also covered in their own mess. The stench almost made him throw up. The kids, covered in gang tattoos, had been reduced to an almost animal state. Del Rayo felt that, if he were left there, they would tear him limb from limb and consume him.

He was relieved when he was taken to another room – this one empty – where he would be kept isolated. But he would not be entirely alone. The *sicario*, who couldn't have been older than twenty, handcuffed himself to del Rayo. He told del Rayo that Capitán Muñeco was second in command in the city of Veracruz and that he was in one of his safe houses. He would be in charge of him, he said, until del Rayo paid the $4.5 million.

Two days passed and del Rayo waited for some sign of whether he might live or die. At night, Capitán Muñeco and his lieutenant, a large, fat man, stayed up doing lines of coke and groping prostitutes. The front room was illuminated with Santa Muerte candles, the Grim Reaper-like saint whom many of the Zetas followed, and candles of San Judas Tadeo, the patron saint of lost causes. Del Rayo, a Catholic, was offended by the desecration of San Judas. Everyone who worked at the safe house snorted cocaine day and night. The gunmen were twitchy and paranoid, especially Capitán Muñeco, who was prone to violent, erratic moods. Del Rayo could hear laughter and the screams of people being tortured in other rooms. One day, a coked-up Capitán Muñeco lectured the Central Americans against traveling to the United States. 'What do you want to go there for? You'll only get yourselves killed,' he said, laughing.

Each morning, one of Muñeco's gunmen would take del Rayo's bank card to an ATM and withdraw the maximum amount. He'd also been forced to direct one of his servants to leave his Range Rover and other cars in the parking lot of a strip mall with the keys. The Zetas were bleeding him of whatever assets he had available. But he had still not come up with the $4.5 million. The properties were in his name, he explained to Capitán Muñeco, but his wife couldn't sell anything unless he signed the papers first. 'You've got rich friends, don't you?' Muñeco said. 'Ask them for the money.'

After nearly a week, Capitán Muñeco and his *sicarios* were called to a meeting. Del Rayo wondered whether it was about him. When the young *sicario* returned to the safe house, he seemed to have a secret weighing on him. Back in the room, he handcuffed their wrists together. 'Relax,' he whispered to del Rayo. 'We decided we're not going to kill you. Some people in the organisation are mad because they didn't give the authorisation for you to be kidnapped. Capitán Muñeco wants to get rid of you soon as possible.'

Del Rayo was elated. For the first time, he felt he might live. But when he woke up the next morning, his guard was gone and Capitán Muñeco was in a rage, kicking him as he lay on the ground in the foetal position. 'What did you do?' he screamed. 'Did you offer him money?'

'I don't know anything,' del Rayo grunted between the kicks. 'He never said anything.'

Capitán Muñeco threw del Rayo into the room with the

feral street dealers. The floor was covered in urine and he could only prop himself up against the wall. His wrists and ankles were shackled. All of the hope he'd felt yesterday was gone. Today, they'd kill him for sure, he thought. But as the day progressed, something unusual was going on in the city. Capitán Muñeco and his *sicarios* were even edgier than normal. He could hear military helicopters rumbling low over the neighbourhood. Muñeco had put tinfoil over the antennas of their radios so the military wouldn't pick up his signal. Del Rayo heard chatter coming through the radio from other Zeta safe houses in the city. *Halcones*, or lookouts, were radioing in the locations of the military in case they had to flee. Del Rayo heard the men discussing him in the other room. Coked out and paranoid, they believed that all of the commotion was because of him.

Capitán Muñeco entered and shoved del Rayo back into the adjoining room where he'd been held for the last eight days. 'We're going to let you go,' he said. 'But if for any reason you tell anyone what you've seen here, we'll kill you and your family. Because of the situation, I want to make things up with my boss, so I want $500,000 from you. I want it right away,' he said.

'Of course,' del Rayo said, nodding. He couldn't believe what he was hearing. He refused to believe it until he was out of the house of horrors.

The next afternoon, they led him out of the safe house and into a car. He was surrounded by three heavily armed *sicarios*. They arrived at a shopping mall and, as they entered the parking lot, del Rayo saw a state-police truck with three policemen in the back. They looked at the car and the shirtless del Rayo with his battered, blood-smeared face. One of the gunmen placed the muzzle of his AR–15 in the window so that the police would see it. The policemen looked away and the police truck turned and drove in the opposite direction.

Surprisingly, Capitán Muñeco had left del Rayo's Porsche SUV in the parking lot. He'd already taken four other cars, including two Porsches and a Range Rover. One of the *sicarios* pushed del Rayo out the door. Startled, he ran towards his SUV barefoot and in his underwear. The keys were on top of the front tyre as they had told him. He turned the ignition. He knew it was a miracle he had survived. He wondered, who could have intervened on his behalf, and why?

SEVENTEEN

LAWSON HAD BEEN LIVING IN LAREDO FOR A YEAR AND HE WAS LOOKING FORWARD to spending his Christmas in Tennessee. But in early December, he slipped on a wet patch on a basketball court during a game with some ICE agents and blew out his knee. Two torn ligaments got him a ride to the emergency room. Afterwards, he was sent home with a pair of crutches and a date for surgery in San Antonio in early January.

He was preparing himself for a Christmas alone in Laredo, going over his notes on the Treviño case and drowning his sorrows in old Brad Paisley songs and beer, when he got a phone call from his dad, who said he was coming to visit. Lawson was surprised. His dad had remarried yet again and he was supposed to be hosting Christmas at his house for his new wife's family. In the last decade, other than regularly talking on the phone, they'd rarely seen each other. Lawson had left home at eighteen to go to school, then later moved near Nashville to become a deputy. His new post with the FBI had drawn him even further from home.

When his dad arrived in Laredo, he was his usual outgoing self, making jokes and fetching things for Lawson, who was largely relegated to the new couch he'd just bought. His dad drove, and Lawson gave him a tour of Laredo. His dad especially liked the area north of the Mall del Norte with its nicer, newer neighbourhoods and big-box stores. Lawson lived west of the interstate in an older sub-division but it had green spaces and a small man-made lake that attracted egrets, herons and white-tailed deer. His dad seemed to like his new home, which made him proud.

He invited Pérez over for dinner. She was still on maternity leave until mid-January. He'd already told his dad all about his new partner, who was from the border and spoke fluent Spanish. His dad grilled cheeseburgers for them and thick pieces of bologna, which he jokingly referred to as Tennessee tenderloin. He peppered Pérez with questions about the border but steered clear of talking about the biggest case they were working on, since he knew most of it would be confidential. He'd heard enough already to know that it could be dangerous. 'Just watch your back, son,' he told Lawson one night at the kitchen table.

The week with his father went by too quickly. They drove up to San Antonio for his knee surgery, and his mother and stepfather met them in the parking lot of the hospital. They were going to drive his dad to the airport so he could fly back to Tennessee.

As they said goodbye, it felt unusually emotional, since his dad had never been one to express his feelings and always liked to keep things light.

'The only thing good that's come out of this is that I got to spend so much time with you,' Lawson said, hugging him.

Tears came to his dad's eyes. 'This has meant the world to me,' he said, hugging Lawson back.

Lawson was touched but it also put him on guard. It was not like his dad to come down, spend so much time with him and then be overcome with emotion as they said goodbye. At least twice he'd heard his dad in the bathroom racked by a deep and rattling cough. He'd found a bloody tissue in the wastebasket. His dad smoked at least three packs a day. Lawson knew he'd been to the VA hospital in Memphis but he'd told him it was nothing more than a routine check-up and there was nothing to report. As he watched his mother's car leave the parking lot, he waited to see whether his dad, sitting in the back seat, would turn around one last time to wave goodbye. But he never did. As Lawson watched the car merge into traffic then disappear, he felt a sinking feeling in his chest. He tried to put the worry out of his mind.

EIGHTEEN

WHEN LAWSON RETURNED TO THE OFFICE, HE WAS SURPRISED TO HEAR THAT Hodge's transfer out of Laredo had been suspended until further notice. With the Zetas and the Gulf Cartel still at war in Nuevo Laredo, the bureau couldn't risk being short-staffed. Hodge was sitting at his desk sorting through some paperwork but he couldn't hide his disappointment. He tried not to dump on Laredo in front of the task-force officers and Pérez because they were locals but he had no problem telling Lawson about the unfairness of his still being stuck at the RA.

Lawson opened up the FedEx envelope with the subpoenaed financial statements for Francisco Colorado Cessa's US bank account – the one he'd used to write the $2.2 million cheque at the Ruidoso auction – and Lawson and Hodge got to work examining the documents. From what they could see, Colorado had only recently opened the account at Compass Bank in California. In the month of September 2010, he'd written two cheques totalling $3 million. Besides the Ruidoso auction, he'd written another cheque for close to $1 million to someone named Arian Jaff. When Lawson looked Jaff up online, he discovered that the twenty-five-year-old helped run a family business in San Diego that lent large sums of money at high interest to big-business owners – a sort of payday lender for millionaires. He wrote down Jaff's name and made a mental note to himself to look further into how he might fit into the conspiracy. The network of businessmen entangled in the horse-buying scheme was expanding week by week.

On his computer, Lawson searched through the federal intelligence databases, looking for any information he could find on Colorado's background or business dealings. He found no links with the Zetas. But he did find a brief mention of a connection with Fidel Herrera, the governor of the state of Veracruz, as well as an article about Colorado's brother, who had run for a seat in the Mexican Congress. There wasn't much but what he'd found was intriguing. It was clear Colorado was extremely wealthy and ran what appeared to be a legitimate and successful oil services business. He also had political connections that led all the way to the governor's mansion in Veracruz.

As he gathered the financial data, Lawson also made a point of further educating himself about quarter-horse racing. He had to be careful in his inquiries so that word wouldn't get back to José. Graham gave him a couple of names of trusted and knowledgeable industry insiders and then made the discreet introductions. Once again, Lawson was reminded that a word from the Graham family could open a lot of doors.

He found out quickly, however, that just because they'd agreed to talk to the FBI didn't mean they'd have much to say. They were extremely protective of the sport. They also didn't think it was their job to police it. Lawson's view of cowboys had been shaped mostly by movies and his boyhood love of rodeos and riding. He thought of them as the salt of the earth – plainspoken and honest men.

But he was soon disabused of any Hollywood fantasy he might have had about the nobility of the horsemen involved. Quarter-horse racing, he was starting to discover, was full of handshake deals, cheating and doping. He'd looked into Chevo Huitron, the trainer of Tempting Dash and a friend of Graham's, and found a long list of violations and bans for doping horses. Lawson learned this wasn't uncommon in quarter-horse racing. Injecting race horses with everything from cobra venom to cocaine to Viagra to give them an edge on the track wasn't unusual. Neither was injecting them with cancer drugs or anti-inflammatories to mask the horses' pain from injuries. The doped-up horses broke down on the track at an alarming rate and had to be put down, especially at the casino racetracks in New Mexico where it was like the Wild West of racing.

Because of these practices, quarter horses were 30 per cent more likely to die on the track or be injured than Thoroughbreds, which ran under tighter doping restrictions. In New Mexico, racing promoters blamed the problems on the high altitude of Ruidoso. When pushed, they'd pledge to clean up the doping but nothing changed. It was largely up to the industry to police itself but the industry was more interested in money. And there was less and less of that.

Trainers like Huitron got a slap on the wrist or a small fine, while the owners of the horses feigned ignorance. Even legitimate owners had admitted to Lawson that they felt it was necessary to use the drugs to compete, because everyone else did. As long as they could plead ignorance of what their trainer was up to, their conscience was clear.

A big purse at a race like the All American Futurity could bring untold riches but, more often than not, owners barely broke even in racing. The better bet, Lawson learned, was in breeding. A quarter horse had a crucial three-year window to prove its genetic worth as a champion racer. If it succeeded, it became a valuable breeding commodity. One of the industry's most famous studs, the bay stallion Corona Cartel, was bred at the Lazy E Ranch in Oklahoma for a $35,000 stud fee. Every year, Corona Cartel served close to ninety mares, netting more than $3 million annually. Every horse that contained the name 'cartel' – and there were thousands of them – had been sired by the prolific stallion, which was owned by a flamboyant Mexican American actress and singer from Arizona.

Over the course of a stallion's twenty-five-year life span, it was like owning a golden goose. To continue reaping the rewards, some owners even continued selling the frozen semen of their champions after they had died.

A horse of Corona Cartel's calibre was what every horseman like Graham dreamed of. With such a valuable breeding commodity, everyone got rich, including the farm where the horse was kept, which could charge fees and expenses to the dozens of owners who brought their mares there to be bred. But there were only a handful of these exceptional sires to be had. Which was why Graham had done whatever he could to get Tempting Dash for the family business.

At the All American in Ruidoso, Lawson had been drawn in by the excitement and energy at the racetrack. But the more he learned about the business of racing, the more he understood why the Treviños saw it as such an easy mark for laundering. No one was going to ask any questions as long as the money kept flowing, and Miguel had more than enough of it to go around.

NINTEEN

A LFONSO DEL RAYO HAD SPENT HIS CHRISTMAS HOLIDAY IN THE HOSPITAL.
The top of his head and forehead were still pockmarked
with angry red gashes from the muzzles of AK-47s and AR-
15s. The doctor said he'd need reconstructive surgery to remove
the circular scars. His left pinky and ring finger had also been
broken and were swollen. And his whole body was bruised
and aching.

He and his wife, Carolina, were still trying to piece together
what had happened when del Rayo received a strange phone call
three days before the New Year. It was José Guillermo Herrera,
the secretary of commerce for Fidel Herrera, the powerful
governor of Veracruz. During the kidnapping, Carolina had
reached out to the governor's son, Fidel Jr, an old friend from
school, after other friends in their circle had refused to get
involved. Fidel Jr had immediately contacted his father to ask for
help on her behalf. The governor sent to del Rayo's home his
chief of state investigations, Arturo Bermudez, and another man
who was an expert in kidnap negotiations.

Del Rayo had become acquainted with Fidel Herrera in the late

1990s when he was head of the PRI state committee in Veracruz. Herrera had come from a poor family. But through ruthlessness and cunning, he'd become the most powerful politician in the state. He'd served as a senator and a congressman and, in 2004, he'd been elected governor.

Initially, Carolina had been relieved to receive the help from the governor but, later, she had become alarmed. He insisted that she send her two children with an aunt to Mexico City and then he moved her into a safe house with security cameras and concertina wire ringing the walls. She was instructed not to tell anyone where she was, not even her own family. Alone in the house for several days with Herrera, Bermudez and the kidnapping expert, she had started to feel like she'd been kidnapped too. Herrera sent his people to follow del Rayo's business partners and ex-wife. Inexplicably, her husband's estranged mother was also somehow allegedly involved. The governor's security team hacked phone calls and Herrera listened in. Among Veracruz's political elite, everyone knew that nothing happened in the state without Herrera knowing about it. Carolina began to think he was taking a macabre delight in her family's misfortune.

He'd only permitted Carolina to leave the safe house after del Rayo had been home for several hours. The night of his release, the governor had phoned their house and Carolina had answered. When she heard the unmistakable rasp of Herrera's voice, she started to shake uncontrollably and couldn't speak. Del Rayo had had to take the phone from her hand.

Now the governor's secretary of commerce, José Guillermo Herrera, was calling del Rayo and asking for a meeting at his home. 'I have someone you need to talk to about your kidnapping,' Herrera said. Del Rayo had known José Guillermo for some years as he'd climbed the ladder within the governor's office. It was often assumed that he was a relative of the governor's because they had the same last name but there were no blood ties between them, just a mutual fetish for power.

'When?' del Rayo stammered, caught off guard.

'In two or three days,' Herrera said. He said he'd be in touch as soon as he knew more.

Del Rayo hung up the phone. He couldn't refuse the meeting. He'd been released without paying a ransom. And he was still alive. Most people who were kidnapped were never returned, not even after their families had paid the ransom. Deep down, he'd known his release couldn't have come without a price.

Two days later, José Guillermo Herrera arrived at del Rayo's home accompanied by a well-dressed man in his twenties with dark, slicked-back hair. The man shook del Rayo's hand with gusto and introduced himself as Carlos Nayen. He complimented del Rayo on his beautiful home, then got down to the business at hand. 'You were saved by my boss,' Nayen said. 'As payback, we need you to go to Oklahoma City on January thirteenth to buy a horse.'

'What?' del Rayo said, confused. 'But I don't know anything about horses. Besides, I've got my surgery scheduled that day.' A plastic surgeon was going to remove the circular dents left by the gun muzzles from his forehead. A doctor also had to break his fingers again so they could be reset in a cast.

'Just make sure you're there,' Nayen warned. 'If you don't, you and your family are going to have problems.'

Nayen didn't need to elaborate. Del Rayo had no idea who Nayen's boss might be but he knew it was someone powerful, because he was still alive. He assured them that he would be there. During his nine days in the safe house, it had become clear that the Zetas had eyes and ears in the highest levels of the police and government in Veracruz. The kidnapping had changed him. He didn't trust anyone anymore, not even his

closest friends. Here was Herrera, an adviser of the governor –
someone he had known casually for years – sitting in his living
room and negotiating the ransom for his kidnapping. He was
starting to realise that narcotrafficking and politics were like a
snake devouring its own tail. There was no way to tell anymore
where one began and the other ended.

LAWSON WAS SITTING AT his desk, making a list of the horses he'd
identified so far as being part of José's operation, when he got a
call from Graham. 'Something's up with José,' Graham said.

Lawson sat up in his chair. 'What's going on?'

'He's selling a horse called Blues Ferrari at the next auction at
Heritage Place. It's the first time he's sold a horse at auction.'

'What do you think he's up to?' Lawson asked.

'I don't have a damn idea,' said Graham. 'But he's asked me to
get it ready for sale.'

Graham said the auction would be held on 15 January and
gave him the hip number of the horse. Lawson still had his knee
in a brace and would be on crutches for two more weeks. He
would have to convince Hodge to go in his place, which would
be tough because Hodge always came up with a good reason not
to go. It was starting to get to him whenever anyone in the office
referred to the investigation as Hodge's, especially since Hodge
refused to do any of the travel. But this time, he wouldn't have a
choice. His name was on the case file too.

TWENTY

ALFONSO DEL RAYO TOOK THE FIRST FLIGHT FROM SAN ANTONIO, TEXAS TO Oklahoma City. He still had the muzzle-shaped scars on his forehead and his broken fingers were in a splint. His right eye was bloodshot; the blood vessels had burst in his eye when his abductors had hit him with their rifle butts. His black hair, now down to his shoulders, was slicked back but he hadn't shaved in days. He'd always been an extrovert. Now he looked haunted. He noticed people staring at him in the airport.

He waited for two hours at the Oklahoma City airport before Nayen and two other men arrived. Nayen introduced his younger brother Antonio and Fernando Garcia, who he said was a friend. They drove to an Embassy Suites. The horse auction would be the next morning at a place called Heritage Place, Nayen explained. That night, they stayed together in a two-room suite. Nayen and his brother slept in the same room with del Rayo in case he had any second thoughts.

The next morning, they parked in a massive lot filled with horse trailers and farm trucks, then made their way up to the white colonnades at the entrance of Heritage Place. Behind the building's colonial façade were an indoor exercise ring and an air-conditioned amphitheatre where horses were paraded around a horseshoe-shaped stage for buyers. The building was packed with prospective bidders for the winter mixed sale. Del Rayo had never been to a horse auction. In the clubhouse bar, he saw wealthy Argentines, Mexicans and Brazilians huddled around tables debating bloodlines and racing stats over Bloody Marys and *micheladas*.

Del Rayo found it hard to believe he was there as Fernando Garcia showed him a thick black sales book that listed each horse and its hip number, as well as its breeding lineage and racing record. Garcia explained that the horse they wanted him to bid on was called Blues Ferrari and that he'd be sold near the end of the three-day auction, which would be tomorrow.

Blues Ferrari had a top-of-the-line pedigree but had been a disappointment on the track. Ramiro Villarreal had bought the horse in 2008 for $15,000 at the Lucky 7 Ranch in Oklahoma and named him after Miguel's favourite sports car, then entered the colt in a Los Alamitos futurity trial in California, where he'd failed to qualify. In two years, the horse hadn't won more than $20,000. Then he'd suffered a leg injury.

The stallion had been registered in March 2010 to an LLC called Fast and Furious. Later that same year, Tremor Enterprises purchased the horse for $50,000. Del Rayo had no idea but Miguel, José and Nayen had decided to sell the horse because of his poor performance. Forcing del Rayo to buy Blues Ferrari would inject more clean money into Tremor Enterprises' bank account. Miguel hadn't ordered del Rayo's kidnapping but, once Nayen had told him about it, he'd seen how another wealthy business owner could be useful to their plan and had given the order for him to be spared.

Garcia led del Rayo to the sales arena where the horses were being paraded before the buyers and explained to him how the bidding was done. Del Rayo could scarcely decipher the staccato droning of the auctioneer or the nearly imperceptible gestures of the bidders. A wink of the eye could mean a $10,000 bid or a speck of dust in someone's eye. Garcia told del Rayo not to worry. 'Just raise your hand when the bidding starts,' he instructed. 'Keep bidding until the horse is yours – no matter what.'

The next morning at the auction, Nayen's little brother, Antonio, followed del Rayo everywhere, even when he went to the bathroom or outside to smoke a cigarette. But Nayen and Garcia were taking pains not to be seen anywhere near him. Del Rayo just wanted the bidding to start so he could go home. He had no idea how much he was expected to spend on the horse. He hoped he'd have enough cash to cover the sale. Most of his money was tied up in a golf-resort development in Veracruz.

In the late afternoon, Blues Ferrari was finally brought into the sales ring. The horse's ribs stuck out and they hadn't even bothered to brush the mud off his legs. Every other horse del Rayo had seen in the sales ring had been impeccably groomed but not this one. The auctioneer started it off with a $5,000 bid. Del Rayo raised his hand as he'd been instructed. Soon they were at $175,000. Del Rayo couldn't tell who was bidding against him but, whoever it was, the price was rapidly increasing. He raised his hand again and again as he'd been warned. They were now at $300,000.

'Do I hear three-ten, three-ten . . .' the auctioneer called. Del Rayo raised his hand again.

'I've got three-ten, three-ten . . . how about three-twenty, three-twenty . . .' droned the auctioneer.

Del Rayo looked around for the other bidder but couldn't tell who it might be in the crowd of strangers. Nayen, his brother and Fernando Garcia were nowhere near the sales ring, as far as he could tell, but he knew they had to be watching. 'Sold for three hundred and ten!' the auctioneer yelled and gave a sharp whack with his gavel. Blues Ferrari was his.

JASON HODGE AND ONE of the task-force officers from the squad who had volunteered to go along for the surveillance watched from the sidelines. Two guys who looked too young to have that kind of money were also bidding, driving up the price until the auctioneer struck his gavel at a final sale of $310,000. Graham walked Blues Ferrari out of the sales ring and back towards the stables. They watched as Fernando Garcia and another younger guy led the man who had just bought the horse up a flight of stairs to the sales office. A few minutes later, they were relieved to see Tyler Graham make his way up the stairs after them.

Del Rayo hadn't known how much he was expected to pay for Blues Ferrari, only that he had to buy the horse no matter the cost. Now he'd have to scramble to come up with the $310,000. It was the biggest sale of the auction and Jeff Tebow, manager of Heritage Place, moved to shake del Rayo's hand but stopped when he saw how badly bruised and swollen his fingers were. He took note of the scars on his forehead and his battered appearance.

Del Rayo smiled awkwardly at Tebow, who he could tell was now scrutinising him more closely. He explained to him that he'd need to write two cheques but only one could be deposited that day. The other check would have to wait for at least a week until he could move more funds into the account. Tebow nodded and said that would be fine. Del Rayo wrote out the first cheque for $150,000 but his hand shook and he was having trouble holding the pen because of his damaged fingers.

'Were you in an accident or something?' Graham asked.

'Um . . . yeah, a golfing accident,' del Rayo stammered, keeping his eyes on the cheque he was filling out.

Graham and Tebow looked at one another. Tebow had gone from being excited about the sale to being alarmed. It was an awful lot of money for a horse that hadn't run well and looked underweight. One horseman watching the auction that day would later say that Blues Ferrari had looked like 'death eating a cracker' in the sales ring. And Tebow had never seen del Rayo at Heritage Place before. He was starting to worry that the cheque might not clear the bank. Without del Rayo noticing, Tebow snapped a photo with his mobile phone of him writing out the cheque. He could feel that something wasn't right with the sale. And he wanted some kind of evidence if the money never materialised.

The winter mixed sale of 2011 would turn out to be the highest-grossing auction in thirty-three years for Heritage Place. 'The International demand for the Racing American Quarter Horse is unbelievable,' noted Tebow afterwards in a triumphant press release. Tyler Graham, who had served not only as the selling agent for Blues Ferrari at the auction, but also as a bidder for José, was heralded as the sale's top buyer in the same release. But later, he would complain to Lawson that he wasn't given enough time to prepare Blues Ferrari for the sale, nor did he have any idea that José was going to sell the horse to himself. They both suspected that Alfonso del Rayo was yet another Mexican businessman doing Miguel's bidding and helping him build his racing empire in America. In Laredo, Lawson added Alfonso del Rayo to the growing list of suspects in the case file.

THE MORNING AFTER THE auction, del Rayo flew back to San Antonio with Nayen, Antonio and Garcia. Del Rayo owned a large home in a gated community in San Antonio, which he kept as an investment and a place for his family to vacation. He'd left his wife and kids there for safety while he was in Oklahoma. When they arrived at the airport, Nayen told del Rayo he wanted to see his home in San Antonio. Del Rayo felt it would be unwise to say no — he was still thankful to Nayen for saving his life. He knew he'd be dead if Nayen and his boss — whoever he was — hadn't intervened. He drove them to his house in his rented mini-van and Carolina served the men drinks while they looked around the well-appointed home. When they were done with the tour, Nayen smiled. 'Now I know where you live,' he said in such a way that it could only have been interpreted as a threat. Then he asked del Rayo to drive them to Retama Park, a nearby racetrack.

Anxious to be rid of them, del Rayo did as they asked. When they pulled up to the front of the track, a group of men were waiting for them at the curb. Nayen got out from the front passenger seat and immediately began giving orders to them in Spanish. They walked away in a pack, trailed by Garcia and Antonio. As del Rayo pulled away from the curb, he took a deep breath. He hoped that whatever debt Nayen's boss felt he was owed had now been paid in full. But he couldn't shake the feeling that he'd soon see Nayen again.

TWENTY-ONE

AFTER THE HERITAGE PLACE WINTER AUCTION, GRAHAM HAULED BLUES FERRARI and the other horses José had bought at auction back to his farm in Elgin. It had been more than a year since he'd first met José Treviño at Lone Star Park in Grand Prairie, when Tempting Dash had set a track record and caught the industry's imagination.

The breeding of the champion had not been as smooth as he'd hoped. Not long after arriving at the farm, the stallion was diagnosed with a rare blood-borne disease called piroplasmosis, which the vet surmised had probably been transmitted from a contaminated needle or another infected horse. The news was a shock for José. The most valuable horse he owned was now under quarantine. The Texas Animal Health Commission had banned Tempting Dash from the racetrack to avoid infecting other racehorses with the disease. The champion stallion, the cornerstone of Tremor Enterprises, would never race again.

José wanted to bribe the commission to lift the quarantine. 'What if we gave them a couple hundred thousand to forget the whole thing?' he told Graham.

But Graham said they had no choice but to obey the commission's ruling. The horse was still a champion. The disease didn't change that. But now the best José could hope for was that the stallion could still be bred.

Within days, José sent a worker to Graham's farm to load Tempting Dash into a trailer. He wouldn't tell him where he was sending the horse. Graham couldn't help but wonder if the horse would be hauled south to Mexico and Miguel.

Graham was angry he'd lost Tempting Dash – the champion sire that was going to put his family's stud farm back in business. Now the horse was gone and he was still ensnared in José's operation, which had at least forty horses at his farm.

Carlos Nayen was still in charge of the rapidly growing expenses for everything from horseshoeing to boarding and breeding. But the payments came in fits and starts. Sometimes it was cash, other times by wire from ADT Petroservicios or Grupo Aduanero Integral in Veracruz. Nayen was also instructing Graham to list the horses and their accounts under various owners' names, including Hernando Guerra, Francisco Colorado and Pedro Alcala. Nayen and Garcia also continued to change the horses' names to new monikers that weren't exactly subtle, like Forty Force, Break Out the Bullets, and Number One Cartel.

Graham noticed that the various owners listed never visited his farm. But José showed up weekly to check on the horses, ask questions and make sure everything was running smoothly. His path seldom crossed with Nayen's, whom he seemed barely able to tolerate. Graham's dealings with Nayen were also becoming frayed. The ballooning debt was becoming a constant point of contention between them. 'I'm not a bank,' Graham would often remind him. 'I've got to be paid for my services.'

LAWSON STILL HADN'T BROUGHT up the DEA's bank account to Graham. He could sense that Graham was on edge and growing weary of their arrangement. Graham had recently married his high-school sweetheart and had more to worry about now than just himself.

So when Lawson saw the DEA's number come up on his office phone, he couldn't help but feel a sense of dread. He'd been avoiding Hathaway since before Christmas, while he and Pérez worked on the Title 3. But now he would have to give him an update and there was little to report.

He picked up the handset. 'How's it going?' he said.

Hathaway got straight to it. 'Me and Rene are going to Elgin tomorrow to get Tyler Graham to sign up with us.'

The information was like a kick in the gut. He knew Hathaway was bold but he'd never imagined he'd roll right over him. 'If you want to talk to him, you need to talk to me first,' he said. 'We can set up a meeting with him at our office. That's the way the protocol works.'

'Look, the way we see it, the guy is indictable. You need to push him harder, tap his phone, make him use the bank account we set up, or else,' said Hathaway.

'You can't pull this bullshit,' Lawson said.

They were going to play rough with Graham to get him to co-operate. But Lawson doubted the aggressive move would work. There was little they could indict him on. It would be too difficult to prove to a judge that Graham had prior knowledge of whom he was getting involved with when he'd agreed to bid for José at that first Heritage Place auction. Lawson had seen the look on his face when they'd first met and he'd brought up the Zetas. Graham had had no idea who was pulling the levers behind José.

'He's not going to talk to you,' Lawson said. Before Hathaway could answer, he slammed the phone down, walked back to Villarreal's office and knocked on the door. When he told Villarreal about the call, his boss looked like he might break something too. Then he reached for his phone. Lawson knew Villarreal was working up a righteous fury that would soon be unleashed on Hathaway's boss upstairs.

While Villarreal traded harsh words with the DEA, Lawson dialled Graham to warn him about the impending visit to his farm. He had no choice but to try to head off the two DEA agents and salvage their agreement.

Graham answered after the second ring. 'What's going on?' he said in his typical laid-back style.

'Look, there's something that's come up.' Lawson knew he sounded tense and he tried to relax. He didn't want to alarm Graham but it was hard to contain the mixture of panic and anger welling up inside of him. His worst fear was coming true. The DEA was going to hijack Graham and, without him, Lawson didn't have a case.

'What is it?' Graham said, his tone turning more serious now.

'There's two DEA agents that are going to show up at your ranch tomorrow. They want to flip you so you work for them. You're a grown man – you do what you want to do – but I suggest you don't answer the door.'

Graham was quiet for a moment, taking it all in. 'I won't,' he said finally. 'I don't plan on changing our arrangement.'

'That's good to hear,' Lawson said.

Graham thanked him for the warning, then hung up the phone. All that Lawson could do now was wait. He buried himself in the facts of the case and tried not to think about the DEA knocking on Graham's door. He'd been working the investigation for little more than a year. With the help of Hodge and Pérez, he'd been able to navigate the surveillance warrants, the 1023 reports and other paperwork they needed to build a prosecutable case. They had a growing list of suspects that included Francisco Colorado, Alfonso del Rayo and Alejandro Barradas, who were wiring money from Mexico or writing personal cheques to pay for the horses. He had the photos of Carlos Nayen, Fernando Garcia, José and his crew at the All American. He'd also done surveillance at auctions at Heritage Place, tracing the horses through the various LLCs and straw buyers back to José. All of it pointed to a rapidly growing money-laundering conspiracy.

Lawson scarcely slept that night and he tried to keep himself busy with other work until late in the afternoon, when he finally phoned Graham.

He didn't bother with a greeting. 'So did you answer the door?' he asked, trying to sound casual even though the entire investigation was riding on Graham's answer.

'I've been gone all day,' Graham said. 'I'm not even at the farm.'

Lawson relaxed with the good news. 'Hey, can you meet me at the Omni Hotel in a week . . . maybe Tuesday or Wednesday?'

'Yeah, I think so,' Graham said. 'But let me check with my secretary first. I'll get back to you.'

Lawson was comforted that Graham had stuck with him but he also knew that their partnership had already been strained before the incident with the DEA, which had only jeopardised it further. He was going to have to work to rebuild the trust between them. Establishing rapport with a source and then keeping them close was something they couldn't teach you at Quantico. You had to learn it through trial and error. But losing Graham was not a risk he could afford to take. He needed to see him face-to-face and dispel any second thoughts the horse breeder might be having about working with the FBI.

THE LOBBY OF THE Omni Hotel in downtown Austin was filled with women and men in business suits, wearing conference badges

on lanyards and hauling roller bags. It was about as anonymous a
meeting place as an airport, which was why Lawson had chosen
it. Inside the cavernous and sun-filled glass atrium lobby, it was
nearly impossible to overhear the conversation of a neighbouring
table among the potted plants and din of dozens of conversations
all taking place at once.

Graham sat down across from Lawson in one of the hotel's
overstuffed chairs and ordered an iced tea from the cocktail
waitress, since it was early afternoon. After they were done, he'd
have a forty-five-minute drive back to the farm. Lawson ordered
the same.

'Thanks for coming down,' Lawson said.

'Did I have a choice?' Graham said.

Lawson and Hodge had brought Ernie Elizondo, one of the
task-force officers, along with them to the meeting. Elizondo
sat to the side of Lawson pouring packets of Sweet'N Low into
his iced tea while Lawson did the talking. Hodge sat next to
Graham.

'The DEA thinks you're indictable,' Lawson said. 'Their plan
was to make you work for them, or they'd threaten you with an
indictment. So you're lucky you're with us. We're not going to
go down that road.'

'What the fuck?' Graham said, slamming his iced tea down on
the table. 'You don't think I haven't spoken with my attorneys?
I know I'm not indictable!'

Lawson noticed the cocktail waitress look in their direction
and he instinctively moved closer to the table. Elizondo pulled
his chair in too, as if trying to minimise the collateral zone for an
impending explosion.

'Don't get all twisted,' Lawson said, lowering his voice. 'I'm
telling you, we got your back. But we're also doing you a favour.'

Graham's face flushed with anger. 'Shit,' he said, shaking

his head. 'You think I'm doing this because I'm scared of an indictment? I'm doing this because I messed up and I wanted to make amends.'

'And I'm telling you we got your back.' Lawson's voice was getting louder now as he grew angry. This wasn't how he'd planned the conversation to go. He'd thought Graham would be thankful that they were looking out for him, and it would help shore up any misgivings between them. But Lawson hadn't accounted for the rich-boy entitlement to kick in. The way Graham looked at it, he was doing the FBI a favour, not the other way around.

'Anyone want more iced tea?' Hodge asked, trying to cut through the mounting tension. The cocktail waitress hovered nearby with a half-filled pitcher of iced tea, looking nervous.

'Yeah, I could use some,' Lawson said, thankful for the diversion.

He realised he'd let the conversation get out of hand and now he needed to do damage control before Graham walked out the door. 'Look, I want to thank you for everything you've done,' he said. 'And I want us to keep working together.'

Graham sat back in his chair and looked off in the distance. Lawson followed his gaze to a TV screen showing a football game near the bar. He knew Graham was taking his time, using the same hard-nosed tactics he'd learned from his grandfather, before he gave him an answer. If he wanted to play tough, Lawson thought, he'd remind Graham of the agreement he'd signed.

'Yeah, we're good,' Graham said, turning back toward Lawson finally. 'Don't worry about it.'

'All right, so we're good?' Lawson said.

'Yeah.' Graham nodded. 'I guess I better be getting back to work.' He stood up. Lawson stood also and held his hand out, and they shook hands awkwardly. Then Graham nodded to

Hodge and Elizondo, who also got up from their chairs. They remained standing and watched as Graham walked towards the exit and through the glass revolving door to the street outside.

'Well, that went well,' Elizondo said with a wry smile.

TWENTY-TWO

GRAHAM HAD LOST TEMPTING DASH. EVEN WORSE, HE'D BEEN FLOATING THE bill for feed and boarding for José's horses for several weeks. His frustration over the overdue bill, which had already reached $36,000, was mounting when he received a call from a man in Laredo who said his name was Victor López and that from now on he would be helping Nayen. López said he had the money they owed him. But Graham would have to come to Laredo to pick it up. He told López he'd take a look at his schedule and then get back to him. But he had no intention of going anywhere near the border; it was too close to Miguel and the Zetas for his comfort. As soon as he hung up the phone he called Lawson.

Lawson picked up the vibrating mobile phone on his desk. Since their argument at the Omni, he and Graham were still nursing some raw feelings. But Graham had dropped any pretence of leaving, much to his relief. Lawson listened closely as Graham told him about the call from a new guy named Victor López summoning him to the border. He wanted guidance on what to do. It would be suspicious if he refused to pick up the money, especially after he'd been complaining to José and Nayen for weeks about not getting paid.

Any chance that the DEA was going to help the FBI connect the drug money in Mexico with the horses was now definitely off the table. Lawson hadn't spoken with Hathaway since their heated exchange on the phone. But now they had this new guy, Victor López, promising to deliver $36,000 in cash to Graham. Lawson could see the potential. It would be solid evidence to help them make the link between the drug money and José. 'Tell him you'll do it but you can't go yourself because you're too busy,' he told him. 'You'll be sending a trusted employee instead. We'll take care of the rest.' Graham readily agreed to the plan, no doubt relieved that he didn't have to go himself.

After Lawson hung up the phone, he turned around in his chair to run it past Hodge. He was encouraged by the new development because evidence from the money drop would help get a busy prosecutor's attention when they pitched the investigation at the US attorney's office later in the month.

It hadn't been easy to convince Hodge to go to Oklahoma City to do the surveillance on Blues Ferrari. Lawson was beginning to worry that, once Hodge left, Villarreal would assign another agent as lead on the investigation. Lawson wanted Pérez but Villarreal had yet to appreciate her many strengths.

Lawson told Hodge all about his conversation with Graham and about Victor López and the money drop. But Hodge was less than encouraging. He didn't think they could get the approvals they needed in time for the surveillance. 'That dog ain't going to hunt,' was how he put it to Lawson. This was one of Hodge's favourite phrases, which he repeated often when he thought something was insurmountable.

But Lawson wasn't going to give up that easily. He walked over to Pérez's desk on the other side of the office. She was sitting at her computer, working on the Title 3. He was glad to have her back from maternity leave.

'*¿Qué onda, güey?*' Lawson said, smiling. His greeting was northern Mexican slang for 'What's up, dude?' The phrase was so commonly used in day-to-day Spanish on the border that he'd picked it up and now used it whenever he felt like it, to the amusement of the rest of the squad.

'Oh no.' She laughed. 'I hope you're not saying that to all the girls at the clubs.'

Lawson propped himself up against her desk. 'What? You mean they won't find it sexy?' he said.

'Oh yeah, you should definitely use it,' she said, laughing again. '*Pinche güey* is also very sexy.'

'How's the Title 3 coming?' he said.

'It'd be a lot easier if Fernando Garcia didn't drop his phone every couple of weeks. By the time I pull the phone records, he's changed his number.'

'I've got some good news,' he said.

'It's about time.' She smiled again.

Lawson told her about the phone call with Graham and the set-up to have Victor López deliver the money. The problem was, Hodge didn't think it was possible to get the approvals in just a couple of weeks.

'Let me guess,' she said. 'That dog ain't going to hunt.' Lawson nodded and smiled. Hodge said it so often that it had become a joke around the squad room.

'We used to do this kind of thing all the time in Miami,' she said. 'You could get an undercover to pretend he works for Graham.'

'Yeah, that's what I was thinking.' Lawson nodded. 'Then we bring the cash back to the office and document it.'

'We follow the money,' Pérez said, 'and it will lead us to Miguel.'

FOR SOMEONE COMING FROM across the river in Nuevo Laredo, the plaza in front of La Posada Hotel was a logical place to meet. The historic and imposing Spanish-style hotel clung to the bluff above the Rio Grande like an ancient citadel. In the nineteenth century, it had served as a convent and its white stucco walls had withstood bullets in the Mexican Revolution. Now La Posada served as a point of pride in Laredo – it was the closest thing the city had to a fancy hotel. It was also within walking distance of the bridge into Nuevo Laredo. And the plaza across the street, ringed by palm trees, had been a meeting place for countless border transactions since before Texas had joined the Union.

Victor López had designated the time and place. Graham told López that his farmhand, in a dark-blue pick-up truck, would be there at the plaza waiting. There would be bales of hay in the bed of the truck, so López couldn't miss him.

Lawson sat nearby in his unmarked Chevy keeping his eye on the undercover and waiting for López to appear. An agent from another RA had volunteered to be the undercover. He wore a transmitter so Lawson would overhear everything that was said during the transaction. Pérez, in another unmarked vehicle parked near the Catholic church on the far end of the plaza, also kept watch. If the undercover got hurt or the money got ripped, they would move in fast to pull him out.

It was late January and unusually cold, so Pérez had to keep the car and the heater running to stay warm. Three undercover task-force officers circulated around the plaza, sitting on benches or pretending to wait for a taxi or bus at the curb. But mostly they kept moving just to stay warm.

Perdomo and Hodge had parked near the international bridge, where they would alert the team once they spotted López crossing the bridge into Laredo. An hour and a half passed but there was still no sign of him. 'What the hell?' Lawson said over the radio to the guys near the bridge. 'Have you seen him yet?'

'*Nada,*' said Perdomo.

Lawson phoned Tyler Graham in Elgin to ask for his help. 'Hey, could you phone Victor and ask him what's going on? He's almost two hours late.'

'All right,' Graham said. In a few minutes, he called back.

'He says one of his friends was stopped by a Customs and Border Protection agent on the bridge. But Victor says she's only got $9,000 on her so there's nothing they can do to her.'

'Shit,' Lawson said. Now was not the time for US Customs and Border Protection to be doing its job. From what Graham had told him, he guessed that López was using several women as mules to bring the money across the bridge. Each one of López's 'friends' was carrying cash under the $10,000 limit, which meant they weren't required by law to declare it to a US customs agent at the bridge. Concealing the cash and bringing it across in $9,900 increments or less was what the feds called 'structuring of funds' and it was illegal. This was why the customs agent was suspicious. If another one of López's friends got popped on the bridge with $9,000 in cash in her purse, their money drop would never happen. They needed to do something quick. Lawson radioed the others with the update.

Perdomo's voice crackled over the radio: 'I'll go talk to CBP.' Through his binoculars, Lawson could see him walking fast towards the bridge, which was choked with cars and pedestrians waiting in line to enter the United States. He knew it would take time to convince the CBP agent on the bridge to let his quarry go. It could be another thirty minutes, easy.

Finally, Pérez and Lawson spotted someone who they suspected was López walking swiftly towards the plaza. Stocky and in his late twenties, with a buzz cut, López was wearing a navy-blue windbreaker over a red hoodie and lugging a dark duffel bag.

'Here he comes,' Lawson said over the radio. Pérez peered through her binoculars to get a better look as López walked briskly towards the hotel. The undercover agent was sitting in his blue pick-up at the curb. Lawson snapped photos as López approached. The agent unlocked the passenger door and López ducked inside the cab of the truck and dropped the duffel bag on the passenger side floor. The undercover nodded and said, 'Thanks.' There wasn't anything else for Lawson to hear on the transmitter other than the muffled noises of the agent checking inside the duffel bag for the money. After waiting for hours, it was all over in less than five minutes. López turned and quickly walked south towards the bridge and Mexico.

Lawson, Pérez and the others followed the undercover back to their office. When they got there, they counted the money in the duffel bag, which came out to $36,000, just as López had promised. Pérez photographed the cash and then they put it in the safe. In the morning, they would deliver the money to Graham in Austin. And Nayen and José would never suspect that their new employee had just handed Miguel's money over to the FBI. The money drop had worked out better than Lawson had hoped, with the mules bringing the cash across the bridge to López in Laredo. Now they had proof that José had used structured funds from Mexico to pay his mounting expenses at Graham's farm.

TWENTY-THREE

THE LAREDO DIVISION IN THE SOUTHERN DISTRICT OF TEXAS WAS ONE OF THE busiest in the country, with little more than a dozen federal prosecutors filing more than two thousand cases a year. Most of these were bridge cases: drug dealers and smugglers caught moving people or kilos across the river. As Lawson and Hodge showed their FBI shields to the security guards at the entrance of the federal courthouse, they knew they had a high bar to overcome. They would be asking an already over-taxed prosecutor to invest several months, maybe even years, in a complex money-laundering case involving racehorses.

But without a federal prosecutor signed on to the case, they couldn't expand their investigation. They needed authorisation from an assistant US attorney for the subpoena for the Title 3 and, more important, they needed an aggressive prosecutor who would help them build a body of evidence they could bring before a grand jury to secure an indictment.

As they took the lift up to the second floor, Lawson felt his anxiety building. He'd put everything he had into this case and today would determine whether they could take it to the next level.

Lawson and Hodge sat down before a desk piled high with manila folders and documents. The assistant US attorney sitting behind the desk, the owner of the piles, scarcely looked up from the paper she was signing as they took their seats. A legal assistant stood at her side, waiting to whisk the document away to a federal judge somewhere within the bowels of the courthouse.

'How can I help you gentlemen?' she said finally, handing the document to the assistant, who quickly left the room, shutting the door behind her. The prosecutor looked tired and as if she had much more important things to do.

Hodge introduced them and then Lawson started to pitch the evidence they'd gathered so far. He told her about their source, Tyler Graham, who was inside the operation, and the money that was being paid to him through structured funds, and the backpack filled with cash. He was about five minutes into his pitch when he heard the prosecutor clear her throat.

'No venue,' she said.

'Excuse me?' said Lawson, confused.

'Sounds like your source and your money are in Austin. That's the Western District. It's out of our venue,' she said.

Lawson looked at Hodge. He wasn't sure what to do. Should he try to argue that it wasn't out of her venue because Miguel Treviño and the Zetas were from the border, or was there any point?

But the prosecutor was already rifling through more papers on her desk as if the matter was settled. She'd moved on to the next task and was just waiting for the two agents to remove themselves from her office.

'Thank you for your time,' Hodge said, standing up.

Lawson was still sitting in his chair, dazed. He'd expected more than five minutes, maybe a few questions about the case at least. Hodge tapped him on the shoulder.

'Let's go,' he said, motioning with his head towards the door. The prosecutor was already fully absorbed in another document she'd pulled from a file.

Lawson got up from the chair and followed Hodge to the door. 'Please close the door on your way out,' the prosecutor said, without looking up.

When they got out into the hallway, Lawson exploded. 'What in the hell was that?' he said. He could see that Hodge was agitated too but taking the rejection much better than he was.

'It's better not to make enemies,' Hodge said. 'You'll have other cases.'

Lawson tried to calm down. The worst thing was that Hodge was right. He'd be back in her office again before he knew it. And he couldn't risk getting on her bad side.

'You know, Austin isn't a terrible idea,' Hodge said, pressing the down button on the lift.

TWENTY-FOUR

IT WAS HARD FOR LAWSON NOT TO TAKE THEIR REJECTION AT THE FEDERAL prosecutor's office as a crushing setback. The case's future now seemed uncertain and, during his worst moments dwelling on it, even hopeless. But a few days after the failed meeting with the Laredo division, Hodge swivelled around in his chair to share some encouraging news. 'I got us a meeting later this week with a prosecutor in Austin,' he said.

'Who is it?' Lawson asked.

'His name's Doug Gardner. He wants us to come up and present the case to him.'

'Goddamn, that's good news,' Lawson said. He felt like hugging Hodge. He swore to himself he'd never complain again to Pérez about how Hodge never helped enough on the investigation.

THE US ATTORNEY'S OFFICE in Austin was in a high-rise with an impressive view of the Texas Capitol's pink granite dome in the distance. Doug Gardner, the federal prosecutor, received the two agents in a large conference room. Lawson and Hodge laid out their documents from the case on the conference table. They had Gardner's undivided attention, which was encouraging after their experience in Laredo. Gardner had a wiry build and was in his mid-forties, with close-cropped dark hair flecked with grey. Still active in the Marine Reserve, he'd been a military prosecutor before taking the Justice Department job in Austin.

Hodge briefed Gardner on the horses, Miguel Treviño and his brother José, then Lawson explained how their case had its nexus in Austin because of their source, Tyler Graham, who was being paid to board and breed several of José's horses at his farm near Austin. As Lawson was making his pitch about venue, he felt a growing anxiety overtaking him. What if Gardner and the Western District also passed?

But Gardner appeared to be fully engaged in the briefing and asked a lot of questions. As the OCDETF co-ordinator for Austin, Gardner handled a majority of the cartel and money-laundering cases that came through their office. OCDETF was a long acronym for a Justice Department programme with an equally long title: the Organized Crime Drug Enforcement Task Force. The programme had been created in the 1980s to encourage federal law-enforcement agencies to work together by offering funding from the US Treasury for overtime and other perks so they could do longer, more complex organised-crime cases.

Gardner was intrigued by the direct link to Miguel Treviño through his brother José. He'd prosecuted numerous cases targeting mid-level smugglers and dealers but it was a rare case that led all the way to a major drug kingpin like Miguel. But what gave him concern, he said, was the racehorses. What would happen when they needed to seize the assets − in this case, hundreds of expensive racehorses?

Lawson had been through this before with his boss, Villarreal.

To anyone at management level or higher, it was tough to look past the problem of seizing hundreds of racehorses, which would be an expensive bureaucratic nightmare. All those horses would have to be cared for and later sold. He suspected that this was one reason why other agencies hadn't pursued the racehorse angle. Maybe he was the only one crazy enough to go down that road. 'We'll have to come up with some kind of plan,' Lawson said. 'I've got a background with horses.'

Gardner smiled as if he appreciated Lawson's naïve commitment to the case. There was an awkward silence as the prosecutor thought it through.

'If we're going to do this, you'll need to open a new case in the Western District,' Gardner said finally.

Lawson couldn't contain his grin. 'You've got it,' Hodge said excitedly.

'It's an OCDETF case, so you're going to need to collaborate with another agency on this,' Gardner said. 'Who do you have in mind?'

There was one agency Lawson wasn't going to mention. He'd already been burned once by the DEA.

'It's a money-laundering case,' said Hodge. 'What about Steve Pennington at the IRS?'

Gardner nodded. 'Steve's a good, experienced agent.'

Lawson was relieved that Gardner was running with the idea of Pennington. He hadn't realised the IRS had its own team of criminal investigators until Pennington had showed up in Laredo to work with Hodge, who had been stalled on his drug case for more than a year when Pennington found him.

The IRS criminal investigator was somewhat of a maverick because he ran his own task force in the city of Waco, north of Austin, called the Waco Treasury Taskforce, which dealt exclusively with money-laundering and drug-trafficking cases.

He'd been investigating one of the drug gang's dealers in Waco and, when Pennington ran his name through the deconfliction database, Hodge and the FBI had popped up in the search. Within a few days, he'd arrived in Laredo with the missing pieces of the conspiracy. Pennington helped crank out five document search warrants in one afternoon. It would have taken most agents a couple of days. In less than two weeks, Hodge had his indictment.

Pennington was also old school, which reminded Lawson of his dad. When they'd gone out to do the arrests on the case, Lawson and the others had suited up in their black tactical gear while Pennington had put on a bulletproof vest and plunked onto his head a well-worn blue baseball cap with 'IRS' in yellow lettering. He carried his long rifle in a battered case that looked like it had seen a war or two. Pennington had more than two decades under his belt as an agent but, when he was in Laredo, he'd worked as hard as any rookie. If anyone could help them take down José and Tremor Enterprises, thought Lawson, it would be Pennington.

'I'll give Steve a call,' Hodge said.

TWENTY-FIVE

IN TWENTY-FIVE YEARS, PENNINGTON HAD ARRESTED TOO MANY CARTEL members to count. But he'd never worked an investigation that reached into the very top of the cartel leadership. And the Zetas were the most violent, most notorious of the drug organisations in Mexico. If José Treviño led them to his brothers, it would be the biggest cartel case he'd ever worked.

As Hodge laid out the case over the phone, Pennington's mind was already racing through the next steps of the investigation. Tall and weathered, with short brown hair, a square jaw and silver-rimmed glasses, the forty-seven-year-old lived for his work. And he didn't like to waste time.

The IRS had fewer than three thousand criminal-investigative agents nationwide and they pursued some of the toughest, most complex money-laundering cases, yet they suffered from a chronic public-relations problem that had plagued them since the days of Al Capone. In that case, it was Frank Wilson, a persistent tax agent with the IRS, who'd convinced a racetrack owner to give him vital evidence to go after the famous gangster for tax fraud. But Eliot Ness with his blazing Tommy gun had got all the glory. The story hadn't changed much since. The IRS agents were always the ones with glasses in the back row in the newspaper photos behind the FBI or DEA. They'd spend painstaking months, sometimes years, collecting bank documents, business records and invoices, following the money until they had an air-tight case in federal court, only to have another agency with three times as many agents and a first-rate publicity machine sweep in to claim the victory.

Pennington was one of only a few IRS special agents who still focused exclusively on drug trafficking and money laundering. The agency had moved on from these types of cases in the 1990s, leaving them to the ever-expanding DEA. But Pennington had held out at his remote outpost in Waco. He figured, if he worked hard enough, kept making busts, he'd be left alone. And since the drug trafficking cases always brought the IRS some much-needed publicity, his plan had largely worked.

From his office in Waco, he pursued cases around Dallas and along the Interstate 35 corridor all the way south to Laredo. The major trade route linking Mexico and the United States was a rich target saturated with cash, drugs and guns, especially after the passage of the North American Free Trade Agreement, or NAFTA, in 1994, which had turned the steady drip of international trade into a torrent of tractor-trailers, trains and planes shipping cargo across the border. Among the car parts, household appliances and other goods, there was another booming billion-dollar trade in bricks of cocaine and bales of marijuana stashed in hidden compartments as the Mexicans and Colombians scrambled to keep up with demand in the States. The 'cocaine corridor', as a lot of cops called it, guaranteed that Pennington always had more work than he could handle.

Not surprisingly, Pennington had already heard about José Treviño and his unlikely rags-to-riches story through another

IRS agent, Billy Williams. Pennington often tag-teamed on cases with Williams, who worked out of the grey fortress-like federal building in Dallas. Williams had subpoenaed Treviño's bank records in Dallas, which showed a sudden and unexplainable spike in wealth. The Treviños had been on Pennington's radar for years. The Gulf Cartel and then the Zetas had controlled Nuevo Laredo for more than a decade. Most of the drugs, guns and money running up and down the I-35 corridor had been either touched or controlled by Miguel and Omar since at least 2004. They also had relatives living in the Dallas area, and their elderly mother often visited from her home in Nuevo Laredo.

As Pennington listened to Hodge try to recruit him to the FBI's investigation, he could already see the challenges ahead of them – one of the biggest being the businesses in Mexico wiring money to the US horse auctions. It was a clever move and it made it harder for them to prove that Miguel was using drug money to buy the horses through his brother. Pennington would need access to bank statements and other financial documents from the Mexican businesses to prove their case. The IRS had an attaché at the US embassy in Mexico City. In the late 1980s, the two countries had signed something called a mutual legal assistance treaty, or MLAT, which was supposed to encourage the sharing of financial documents and other information in organised-crime cases. But neither country liked to share the seized assets, which could run into tens of millions of dollars. In the past, Pennington had made a couple of MLAT requests on other drug investigations but had never got any response from Mexico.

But Pennington didn't see this as a deal breaker. Hodge had piqued his interest and the IRS had already taken a look into José's finances in Dallas. So he had one foot in the investigation already. With only a few years left to retirement, the case could be the pinnacle of his career. It would also be the most dangerous. He was well aware of Miguel Treviño's reputation for bloodshed. Still, the thought of going out at the top of his game was more appealing than biding his time with a few more middling cases until they cut him loose with a government pension. When Hodge finally took a breath, Pennington jumped in. 'Hell yeah, I'll do it,' he said.

TWENTY-SIX

AT HIS OFFICE IN WACO, PENNINGTON PORED OVER THE PURCHASE RECORDS and bank statements from the stack of boxes Lawson had given him. He could see that a company called Grupo Aduanero Integral had made at least ten money wires in the amount of $935,000 to Heritage Place after Graham bought Dashin Follies and three other horses for José Treviño. Six months later, Graham paid the remaining $100,000 balance on the horses. This was Carlos Nayen's backpack filled with cash that Lawson had told him about. Pennington noticed two other Mexican companies also wiring money for Treviño's horses: Basic Enterprises and ADT Petroservicios. The money wires from Basic Enterprises had come from Monterrey, Mexico and were associated with the horse agent Ramiro Villarreal. But by early 2010, the activity from Basic Enterprises had dried up.

He also had the BBVA Compass bank records for Francisco Colorado Cessa, the owner of ADT Petroservicios, who'd spent millions in Ruidoso. Lawson and Pérez said they still knew little about the wealthy businessman but that his company, ADT

Petroservicios, appeared to make its money from government oil contracts.

On the surface, the businesses seemed legitimate and the money looked clean. It would be his job to dig deeper until he found the truth. He would work in reverse, starting with the assets – the racehorses – and subpoena more auction houses to figure out how each horse had been purchased. He supposed there could be hundreds of racehorses from Oklahoma to California. It would be a massive undertaking.

For this he would need the help of his long-time partners Steve Junker and Brian Schutt. He'd been working with the two narcotics investigators from the Irving Police Department, in the suburbs of Dallas, for more than a decade. Unlike most cops, Schutt and Junker were willing to wade through boxes of bank records and stacks of documents as long as it paid off in the end.

Over the years, the three of them had formed the core of the Waco Treasury Task Force and were known as 'Steve P and the Two Irving Boys' in law-enforcement circles. Schutt sported a biker moustache and was the quiet sceptic, while Junker, a bodybuilder, was the extrovert. They were both workaholics with an encyclopaedic knowledge going back decades of street dealers and smugglers in the sprawling Dallas–Fort Worth metroplex. Another thing they shared was that everyone mispronounced their last names. Schutt was pronounced 'Skut', not 'Shut'. Junker had it worse. His last name was actually pronounced 'Yunker' but he'd resigned himself a long time ago to the fact that no one was ever going to get it right.

The three made an effective team. Pennington was intense and felt the weight of each investigation on his shoulders as the lead agent, while Schutt was a pragmatic sounding board and Junker would motivate the other two whenever they hit a snag. They looked forward to working with Doug Gardner. Pennington had helped the prosecutor on cases in the past but had never been through a trial with him. He admired Gardner's work ethic and he trusted that the diligent prosecutor would make sure their evidence and case were solid. Any holes and the defence would drive a spike right through their case. Pennington had discovered this the hard way during his first money-laundering trial in the 1980s, when the defence attorney had raked him over on the stand during his testimony. Unnerved, he'd felt that their case was unravelling and, by the time he stepped down from the witness stand, he was sure they'd lost. But much to his surprise, they'd prevailed. That day, he'd learned the value of having an experienced prosecutor on his side in the courtroom.

TWENTY-SEVEN

DURING THEIR MEETING WITH GARDNER, LAWSON HAD TOLD THE PROSECUTOR about the Title 3 they were working on in Laredo. Now Gardner was urging Lawson to get the wiretap done, because it could provide crucial evidence. The goal was to put a wire on Fernando Garcia's phone so they could listen in on his calls with José, Carlos Nayen and the others. But every time Pérez and the FBI's technicians were close to getting the wire up, Garcia would swap his mobile phone for a different one.

Lawson had another idea. Hathaway had been pushing him to get Graham to agree to a consensual wiretap. But so much of the case was on Graham's shoulders that he'd been overly cautious. Their meeting at the Omni when Graham had threatened to leave was still fresh in his mind. But now he knew he was going to have to push and take a chance.

Lawson phoned Graham and asked whether they could record all of his phone calls with José, Nayen and the others. He knew he'd be asking Graham to engage in yet another layer of deception as his source.

'What do you need me to do?' Graham asked with hesitation. Lawson was encouraged that he hadn't said no right away.

'We'll give you the money to buy a phone, then we'll set it up. You won't even notice that the calls are being recorded.'

Graham agreed to give it a try, which took Lawson by surprise. He thought he'd balk at the FBI's further intrusion into his life. He instructed him to go out and buy a Nextel phone, and they would set up the monitoring.

They had a wire room at the Laredo RA where agents sat day and night listening in on wiretaps. In Graham's case, since it was a consensual wire, his phone calls would be recorded and stored in a database. Whenever Lawson wanted, he could log in and listen to the recordings, marking whatever calls were pertinent for evidence. It was nearly as good as the wiretap when it came to evidence pointing to money laundering. But Lawson doubted they'd get the evidence of drug smuggling that they needed. He didn't think Nayen was going to start discussing kilos of cocaine with Tyler Graham. This would still be a hurdle they'd need to overcome.

A few days later, Graham called Lawson on his new phone. The FBI's tech team had quickly set it up. Graham wanted him to know that José had just sent another trailer of horses to Mexico. Lawson estimated he had three hours or less before it arrived on the outskirts of Laredo. Graham told him to look for a blue Ford F-250 truck hauling a white horse trailer. To make spotting the trailer even easier, he emailed Lawson a photo of the licence plate he'd taken with his mobile phone when José and the others weren't looking.

This time, Lawson asked Pérez to ride along on the surveillance. Two of the task-force officers would stake out the bridge to monitor the trailer once it entered the southbound flow of traffic into Nuevo Laredo.

They parked at the same turnout above Interstate 35 and Pérez trained her binoculars on the southbound lanes. When the driver approached, she would signal and Lawson would snap photos of the driver, then they'd follow the trailer and see whether the driver met with anyone else. While they waited, Lawson opened his can of chewing tobacco and Pérez made a face.

'Are you still doing that?' she said. 'I thought you'd given it up.'

'It helps the time pass,' he said, shrugging. They had nothing else to do but wait for the trailer.

Lawson had a girlfriend now, named Elena, whom he'd met at a nightclub, and Pérez liked to tease him about it. 'Watch out,' she warned jokingly. 'A *güero* like you, with a good job . . . she'll never let you go.'

He enjoyed spending time with Elena, he told Pérez, but he'd never fall in love. When his five years was up, he was making a clean break back to Tennessee. Pérez rolled her eyes at this. 'We'll see, we'll see,' she said knowingly. She always found his dating stories entertaining, since she spent most of her hours working or taking care of her kids at home. 'Do you know how long it's been since my husband and I went out on a date?' she said. 'God, I can't even remember.'

Lawson changed the subject to a topic that had been on his mind for a while. He wanted Pérez to work the case with him full time, since Hodge already had one foot out the door. As soon as Hodge got his transfer notice, he'd ask Villarreal if they could put her name on the case file.

'You know Hodge will be leaving soon,' Lawson said. 'Would you be co-agent on the case? I know you've got kids but I need your help.'

Pérez was looking through the binoculars at the southbound lanes of the interstate, waiting for the trailer to appear. For her, the case was also personal. As a first-generation Mexican American, she still had strong ties to her parents' homeland.

Arresting Miguel and his brothers would show her family, and other Mexicans, that there was still such a thing as justice.

She wanted to sign on to the case more than anything. Her work in Miami had never reached into the very highest levels of the cartel, where the real money was made and the orders to kill were despatched. At the root of Mexico's destruction was the money. Miguel could always replace a seized drug load and pass his losses down to the drug's consumers. But Tremor Enterprises was different. They would be targeting his money, some of his most prized assets. And that couldn't be replaced so easily.

But if she took on the investigation full time, she knew there would be sacrifices. Her youngest daughter wasn't even a year old yet. It would mean months away from home on surveillances, and meeting with Graham and the federal prosecutor in Austin, which was one reason why Hodge had been so lukewarm about the case. It would also be dangerous. Lawson would be back in Tennessee in a few years but the border was her home.

'I'll need to talk it over with Juan and Lydia first,' she said. Her husband's aunt was the one who cared for their three children while she and her husband worked. She made it possible for Pérez to put in the long hours on the squad. 'What about Villarreal?' she said. She expected she wouldn't be their boss's first choice.

'I'll talk to him,' Lawson said.

Pérez nodded but looked unconvinced. She didn't think Villarreal was going to be an easy sell. She felt like he'd had it in for her since she'd arrived. She'd made a point of never sitting out any surveillance she was asked to join and she'd gone to every callout, even when she was heavily pregnant. She was also usually one of the last to leave the squad room at night. Despite this, it seemed to her that Villarreal was often monitoring her hours at the office, even when there were guys on her squad who left early and never went on surveillance.

She'd finally called him on it one day but he'd only seemed mystified by her frustration.

'Here comes the trailer,' she said excitedly. The blue Ford and trailer were coming around the bend. Lawson radioed the others. The driver, a dark-skinned Mexican man in a white cowboy hat, was carefully sticking to the speed limit in the slow lane. Through the telephoto lens, Lawson could see that it was the same man who'd been acting as José's bodyguard in Ruidoso. Graham had said they called him Saltillo or sometimes 'El Negro' because of his dark complexion. Lawson snapped some quick photos. Then they drove off after the truck at a distance.

They expected him to keep travelling south and straight into Nuevo Laredo. But instead he took a left heading east. Pérez and Lawson followed behind and Pérez radioed to the other agents that they were on the highway that led to Hebbronville. After a few miles, they found themselves in wide-open ranch land with nothing but mesquite brush and a few trailer homes. The traffic had dwindled to almost nothing as they got further away from Laredo. Lawson slowed down so they wouldn't raise any suspicion with the driver. 'Where do you think he's going?' he asked Pérez.

'I don't know,' she said.

The truck slowed suddenly, then pulled onto a caliche road. White plumes of dust followed the trailer as it made its way down the dirt road and away from them. It would be foolish to follow because they would immediately look suspicious. So Lawson kept heading east on the highway, though it was all he could do not to put his foot on the brake. 'Damn,' he said.

Pérez craned her head around to try to get a better look at where the truck was headed. 'It looks like a ranch,' she said.

It was hard not to be disappointed. All that waiting by the

interstate and they'd come up with little other than the photos he'd snapped of the driver and the trailer. He wanted to get a closer look at the ranch. 'Shit,' he said, hitting the steering wheel.

But Pérez was more pragmatic. At least they had the photos, and that was better than nothing. *'Calmate, güero,'* she said, trying to inject a little levity into the tense mood that had entered the Chevy. 'We've got the photos. Let's go back to the office and figure out who owns the ranch.'

TWENTY-EIGHT

LAWSON'S FRUSTRATION WAS ONLY HEIGHTENED A FEW DAYS LATER WHEN he learned in an intel briefing that Ramiro Villarreal had died in an accident. There were few details but he was sure Miguel was behind it. He searched on his computer for any news reports about the accident. He didn't expect he'd find much. The Zetas had established total censorship over the media in Nuevo Laredo, killing reporters and leaving their decapitated bodies in the street with crudely lettered signs warning that the same would befall anyone who dared report on anything not sanctioned by the drug lord.

After searching for a few minutes, Lawson found a short bulletin in an online news outlet from Nuevo Laredo. The article didn't mention Villarreal by name but, because of the date, 11 March, and the location of the accident on a road that led to Monterrey on the outskirts of Nuevo Laredo, he knew it must be him. He sent the link in an email to Pérez and asked if she'd take a second look, since the article was in Spanish.

Lawson walked over to her cubicle and Pérez was already scrutinising the story on her computer.

'What do you think?' he asked.

'It says he was burned alive in his car. It was a one-vehicle accident.' Pérez raised an eyebrow.

'Yeah, just imagine?' Lawson said with sarcasm.

Pérez clicked on the photos that accompanied the article. The intensity of the fire had incinerated the interior of the Volkswagen sedan and it was nothing more than a grey husk.

'Jesus,' Lawson said. 'So Miguel made sure it was reported as a traffic accident.'

Pérez nodded. 'Looks like it.'

After he was done going through the photos with Pérez, Lawson phoned Graham to see if he'd heard about the accident. Graham sounded rattled by the news of Villarreal's death and said he'd call his friend Chevo Huitron to see if he knew anything more. Villarreal had left one of his horses at Chevo's stable and the horse trainer had been trying to reach him for weeks to collect the money he was owed.

Chevo answered after a couple of rings. He didn't sound surprised when Graham brought up Villarreal's death. 'You didn't hear?' Chevo barked into the phone. Villarreal's charred remains had been found inside a smouldering car on the outskirts of Nuevo Laredo. The newspapers had reported it as a car accident but Chevo said he had his doubts.

Graham relayed the news to Lawson. All that was left of Villarreal was a pile of ashes. Knowing what they did about Miguel and his appetite for violence, the whole set-up couldn't have looked anything but suspicious. Lawson imagined the DEA would be angry now that they'd lost their valuable informant. He would soon find out just how angry.

TWENTY-NINE

HORSE RACING IN MEXICO HAD ALWAYS HAD ITS UNDERWORLD PLAYERS BUT, in the spring of 2011, gun battles and vendetta killings threatened to destroy the industry, as the Zetas pushed deeper west into the Golden Triangle, the cradle of opium and marijuana production and a stronghold of Joaquín 'El Chapo' Guzmán, leader of the Sinaloa Cartel. In the state of Durango, the Zetas extorted race organisers and kidnapped owners of racetracks or their family members, demanding enormous ransoms and control over their businesses. At one racetrack, the owner died, some said from fear, after his two sons were kidnapped and never returned. Corpses swung from bridges – a message to anyone who dared defy the cartel. The stucco walls of police stations were sprayed with bullets from AK–47s, and others were burned to the ground. At night, families slept on the floor to avoid stray bullets from the gun battles between the Sinaloa and Zeta gunmen. Durango had not seen such violence in nearly a century, not since the Mexican Revolution.

Miguel and Omar held races in the Zetas' new territory at ranches commandeered by the cartel. They also took over public racetracks for special occasions like Miguel's birthday. Top cartel leaders and their associates attended a race in his honour at the La Cañada racetrack in Saltillo, Coahuila. Miguel sat near the finish line surrounded by his bodyguards bristling with AK-47s and AR-15s. Bets ran into the millions.

One rancher from Monterrey was foolish enough to let his horse win against Miguel's. Afterwards, Miguel offered to buy his horse but the man refused. A few days later, his stables were attacked, the man killed and his horses seized by Miguel's gunmen. When the unfortunate rancher's family gathered for his funeral a few days later, the gunmen returned, killing everyone at the man's grave. After that, Miguel never lost another race.

Jockeys and others who had legal residency in the United States or could get a tourist visa fled to *el norte* to wait out the bloodshed. Others without papers, in desperation, paid a human smuggler to get them across the border to safety.

Mexico's misfortune benefited the struggling US quarter-horse industry as talented trainers, jockeys and horse owners fled, looking for a fairer, less deadly playing field. But now the Zetas were making their presence known in the United States too. It was already an open secret that they kept horses at racetracks throughout the American Southwest. The Zetas were so feared that the Mexican jockeys, grooms and hot walkers, who cooled off the horses after their runs, would only refer to them as *la última letra*, the last letter.

So it was a lucky break when Lawson got word that a Mexican man who'd recently started working for José's racing operation wanted to talk. The man had phoned a sheriff's office in New Mexico, saying he had information about some shady cartel business going on at the racetracks. At first the sheriff had been unsure about what to do with the caller's tip but then he'd checked the deconfliction database and, to his relief, saw that the FBI in Texas had already opened an investigation.

The sheriff passed on the man's contact information to Lawson. Since the potential source was a Spanish speaker, Pérez set up the meeting. By now, Lawson and Pérez had fallen into a familiar routine. Lawson worked with Graham and other Anglos in the business, while Pérez gathered information from their Spanish-speaking sources.

About twenty minutes into their meeting, Pérez could already tell that the man's information was legitimate. Everything he told her checked out with what they already knew about José's network. But the man was a bundle of nerves, sweating and sometimes speaking in a whisper. He was sure the Zetas would find out about his meeting with the FBI. He was from Mexico, he told her, and he knew what the Zetas were capable of. With its billions, the cartel could buy total impunity. They could kill anyone, torch houses and businesses, and the authorities would do nothing.

She tried to assure him that in the United States it was different. The cartel did not enjoy the same freedom it did in Mexico. 'They could kill you too,' the man said, wringing his hands. Still, he said, he felt compelled to do something. That was why he had called the sheriff. Pérez asked if he would agree to have his phone calls recorded by the FBI. They could also speak by phone regularly and he could keep her apprised of José's plans. After some hesitation, the man finally agreed.

Pérez gave her new source the code name 'Parlay'. From inside José's operation, he'd be able to provide her with invaluable information that not even Tyler Graham was privy to. There would be very little he wouldn't hear or see at the racetrack on the backside, where the horses were kept in long rows of stalls called shed rows and trained to race.

From talking to others in the industry, she'd learned that men like Parlay lived difficult, cloistered lives, sleeping in drafty tack rooms in the horse barns or crumbling dormitory buildings on the backside. The grooms, hot walkers and exercise riders were crucial to the racing industry but they often lived on poverty wages, sometimes working seven days a week. Isolated and their bodies crippled from bone-shattering kicks and spills on the track, they relied on the bottle, drugs and whatever faith they had to keep working.

Most of the denizens of the backside were men and, like her new source, immigrants from Mexico who closely followed the news from home. Quarter-horse racing in Mexico was a small world, just like in the United States, where rumours travelled quickly. Everyone knew the stables owned by the men with too much money, flashy women and cars, and no honest explanation for their wealth.

Pérez would have to work diligently to keep Parlay from losing his nerve, which she knew would be difficult. For someone with relatives still in Mexico, speaking against the Zetas could be a death sentence, not only for her source, but for his family as well. As they spoke, Pérez could see real fear in the man's eyes and couldn't help but share some of it for herself and her own family.

THIRTY

ONCE PENNINGTON AND THE WACO TREASURY TASK FORCE JOINED UP WITH THE investigation, everything fell into place. They had a federal prosecutor signed on, and Lawson, Hodge and Pérez had even got a visit from Armando Fernandez, the special agent in charge from the San Antonio headquarters, which oversaw their smaller regional office. This meant the Treviño case was finally becoming something bigger in the eyes of their bosses in San Antonio and Washington, and they were now starting to pay close attention. It was a lot of pressure for the two younger agents, who were determined not to disappoint them.

In April 2011, Doug Gardner called a meeting at his office in Austin. The federal prosecutor wanted to go over their next steps and probe for any weaknesses in the investigation.

Lawson and Pérez had been scrambling to get more proactive evidence, setting up surveillances and collecting information from sources. Lawson told Gardner and the rest of the agents seated around the conference table the good news about the consensual wiretap on Graham's phone. The recordings were already providing valuable information about Nayen's and

Garcia's activities. They still didn't hear as much as they'd like from José, however, who mostly left the day-to-day operations with Graham up to his two younger associates. José had been especially tough to monitor. He rarely spent more than one night in the same hotel and switched out his mobile phone every couple of weeks. Pérez explained their difficulties in setting up the Title 3. Without the wiretap, it would be difficult to gather the evidence they needed to link the drug proceeds to the purchase of the horses.

Pennington, sitting next to Brian Schutt at the conference table, listened to the two younger agents run through what they had for Gardner, and understood the difficulties before them. They would need to prove to a jury that the businessmen involved knew beyond a reasonable doubt that they were laundering Miguel's drug money. Most federal prosecutors practically wanted to see the kilos of coke piled up on the courtroom table to feel they could overcome that hurdle.

He suspected José was smart enough not to mix his racing business with his brothers' drug trafficking – at least not directly. On the surface, José's business appeared legitimate. He'd even hired an accountant and made sure to pay his taxes on time. They weren't going to find kilos of cocaine stuffed inside the horse trailers at Tremor Enterprises.

Pennington had a solution. 'Why don't we do a historical money-laundering case?' This wasn't official terminology, just a term Pennington had come up with on his own to describe his more unusual approach.

Lawson had no idea what the older agent was talking about. But Gardner looked intrigued. 'That might be a possibility,' he said, mulling it over.

'What's a possibility?' Lawson asked. He was waiting for someone to fill him in.

If the idea had come from anyone other than Pennington, Gardner probably would have passed. But the prosecutor was well aware of Pennington's reputation as a seasoned investigator with knowledge of drug busts and dealers that went back nearly three decades.

Over the years, Pennington, Schutt and Junker had arrested a lot of money couriers and smugglers who had worked for the Treviños. 'We have all of these past cases,' Pennington explained. 'What's done is done. It's a fact.' Why not take the evidence from some of those other cases and use it to bolster their own evidence showing the link between the cocaine proceeds and the horses? The documents would help illustrate how the brothers had been invested in smuggling drugs, money and guns up and down the cocaine corridor for years. It would be tedious and time-consuming to dig up all the former cases and the salient evidence, Pennington said, but that was their specialty.

'Let's do it,' Gardner said. The way he saw it, they had the best of both worlds. Pérez and Lawson would work the proactive evidence – the surveillance, the informants and the consensual wiretap – while Pennington and his task force would weave in the history of the Treviño brothers' drug running and money laundering with the current facts of the case.

It wouldn't be easy. And the team knew they needed to move quickly. One informant, Ramiro Villarreal, was already dead. Miguel and Omar wouldn't hesitate to kill another, even in Texas. If Tyler Graham were found out, he'd be next on their list. Most cartel leaders avoided doing hits in the United States because the fallout was too heavy. But Miguel didn't have a problem sending his *sicarios* across the river. He'd done it before and there was no reason why he wouldn't do it again.

AFTER THE MEETING in Austin, Lawson was feeling energised. The investigation was picking up momentum now and he was further encouraged when Pérez told him there had been a development in the Garcia kidnapping case.

'Good news,' she said, ducking into his cubicle. 'Our source called from Zapata. She says our target is coming across tomorrow.'

Lawson put down his pen. 'It's about time,' he said. He wanted nothing more than to see the Garcia brothers' killer be put away. In the past months, he'd watched his neighbour's world unravel. Her husband had been the breadwinner and now she was struggling to hold on to their home. About a week after he'd panicked, thinking she was following him, she'd realised they lived two doors down from one another. One day, she knocked on his door in tears, asking if she could borrow a gallon of water. The city had just shut off their service. After he'd filled up her pitcher, he'd offered to show her fifteen-year-old son some moves on the basketball court to take his mind off his missing dad but he'd never gotten around to following through with it. The truth was, every time he saw the family, it tore him up.

He'd noticed that some of the other agents working kidnapping cases would make a few calls to their sources in Mexico and then tell the families there was nothing more they could do for them. They'd mark the cases down as 'pending inactive unless other leads develop' and file them away, never to be reopened. Lawson didn't know if it was because they'd been beaten down too many times already by defeat, or if they just didn't care anymore. Maybe he was naïve but he couldn't let the Garcia case go that easily. He wanted justice for the family. So did Pérez, which was another reason why he was glad they'd become partners. They often had long philosophical talks about it while at lunch or on surveillance. Whenever they were called in on the weekends because of a kidnapping, there were always agents who made excuses not to show. It made him remember his dad's warning.

Lawson got the warrant and the tech team set up the trace on the Garcia brothers' mobile phone in a matter of hours. The next afternoon, he started to get a series of emails every fifteen minutes with a latitude and longitude co-ordinate. Their target was on the move.

They got into Lawson's Chevy and Pérez punched the co-ordinates into their GPS tracker. They assumed the co-ordinates would lead them to neighbouring Zapata County, where their source lived. But they were pointed south instead. Lawson kept driving until they were two blocks from the Rio Grande. It was getting dark and Pérez wondered whether they should call for more back-up. She got the next email with another set of co-ordinates – the gunman was less than three hundred yards away now, tantalisingly close. They pulled into an H-E-B grocery store parking lot on the bluff overlooking the river.

Lawson scanned the parked cars for their target – they'd been given a rough description of what he looked like – as Pérez punched in the next set of co-ordinates.

'He's not here,' Pérez said.

Lawson felt a sinking in his gut. 'What do you mean?'

'He's there.' Pérez pointed towards the distant bluff in Mexico. Beyond the chain-link fence of the parking lot they could see the lights flickering on in the humble stucco and concrete homes as night-time fell. Lawson got out of the car and walked to the fence, staring at the tall fronds of the Carrizo cane that lined the slow-moving river down below. The waning twilight, the distant sound of Spanish pop music from one of the houses on the bluff and the dark swallows skimming over the river made him feel like he was in a dream suddenly gone sour. Pérez came up from behind and stood next to him. *'Chingao,'* she said, hitting the fence. They'd given the information about the gunman to the police in Nuevo Laredo but they'd done nothing. As long as the killer stayed south of the river, he'd go free. What would they tell the Garcias? He imagined the killer in one of those houses on the bluff watching them, his mouth curling into a smile. It was like standing next to a black hole. And there was nothing they could do about it.

THE NEXT MORNING, Lawson woke up with a hangover. He reminded himself he'd wanted to work the violent-crimes squad because there was a personal satisfaction in solving a homicide or a kidnapping. You caught your suspect, closed the case and moved on to the next one. And another bad guy was off the streets. But now with the Garcia kidnapping and his other cases along the border, he was beginning to realise it wasn't that simple. In the righteous evangelical faith his mother had brought him up in, bad people were always punished and good people rewarded. But in real life, it didn't always turn out that way. His dad, he supposed, in one way or another, had been trying to teach him this all his life.

Lawson poured himself a cup of black coffee in the break room. His mobile phone wouldn't power up, so he left it with a tech person at the office and went down to the federal courthouse to see about another case. When he got back two hours later, the phone was sitting on his desk. He sat down and turned it on; there were thirteen messages from his older half-brother, Chad. A feeling of dread coursed through him as he listened to the first one. His brother sounded despondent. 'It's Dad. They're doing CPR on him right now.'

Then the next message: 'He's on a Life Flight to Jackson. We'll be at the ER.'

Time seemed to slow as Lawson listened to message after

message from his brother, each more desperate than the last. 'Where the hell are you?' his brother pleaded in his final call.

He phoned his brother but it went immediately to voice mail. He left a message that he was on his way and then threw the mobile phone down on his desk. A sudden torrent of emotion overtook him. He put his head down on his desk and wept. He didn't know how much time had passed before he felt Pérez's hands on his shoulders.

'Are you okay?' she asked, sounding worried. 'I've got to go,' he said. 'It's my dad.'

'I'll drive you to the airport,' she said. After Lawson told Villarreal what had happened, he quickly gathered his things and headed for the door. Perdomo and the other agents peered around their desks, looking concerned, as they watched him leave with Pérez. At his house, Lawson quickly threw a few things into a duffel bag, then Pérez drove him to the airport. On the way, he beat himself up over missing his brother's calls earlier in the day. 'What if my dad's gone by the time I get there?' he asked Pérez.

By the time Lawson got to the hospital in Jackson, it was nearly midnight. He was relieved to find that his father was still alive. His brother filled him in on everything that had happened. His dad had been with his business partner – they'd recently opened a bail-bond business – when he'd suddenly doubled over from a massive heart attack. Now he was in a coma in the ICU. He was only fifty-eight but he'd lived a hard life. The prognosis for his recovery was not good. Now that Lawson was there at his father's side, he wasn't going to let him out of his sight. He remembered their emotional parting in San Antonio only a few months ago and wondered now if his dad had known then that it would be their last.

PÉREZ WOULD HAVE TO work the case without Lawson. She had no idea when he might be back but she was determined to give him as much time as he needed. 'We've got this,' she'd assured him over the phone when he'd called her after his first night at the hospital. 'The important thing is you spend time with your dad.'

She knew what he was going through. She'd lost her father her first year in the FBI, when she was struggling as a rookie in Miami. Unlike Lawson, her dad had never wanted her to join the bureau. He had hoped she'd become a nurse or a teacher – something less dangerous and closer to home. She'd never felt so alone as when she'd got the call in Miami that her father had died. She'd been far from home and never had the chance to say goodbye. Now she was going to do everything she could to reassure Lawson that the investigation wouldn't lose momentum while he was in Tennessee, so he could be with his father.

Fortunately, her new source, Parlay, was turning out to be as invaluable as she had hoped. Now she could corroborate information from Graham about José's plans and better track the day-to-day activities of Nayen, Garcia and the others. But he was growing increasingly unpredictable. They talked nearly every day and it would sometimes take hours on the phone to calm his fears. His moods cycled between total despair that he would be killed and braggadocio about his work with the US government. She was worried about his deteriorating state of mind.

THIRTY-ONE

STEVE PENNINGTON HAD MADE THE TREVIÑO CASE A PRIORITY FOR HIS TASK force. He and Billy Williams, his Dallas counterpart, went through their list of suspects and split it down the middle. Williams would look into Fernando Garcia and Felipe Quintero, a California-based horse trainer who had helped train Mr. Piloto for the All American Futurity, as well as the young Raúl Ramirez, the younger brother of Esgar Ramirez, the well-known jockey who had ridden Mr. Piloto to victory. Ramirez had been one of the teenagers who'd signed the bidding tickets for the horses at the Ruidoso auction. Williams would also look into Tempting Dash's trainer, Chevo Huitron. Pennington would delve into their suspects from Mexico, including Carlos Nayen, José Treviño and his brothers, Alejandro Barradas, Alfonso del Rayo and Francisco Colorado Cessa.

The two agents got to work sending subpoenas to US banks requesting deposit slips, wire transaction records and cancelled cheques. Their goal was to trace how Treviño's network spent their money and, more important, link it back to the Zetas' cocaine trade.

Pennington would need his long-time partners Junker and Schutt to subpoena the dozens of auction houses and racetracks across the Southwest and in California to start tracing all of the horses. But when he phoned the two Irving cops, he was sideswiped by unexpected news. Junker wouldn't be working the investigation. It was a blow to Pennington, who'd relied on Junker's expertise for years.

The long-time narcotics investigator explained to his friend that at least six teenagers' bodies had been dumped in recent months around Irving. The kids, predominantly Latino and from broken homes, had died from drug overdoses. No one on the police force appeared willing to pursue the cases except Junker. Dallas was a major hub for drug shipments, and its dealers were known for their mercenary entrepreneurialism, mixing American pharmaceuticals with illicit drugs from the Zetas and other cartels into highly addictive and deadly concoctions. One popular product was heroin cut with Tylenol PM, which they called 'cheese'. Junker was determined to find the dealer who had killed these kids. He promised Pennington he'd still serve as back-up on any raids or arrests.

This was some consolation for Pennington. He was also relieved to hear that the two cops had a candidate for Junker's replacement – their younger protégée, Kim Williams. Just thirty-two, Williams had already worked vice and narcotics for nearly a decade. Schutt and Junker had taken her on as their pupil. They called her 'Kimmie' and her playful nickname for Schutt was 'old fucker', which always made him smile. She would be the first woman to work on the Waco Treasury Task Force since it had been formed in 1998.

Williams had another talent that made her uniquely qualified to work on the case. She was an experienced horsewoman who had ridden quarter horses in rodeos in and around Austin as a girl. Schutt had also grown up riding quarter horses on a South Dakota farm.

Schutt and Kim Williams were the only members of the task force looking forward to spending time around stables and horse auctions. Pennington had worked hard to put his Oklahoma farming days behind him and now found it ironic that he'd be spending the next several months mucking around horse barns.

After meeting with Pennington in Waco, Schutt and Kim Williams got to work serving subpoenas to at least a dozen horse auctions and the headquarters of the American Quarter Horse Association, in Amarillo, Texas, which also kept breeding records and other documents for the industry.

But Pennington knew they still needed more. They needed help from the authorities in Mexico. So through the IRS attaché at the US embassy in Mexico City, he submitted MLAT requests for bank documents on Francisco Colorado, Alejandro Barradas and Miguel and Omar Treviño. He hoped that, this time, he might get lucky.

TWO WEEKS AFTER LAWSON had rushed home to Tennessee, his father passed away. He'd never come out of the coma but at least Lawson had been able to say goodbye. He had sat by his bedside and held his hand until he was gone. Even though he'd watched his father die, he still found his death hard to accept. They hadn't lived together since he was a toddler but his dad had remained a central presence in his life. Lawson still expected to pick up his phone and hear the familiar rasp of his dad's voice, as he passed along a joke or a piece of wisdom from his years on the force. Two weeks after the funeral, he returned to Laredo. Pérez and Hodge tried to give him some time alone but the only thing he could think to do was to immerse himself in the investigation once again. He told Pérez it was what his dad would have wanted him to do.

THIRTY-TWO

TYLER GRAHAM HAD WORKED EVERY ANGLE WITH THE TEXAS ANIMAL HEALTH Commission to make sure that Tempting Dash could be bred despite the quarantine. And he'd finally convinced José to ship him back to his farm. Besides Tempting Dash, he now also had the All American winner, Mr. Piloto, and the two champions were drawing the prestige to his farm that he had always hoped for. But so far, there'd been little in the way of money. The two prized stallions were making tens of thousands of dollars in stud fees for José, which Graham was tallying for him. But José would put none of that money towards the rapidly growing bill for boarding, feed and other costs, which had now topped $670,000.

A devastating drought in the summer of 2011 only compounded Graham's problems. Each day was another scorching hundred-degree assault on his farm, and the once green pastures had baked into a fine brown dust. Desperate ranchers had started buying hay and alfalfa from as far away as South Dakota in an effort to save their livestock. Some were abandoning their cattle and horses to die, unable to pay the exorbitant prices for feed. Costs to care for José's horses kept climbing and Graham was running out of money and patience. He needed José to pay his bill.

But Graham hadn't seen Carlos Nayen in several months. Fernando Garcia called to check up on some of their mares at the farm and Graham couldn't help but vent all of his frustrations about their mounting debt.

'What do you think your schedule is on your little brother to start shovelling some money in here?' Graham said, using the nickname they'd given Nayen. They also called him 'Mr Shoes' or 'Mr Pink', mocking his vanity about his clothes.

'He hasn't shown with any money yet?' Garcia said, surprised. 'Zero,' Graham said.

'What the hell? I haven't talked to him in a week. I've only talked to Victor.'

'Yeah. Well, I talked to Victor too,' Graham said. 'Like I told Victor the other day, I'm not in any rush for you all to pick up horses or anything like that, but I'm starting to get pretty far out there. I'm needing to pay some bills myself, you know. Hell, I just bought $70,000 worth of alfalfa, you know.'

'Seventy thousand dollars' worth of alfalfa . . . Man, how many bales is that?'

'Ten eighteen-wheelers.'

'Damn, that's a shitload of alfalfa,' Garcia said.

'Yeah but, when you've got this many horses around here and it's so dry, I got to have it.'

THIRTY-THREE

WHEN ALFONSO DEL RAYO HAD WATCHED CARLOS NAYEN WALK AWAY AT RETAMA Park, he'd hoped it would be for the last time. He'd done what he'd asked and paid the $310,000 to Heritage Place. But a few months after the auction, Nayen called him again. 'Things are bad,' he told del Rayo. 'I need ten million pesos, fast.'

'I don't have that kind of money. I need time,' del Rayo protested. Apparently, this wasn't what Nayen had wanted to hear. The next day, a stranger phoned him and said that, if he didn't come up with the money soon, he and his family would be killed.

Del Rayo phoned Nayen to complain about the anonymous threat. 'I'm working on getting the money,' he said.

'Don't worry,' Nayen said calmly. 'Nothing is going to happen to you as long as you get me the money. I need it in cash.'

What del Rayo didn't know was that José had amassed a $670,000 bill at Graham's Southwest Stallion Station. Graham was losing patience and had told Nayen and José that he needed something, anything to go towards what had become a "monstrous" bill at his ranch.

On paper, del Rayo was wealthy, but he had very little cash on hand. He certainly didn't have ten million pesos (about $700,000 in US dollars). He put two of his properties up for sale at a reduced price in hopes they would move quickly. Meanwhile, strangers kept calling, threatening to kill him if he didn't come up with the money.

After a week of running all over hot and humid Veracruz, del Rayo gathered the ten million pesos. The whole time he was hustling, he thought of nothing but the torture he'd endured in Capitán Muñeco's safe house and what the Zetas would do to his wife and kids if he didn't give Nayen the money. At the bank, he asked for the ten million in cash and the bank teller gave him a surprised look. 'Are you sure?' she asked.

'Yes.' He nodded. 'Put it in these.' He handed over three large duffel bags.

He took the duffel bags stuffed full of cash to his office and shoved them under his desk, then quickly phoned Nayen.

'I've got the money,' he said.

'We don't need it anymore,' Nayen told him.

'What?' Del Rayo said, feeling his stomach churn. He'd just spent the last week running around Veracruz, feeling like the devil was at his heels.

'Put it back in the bank,' Nayen instructed. 'We're going to need you to wire the money to someone in Texas. We'll tell you where to send it.'

Del Rayo felt he was being pulled further into something he wanted no part of, and there was no way out. He'd seen the reach of the Zetas in Veracruz. They controlled everything from the governor's mansion down to the local police. To escape them, he would have to leave Mexico. But how could he leave his home?

IN MID-JULY, GRAHAM BROUGHT up the money again with Garcia. 'Y'all are getting me in a jam with José,' he complained. 'Just pay the bill and I'll give him his stud fees.'

'We will soon,' promised Garcia. But ten more days passed and they still hadn't paid. Garcia called Graham again. 'Did Victor tell you they were sending the money today?' Garcia asked, hopeful.

'Yeah, supposedly they're doing it through Alfonso del Rayo. It's been kind of a clusterfuck, so I don't know. I hope they figure it out today . . . they've wired money to the ranch's account I don't know how many times. I don't know what's so confusing this time.' In Veracruz, del Rayo was under intense pressure to wire the money to Graham, but it wasn't easy to wire such large amounts. There were forms to fill out, restrictions and expensive peso-to-dollar conversion fees. On 28 July, he was finally able to wire $250,000 through a Chase bank account to the Southwest Stallion Station. He sent another $300,000 less than two weeks later. All the while, he kept receiving death threats. He imagined Capitán Muñeco and his hefty lieutenant arriving any day at his home with a convoy of SUVs filled with *sicarios*.

Del Rayo was down to the last $150,000 but then his bank in Mexico flagged the wire transaction for further scrutiny, saying it looked suspicious. He explained his predicament to Nayen over the phone but Nayen seemed not to believe him. Del Rayo promised to figure out another way to get the $150,000 to Tyler Graham. He knew he needed to work fast.

BACK IN LAREDO, LAWSON had been listening to the recorded phone calls between del Rayo and Graham with growing interest. He had imagined del Rayo was just another wealthy businessman, like Francisco Colorado, who had willingly gone into business with the cartel. But something was different about del Rayo.

For one thing, in his phone calls he sounded scared, and Graham had told him about his battered appearance at Heritage Place, which del Rayo had blamed on a golfing accident. He wondered whether del Rayo wasn't such a willing player in the conspiracy after all.

In the first week of August 2011, del Rayo flew to San Antonio.

Once the plane touched down, he phoned Tyler Graham to set up a meeting so he could deliver the money in person.

Graham answered the phone right away. 'Hey, Alfonso, what's going on?'

'I want to explain to you. I need to give you three cheques. The three of them are for 50 [$50,000] each, but you're only going to be able to cash one or deposit one this week and one the next week . . .'

'Okay,' Graham said.

'I just want to make you feel comfortable and secure about the cheques,' del Rayo said, sounding stressed. 'And I want people in Mexico to also feel comfortable and not to be worried about it.'

'Well, if you want me to, I can come down there this afternoon if that makes it easier on you,' Graham offered. He'd waited long enough. The two men agreed to meet at del Rayo's home in San Antonio later in the afternoon. Graham didn't have the same concern about driving to San Antonio as he did about Laredo, which was too close to Miguel Treviño for his comfort.

THIRTY-FOUR

GONE WERE THE SCUFFED WORK BOOTS AND WORN JEANS FROM THE EARLY DAYS when José Treviño had raced Tempting Dash near Dallas. Now he wore expensively tooled cowboy boots, pressed linen shirts and a brand-new white Stetson, and spent much of his time on aeroplanes, jet-setting from the Los Alamitos racetrack in Los Angeles to Ruidoso and Dallas to watch over his expanding racing empire.

Increasingly, whenever he visited Graham's farm, he would pepper him with questions about the breeding business. But it still came as a surprise to Graham when Fernando Garcia casually mentioned in late September 2011 that José was going to open his own stud farm in Oklahoma.

Graham found it hard to believe. José had only been in the industry for less than two years and horse breeding was a science that took years to master. But by the time Graham had heard the news from Garcia, José had already purchased forty acres in Lexington, a small farming community thirty-five miles south of Oklahoma City. And he was trying to convince a neighbouring rancher to sell him sixty acres more.

The next time Graham saw José, he couldn't help but ask why he wanted to leave his farm. 'I thought we had done a good job, been profitable for you,' he said.

José conceded that his new business would be a struggle at first, but 'I want to try and do it on my own,' he told Graham, who was relieved to hear that at least José would leave Tempting Dash at his farm for the foreseeable future. Because of the stallion's blood disease, the horse was more complicated to move and board than the others. But José said he would be sending someone soon to pick up Mr. Piloto and the hundred or so other horses he had at Southwest Stallion Station. José had named his new business Zule Farms, after his wife, Zulema. And he'd already designed a cattle brand for the farm – a Z cradled in two half circles, which he had printed in gold on glossy burgundy-coloured business cards. He was in the process of moving his wife and two younger children from their tiny brick home in the Dallas suburbs to Lexington. His mother, Maria, would also live there with them. 'I feel like I'm living the American dream,' he proudly told Graham.

After José left, Graham phoned Lawson to give him the bad news. If José distanced himself from Graham, it would be disastrous for their investigation. They arranged to meet at a restaurant halfway between Elgin and Austin.

The next afternoon, Lawson and Pérez sat down at a booth at Cafe 290 to wait for Graham. With the help of Pennington and his task force, they'd been able to trace as many as two hundred horses in the Southwest and California that belonged to José. The former bricklayer was becoming more powerful by the day and rapidly dominating American quarter-horse racing. Now it looked like he was positioning himself to take over the more lucrative breeding business too. Lawson had noticed how the same insiders who had at first welcomed José's millions as a salvation for their industry were now starting to become alarmed, as they were forced to sit out auctions because of the spiralling prices that few could afford. They also wondered aloud how Tremor Enterprises, in just two years, could have won all the top races in the industry, netting more than $2.5 million, a feat not even accomplished by veteran racers after a lifetime in the sport. Drought, casino gambling and recession already threatened the beleaguered industry. José and Tremor Enterprises posed a new kind of existential threat.

Lawson spotted Graham from a distance in his familiar burgundy baseball cap. He sat down at their booth and ordered an iced tea. By now, Pérez and Graham had met a couple of times, and Lawson had already explained that Jason Hodge would be leaving Laredo soon, so Pérez had taken his place. Graham didn't seem to mind. The only thing he cared about was that the investigation wrapped up as soon as possible so he could be done with the FBI.

Graham explained what he'd learned from José about his new ranch in Oklahoma.

'Do you think he suspects you of anything?' Lawson asked.

'I don't know how he thinks he's going to run a breeding business just like that,' Graham said. He couldn't hide his annoyance with José's thinking he could just start a business like the Southwest Stallion Station, which had taken decades of expertise from his grandfather and himself to build. All of the awards and prize money were going to José's head. 'No, he sees me as his competitor now, that's what's going on.'

Pérez hoped he was right. José cutting Graham off would be nearly as bad as losing the horse breeder as a source. She still had Parlay but he was so anxious, she wasn't sure how much longer he'd hold up. 'So you're not worried he's on to you?'

'No,' Graham said. 'I've still got Tempting Dash.'

'See if you can get yourself a tour of his ranch,' Lawson suggested.

'I'll ask,' Graham said. 'But I can't make any promises.'

THIRTY-FIVE

IN SEPTEMBER 2011, JASON HODGE FINALLY RECEIVED HIS AUTHORISATION TO transfer out of the Laredo RA. He could scarcely hide his joy as he began packing up his desk. Lawson still hadn't got a sense from Villarreal on what he planned to do about Hodge's replacement. He was worried that he'd appoint someone else besides Pérez, who had already been working the case with him for several months.

At home, Pérez had talked with her husband, Juan, and his aunt Lydia, and deliberated over what to do. Signing on as co-agent would mean long hours away from home. Her husband, an accountant, knew she was excited about the case and encouraged her to do it. But ultimately, it was Lydia's approval that would matter most, since she lived with them and looked after their three kids, ages five, three and one, which was no easy task. Pérez knew she owed much to the older woman, who had been essential in helping her have both a career and a family. Without her it would have been nearly impossible to work those long hours on the violent-crimes squad. Now Pérez was asking her for even more time away.

Finally, one night after dinner, Lydia took Pérez aside. 'If you feel it's the right thing to do, then do it,' she said. 'Don't worry about the kids. I'll be here.'

With her blessing, Pérez felt a sense of relief. She knew her kids would be in good hands at home while she plunged further into the pursuit of José Treviño and his brothers.

With Pérez now fully committed to taking on the case, Lawson knocked on the door of Villarreal's office. By now, Hodge was also advocating for Pérez to replace him. All Lawson had to do was convince Villarreal. The blinds were open, as they usually were when his boss was at his desk. Villarreal motioned through the window for him to come inside.

Lawson glanced at the front-page news story in Spanish framed on the wall above Villarreal's desk. As a street agent in the 1990s, Villarreal had cracked open a major police corruption case in San Juan, Puerto Rico, his crowning achievement. Despite whatever issues Lawson had with his boss, Villarreal was an agent's agent and Lawson gave him much of the credit for putting them back on the streets, where they could do real law-enforcement work again.

Lawson sat down in the chair across from Villarreal's desk. 'What's up?' Villarreal said, looking up from a stack of papers. 'Well, Jason is transferring out of Laredo, which means we'll need another agent to sign on to the Treviño case,' Lawson said.

'Yeah, I've been thinking about that,' he said. 'What about Raúl? He's got SWAT training.'

'I was thinking Alma Pérez,' Lawson said.

Villarreal shook his head in the negative. 'She's got kids, and you need someone who's willing to do the travel.'

'She's willing. We've talked about it and she wants to do it.'

'Well,' Villarreal said, shrugging. 'The case agent knows best. It's your decision. But what about Juan? He's worked some cartel cases before. He'd be good.'

'We've already been working the case together for a few months,' Lawson said, growing annoyed that Villarreal was refusing to entertain the idea of Pérez being his co-agent.

'Well, you know best,' Villarreal said, adopting a conciliatory tone. 'But consider Raúl or Juan.'

Lawson sensed that he was being dismissed. It had been a frustrating round, with neither one of them conceding in the ring. But he wasn't about to give up yet. He knew sooner or later Villarreal would see that Pérez was the right choice.

He got up from the chair. 'Thanks for your time,' he said. Villarreal nodded and Lawson closed the door behind him. Pérez's desk was in view of Villarreal's office. Lawson wondered if she'd been able to tell that the conversation hadn't gone well.

'How did it go?' she asked, looking doubtful.

'Let's just say he didn't say no.'

'What's the big deal?' she said. 'We're already working it together anyway.'

'He'll come around,' Lawson said.

THIRTY-SIX

NOT LONG AFTER THEIR MEETING AT CAFE 290, SALTILLO ARRIVED AT GRAHAM'S farm hauling a large ten-horse trailer. He would have to make several trips to Oklahoma, since José had nearly a hundred horses at Graham's farm. Saltillo loaded the babies of Tempting Dash that were listed under Carlos Nayen as owner. Dashin Follies, the most expensive mare ever sold at Heritage Place, was owned on paper by Alejandro Barradas but Saltillo was taking the mare to José's ranch too. For Graham, it was disturbing to see Barradas's name still on the paperwork for several of the horses, since he'd heard through Chevo Huitron that the Veracruz businessman had been kidnapped months ago and never returned. José had never mentioned a word about his disappearance.

Graham hadn't been able to wrangle an invitation to José's new farm yet but Pérez and Lawson were relieved to learn that, while José was distancing himself from Graham, he wasn't severing their business relationship altogether. Continuing to work with the Graham family gave José much-needed credibility in the industry and it encouraged others to do business with Tremor Enterprises. José asked Graham whether he could have the lab equipment for his new breeding facility shipped to Graham's ranch so that Saltillo could pick it up later. In Lexington, everything was still in turmoil, José explained, as he remodelled the house and barns and built his new state-of-the-art breeding facility. As the weeks passed, cardboard boxes filled with ultrasound machines, incubators and other lab equipment began to pile up in Graham's office.

Again, José asked Graham to serve as his agent at an upcoming Heritage Place auction. Graham sold four racehorses for him, including Forty Force and Number One Cartel, at the November 2011 auction. Auctiongoers were dazzled, once again, when José set a new record for a top sales price. Just like Blues Ferrari, his horse Number One Cartel had sold for a price several times over what the stallion was worth. The owners of Heritage Place, including Doc Graham, were so pleased with José's record-setting prices, which would also fatten their bottom line, that they presented him with a trophy to commemorate the day. At the auction, Garcia and Nayen bought mostly breeding mares for José's new farm and the bill was close to a million dollars. By now, record-breaking had become synonymous with Tremor Enterprises.

To many in the industry, Tremor Enterprises appeared unstoppable. One of José's horses, Separate Fire, trained by the industry's top trainer, Paul Jones, would sweep the Ed Burke Million Futurity at Los Alamitos a few months later, winning the million-dollar purse.

The media covering the race couldn't help but note that José Treviño and Tremor Enterprises had now won million-dollar races in New Mexico, Texas and California, and in just two years – a remarkable feat that was rarely accomplished. José, in a black cowboy hat, posed for the cameras with his wife, Zulema, holding the crystal trophy, and reflected on his good fortune for the assembled reporters. 'We're down-to-the-ground people but this is a great moment and we will enjoy it,' he said. '. . . We feel blessed whenever we win a race.'

José could scarcely contain his pride. For decades, he'd worked ten-hour days under the hot Texas sun, earning barely enough to feed his family. Now he was a millionaire and owned his own ranch, which soon would more than double in size. He'd finally convinced his neighbour in Lexington to sell his sixty-acre farm, adjacent to José's forty acres. The property came with a three-bedroom home and three barns. José would pay close to $1 million for both of the properties. It was all part of their American dream – the ranch, the racing empire and the Treviño name synonymous with success.

AS HIS ELDER BROTHER fulfilled their legacy in America, Miguel was conquering Mexico. By the end of 2011, the Zetas controlled the eastern half of the country. The Sinaloa Cartel controlled the other half.

The Zetas, relative newcomers and without the Sinaloa's government contacts or established drug routes, were still in a position of weakness and responded with more violence. Trained in urban guerrilla tactics and counter-insurgency, they ambushed Sinaloa's gunmen, carving further into the powerful cartel's territory.

The Sinaloa Cartel responded by deploying its own armed paramilitary wing – el Cártel Jalisco Nueva Generación, which also called itself the Mata Zetas, or 'Zeta Killers'. In September 2011 in the state of Veracruz, a Zeta stronghold, two truckloads of corpses, handcuffed and partially clothed, were dumped in the middle of a busy highway during rush hour, terrifying onlookers. Nearby, a conference was being held for the country's top federal prosecutors and judiciary officials. The Mata Zetas had carved Zs into the torsos of the bodies as a warning.

Two months later, the Zetas struck back. On 23 November, three cars were set ablaze in Culiacán, the capital of the state of Sinaloa. Sixteen bodies were recovered from the smouldering vehicles, some of them handcuffed and wearing bulletproof vests. Another ten bodies were recovered from charred vehicles in two more towns nearby.

The next day, the Zetas attacked again, in the neighbouring state of Jalisco, territory of the Jalisco New Generation Cartel. The cartel left three SUVs packed with twenty-six bodies, some still with the plastic bags over their heads that had been used to asphyxiate them. The SUVs were abandoned in a major avenue in Guadalajara not far from where hundreds of celebrities and invited guests had gathered for the city's renowned international book festival. Without naming names, Sinaloa's governor told the media the bloodshed was due to a 'bitter fight among criminal groups.'

Miguel and Omar led the offensive. Only Lazcano, one of the original military founders and leader of the Zetas, held more power within the ranks of the cartel. But Miguel was growing tired of his role as second in command. In July 2011, the Mexican army captured Mamito, along with a handful of other high-level operatives. Within days of their capture, signs were hung in Zeta territory blaming Miguel for orchestrating their arrests and warning Lazcano of the 'Judas' within their ranks. Miguel, it was said, would not stop until he alone controlled the Zetas' criminal empire, which now ranged from the Texas border into Central America and as far away as Italy, where the Zetas had formed an alliance with the 'Ndrangheta, which commanded much of Europe's cocaine trade.

FRANCISCO COLORADO KNEW WELL ENOUGH that no one got close to Miguel without eventually paying for it. Shortly before the November

Heritage Place auction, he had made a panicked call in the middle of the night to Arian Jaff, the money-lender in California.

Colorado told Jaff he needed an emergency loan and begged him to come to Mexico right away. When Jaff arrived at his office in Tuxpan, Veracruz, he found the fifty-year-old Colorado unshaven, with dark circles under his eyes, and surrounded by bodyguards. He explained he was no longer able to bid on Pemex contracts because the government was looking into improprieties with his billing at ADT Petroservicios. He was also having security issues, he said. And he needed money right away.

The two worked out a one-month loan of $1.7 million at 10 per cent interest. Now Colorado had another favour to ask: could Jaff wire $773,000 to a horse auction in Oklahoma City? It was an unusual request but Jaff agreed to wire the money. With Colorado's business faltering, he'd no longer be of use to Miguel. Alejandro Barradas was already dead; so was Ramiro Villarreal. The Mexican front men for Miguel's ambitious money-laundering scheme in the United States were starting to fall as fast as the cartel's foot soldiers.

THIRTY-SEVEN

PENNINGTON THOUGHT OF EVERY INVESTIGATION HE WORKED AS A PUZZLE. AFTER twenty-five years, he still relished putting together the pieces and unravelling the conspiracy. He'd devoted his entire career to uncovering what the human mind was capable of when it came to washing clean one's financial sins: tax havens, anonymous trusts, shell companies and bribery. His conclusion was that there was no depth a man would not sink to if there was a pile of cold, hard cash at the bottom of the deep, dark well.

Miguel had been clever in using the Mexican companies to wire the money to the US auction houses because the businesses appeared to be legitimate. Colorado and his ADT Petroservicios had tens of millions in Pemex contracts. The commingling of the dirty money with the clean made it nearly impossible to separate the two, especially if the Mexican banks didn't come through with the financial records they'd requested. So far, there'd been no answer and Pennington knew better than to expect one.

Luckily, the cocaine corridor was about to yield their biggest breakthrough yet. During a routine traffic stop, a state cop had found $462,000 in a hidden compartment inside a car. The courier was heading south towards the city of Eagle Pass. The cop, thinking it might interest Pennington, called to tell him about the incident. What got Pennington's attention immediately was that the courier was on his way to Eagle Pass, which shared a border with the city of Piedras Negras. This was Zeta territory and a stronghold of Miguel and Omar Treviño. That meant the courier worked for them.

Pennington immediately asked for the case file. Right away, he noticed that the courier's car had been recently purchased at a dealership on the north side of San Antonio. He decided to drive down and check it out himself. When he arrived at the dealership, once the car-lot owner understood that the IRS wasn't investigating his business, he was happy to pull the sales documents for the car. In a small notebook, Pennington wrote down the name of the man who had referred the courier to the sales lot. He asked the owner to check if he had any other recent sales that listed the same man as a referral. It turned out there were several.

When Pennington got back to Waco, he entered the name into the deconfliction database and saw that the DEA in San Antonio had already begun an investigation into his suspect. The officer assigned to the case was a San Antonio cop on a DEA task force. Pennington picked up the phone and arranged for a meeting. When he got to the DEA's office in San Antonio, Pennington gave the officer a summary of the money-laundering case, the Treviños and the racehorses. 'I have a feeling this guy is tied into our case somehow,' he told him.

As soon as he mentioned racehorses, the officer's eyes grew wide and he pushed back his chair from his desk. 'I've got someone else you need to meet,' he said. He grabbed the phone and quickly dialled a number.

The officer's reaction gave Pennington hope and he was not disappointed when, about an hour later, a man arrived and introduced himself as Raúl Guadalajara. He explained that, until recently, he'd worked as a drug smuggler and money courier for a man named Mario Alfonso Cuellar, known as Poncho, who was a major player in the Piedras Negras plaza. Cuellar worked for Miguel and Omar, and he was responsible for sending hundreds of tonnes of cocaine to Dallas every year. Occasionally, Guadalajara said, Cuellar had instructed him to deliver drug money to people in the United States to pay for racehorses. 'You should talk to Poncho Cuellar,' he told Pennington.

'Yeah, well, that will be tough since he's in Mexico,' Pennington said.

Guadalajara shook his head. 'No, he's not. He's here.'

'In Texas?' Pennington asked, feeling an edge of excitement. Guadalajara explained that, a few months earlier, there had been trouble in Piedras Negras with Cuellar and his crew. Miguel and Omar wanted them dead. So Cuellar and his right-hand man, a guy named Hector Moreno, had fled to Texas along with their families. Guadalajara worked for Cuellar, so he'd also fled to San Antonio to save his own life. Pennington listened with growing interest. After the informant left, Pennington immediately phoned Lawson and Pérez. 'We just got a huge break,' he told them excitedly. 'You need to get to San Antonio as soon as possible. I'll stay here tonight and wait for you.'

Pérez and Lawson drove up first thing in the morning. Pennington's excitement fuelled their expectations. They were not disappointed. The three agents met with Guadalajara once again at the DEA's office and he explained how he'd delivered money to José to pay for Miguel's racehorses. Guadalajara told them that both Cuellar and Moreno were in Dallas. They had turned themselves in to the DEA and asked for protection in exchange for information on the Treviños.

Both Lawson and Pérez realised that Cuellar was the crucial

link they had been searching for between the drug money in Mexico and José's burgeoning racing empire in the United States. It was better than a Title 3. Now they had witnesses who could testify on the stand that it was Miguel's money behind Tremor Enterprises. But first they'd need to convince the DEA to give them access.

EIGHT MONTHS AFTER THE DEATH of Ramiro Villarreal, DEA special agent Rene Amarillas and the Houston office were still trying to reassemble the pieces of their investigation. But now they had Poncho Cuellar and Hector Moreno in Dallas. Their defection was a coup for the DEA. Cuellar and Moreno were key money men in Miguel and Omar Treviño's empire. Moreno was in charge of logistics and smuggling operations for the Piedras Negras plaza where they sent across up to a tonne of cocaine every month to wholesale dealers in Dallas. Cuellar was in charge of the money, making sure the hundreds of millions in US drug proceeds got to the right people: corrupt law enforcement and military, the Colombian suppliers of the cocaine, and Miguel and Omar. They also knew all the key players within the cartel. They were highly valuable sources and the DEA was in no mood to share, especially with the FBI.

In Dallas, IRS special agent Billy Williams tried to gain access to Cuellar and Moreno through a DEA agent he often worked with but was unsuccessful. Next, Lawson and Pérez asked their boss, Villarreal, if he could appeal to the head of the Dallas DEA but he didn't get anywhere either. The team were running out of ideas. Lawson had tried to employ the patience that Pérez always preached but he felt the old frustration and doubt of his early days in Laredo. The various agencies tasked to fight the war on drugs were now fighting among themselves.

WHILE PEOPLE ABOVE THEIR pay grade argued over access to the key informants in Dallas, Pennington and his task force sifted through the growing number of financial records they had collected.

To the untrained eye, everything that José was doing would appear legal at first glance. Pennington had to give them credit. It was a fairly sophisticated operation. Obviously, Miguel and Omar had their own team of financial experts advising them.

But the task force had diagnosed a couple of weaknesses that would help them make their case. Ironically, the biggest was José. While the now forty-four-year-old bricklayer had a clean criminal record, he also had a financial history in the United States that they could access. When Williams subpoenaed the records for José's personal account at Bank of America, they could see that the family's annual household income had never topped more than $50,000. But in less than a year, they'd become millionaires.

In December 2009, José had formed his racing company, Tremor Enterprises LLC, and opened a business account with Bank of America, where he deposited the $445,000 Tempting Dash had won in Grand Prairie. There was also the $968,440 deposited after Mr. Piloto won the All American Futurity race in 2010.

In October 2011, José registered two more companies, Zule Farms LLC and 66 Land LLC, for his new breeding business in Oklahoma, and he opened two more business accounts at Bank of America. Through the diligent work of Kim Williams and Brian Schutt, who were combing through thousands of pages of horse documents, they found that at least a dozen of the mares that had been transferred to José's farm in Lexington had been paid for through money wires from Basic Enterprises in Monterrey at a cost totalling nearly $1 million.

But the curious thing was there were no cheques going out

from José's accounts to pay for any of these horses. His crew appeared to be generating new LLCs as fast as they bought horses, then passing the horses from one LLC to the next in an intricate shell game, so it looked like José only owned a few of the horses on his Lexington ranch. Ownership of the mares was listed under various names, including Carlos Nayen, who had started an LLC called Carmina, and Fernando Garcia, who had Poker Ranch.

Working with Tyler Graham, Lawson had diagnosed the brothers' other weakness. They were sitting on piles of cash in Mexico but it was no use to them until they could launder it through US banks. They treated the businessmen, Alfonso del Rayo, Francisco Colorado and Alejandro Barradas, like ATMs and they were useful for wiring large amounts of cash.

What they hadn't taken into account were the rapidly mounting expenses for everything from vets to blacksmiths for their growing number of horses. Graham would wait for months before he got paid. The money often had to be smuggled across the border by Victor López. Several of the top breeding and training facilities in the United States, including Lazy E in Oklahoma and trainer Paul Jones, were also becoming increasingly frustrated with their slow payments.

In August 2011, Lawson and Pérez had done another surveillance of Victor López – this time in the parking lot of the Mall del Norte in Laredo. López handed another undercover agent $56,000 in a plastic K-Mart shopping bag.

Through the calls between Graham and the various members of José's network that were being recorded, Lawson could see that the conspiracy was growing so large that it was becoming complicated for them to manage. Through their conversations with Graham, it seemed Nayen and Garcia were starting to have difficulties tracking the enormous number of horses they had purchased. With the help of Pennington's task force, the agents had been able to estimate that Miguel now had as many as four hundred horses boarded at racetracks and training facilities throughout Oklahoma, the Southwest and California.

THIRTY-EIGHT

IT WAS LIKE THE DEA WAS TOYING WITH THEM. THE DALLAS OFFICE WOULD agree to a day and time they could meet with Poncho Cuellar, then they'd cancel the meeting at the last minute. Five months had passed and Lawson and Pérez still hadn't been allowed to interview the man who could be so vital to their case. Lawson was anxiously searching for a solution but he knew he wouldn't be getting any help from Jeff Hathaway, not after their blow-up over Tyler Graham.

Doug Gardner finally appealed directly to his counterpart in Plano who was prosecuting the case against Cuellar and Moreno. It turned out this was the right move. Within days, the prosecutor put Gardner in touch with the men's lawyer in Dallas and they set up a meeting.

Six months after Pennington had made his breakthrough discovery in San Antonio, they finally got their interview. The DEA made it a condition, however, that one of its agents from Dallas be present during the debriefing. They also wanted to see a list of the FBI's targets in their investigation. Lawson hesitantly handed over his list, which included Carlos Nayen.

The team was eager to meet with Cuellar first, since he would possess the most knowledge about how Miguel's business was run. In mid-November 2011, Cuellar and his lawyer filed into the federal prosecutor's office in Plano and sat down at the conference table across from Lawson, Pérez, Pennington and Gardner. Cuellar, who was out on bond, was dressed in an expensive dress shirt and clean-shaven, but looked pale and tired as his lawyer introduced them one by one. A DEA agent who remained silent sat behind them with a notebook, ready to write down anything that piqued his interest.

The move by the DEA annoyed Lawson but he knew there was nothing he could do about it. Every detail of this meeting had been carefully negotiated between the two agencies beforehand. He was encouraged, however, when they learned they'd be able to speak with four more of Cuellar's workers, in addition to Hector Moreno, who had also turned themselves in to the DEA. It seemed half of the Piedras Negras plaza had fled to Texas. Once they heard what Cuellar and the others had to say, they would understand why.

Pérez found it difficult to look at Cuellar without feeling revulsion. She had something more personal she needed to ask him regarding a friend of the family who had gone missing in Piedras Negras. Veronica, in her mid-forties, was the mother of two small children and had become good friends with Pérez's aunt. When she'd graduated from the FBI academy, Veronica had given her a painted statue of an angel. 'This will guard over you and keep you safe,' she'd told Pérez. She had always liked Veronica and considered her a kind person, devoted to her family.

One afternoon in March, Veronica had driven across the bridge to Piedras Negras to pick up her young niece at the bus station. Neither one of them was ever seen again. In her own investigation, Pérez had discovered Veronica had been a friend of Cuellar's wife, who worked as a notary public in Piedras Negras. Through her sources, Pérez had learned about the massacres in the region after Cuellar and his men had fled Mexico in March. Miguel and Omar had unleashed their vengeance on anyone remotely related to the men, and Pérez feared that Veronica and her young niece had been swept up in the killing. She'd come up with few clues and now Pérez was anxious to learn what Cuellar knew about the two missing women, and if he could provide any closure to their families and her aunt, but she knew she'd have to wait until the end of their debriefing. She'd told Lawson and the others about Veronica before the meeting with Cuellar and they'd agreed on a plan. The investigation would come first and then Pérez could ask him about Veronica.

Pérez would translate for the team, since Cuellar spoke only Spanish. She began the debriefing by asking him how he'd come to work for the Zetas. Cuellar explained that, in 2007, the Zetas had begun picking up anyone involved in the drug business in his hometown of Piedras Negras. The cartel offered two choices: work for them or die.

Piedras Negras was a small city of about 150,000 residents. On the other side of the river was Eagle Pass, an even smaller Texas border town that was a convenient two-hour drive to San Antonio, a major stop on the cocaine corridor. When the Zetas picked up Cuellar, he was told that he would now work for one of their men, called Comandante Moy. One day, Cuellar called Moy for instructions but someone else answered his phone. 'Who is this?' the man barked. Cuellar gave him his name. And the man told Cuellar his name was Comandante 42.

Within a few hours, Comandante 42 pulled up to his front door in a Hummer, with another Zeta called Mamito. Let's go for a ride, 42 said. Mamito got in the backseat behind Cuellar.

As they drove around town, Cuellar knew it might be his last ride, especially when he discovered that 42 was Omar Treviño, the younger brother of Miguel Treviño. 'We have a shortfall of $750,000,' Omar told him. But Cuellar was sure he didn't owe the Zetas anything. They went to see a man called Cuno, an accountant who tracked finances for Miguel and Omar's growing empire. Cuno told Cuellar he owed $18,000.

Cuellar quickly paid the $18,000. But Omar wasn't ready to let him go just yet. They drove around town all night in a convoy, Cuellar now sandwiched between Mamito and another dead-eyed *sicario* in the backseat of 42's Hummer. Omar's convoy of *sicarios* circled the city making stops, bundling terrified men out of their homes. Stripped to their boxer shorts, they were blindfolded and handcuffed, some praying and trembling as they were shoved into the SUVs.

By morning, Cuellar said, Omar's convoy had picked up twenty people, including two of his friends. Omar said they were *contras*, men who worked for other cartels or who had tried to remain independent. They would be taken to a ranch commandeered by the Zetas, where they'd be shot. Then their bodies would be burned in fifty-five-gallon drums filled with diesel. 'By the way,' Omar said to Cuellar, 'Comandante Moy is dead. I killed him because he was stealing from me.'

Lawson was taking notes as Pérez translated. It still never failed to shock him when he heard stories like Cuellar's – and he had heard others – about how the Zetas operated so brazenly. Cuellar told them it was the horses that had saved his life. During that long night, he had listened to Mamito talk about racing bloodlines to Omar – it was nearly all he talked about. Cuellar mentioned that he owned quarter horses and liked to race. Suddenly, the taciturn *sicario* took an interest in him, quizzing him about various champions. Mamito threw out a couple of the top bloodlines –

Royal Dutch, Corona Cartel – and Cuellar nodded his head in recognition. Mamito started to relax. 'Omar,' he said, 'I think we've found someone for you.'

After that, Cuellar said, the tension in the SUV seemed to dissipate. You're safe here, Mamito told him. Nothing's going to happen to you. They dropped him in front of his house as the sun was coming up. He was lucky to be alive and glad not to be one of those men picked up by Omar's *sicarios*, begging for their lives.

About six weeks later, Omar summoned him to a safe house. He said he wanted to race some of his horses against Cuellar's. In the span of four months, they held two races and Cuellar always made sure that Omar's horses won, because he was Miguel's brother and because he was known to fly into a rage whenever his horse lost, often killing the owner of the winner. Omar seemed pleased with all of the money Cuellar was letting him win at the races. 'From now on, you're going to work for me,' he told him.

But Cuellar soon learned that Omar didn't do small-time drug loads, like he'd worked with in the past. A Zeta at his level worked in kilos and tonnes. He would give Cuellar anywhere from 250 to 500 kilos of Colombian cocaine at a time to move across the border. But Cuellar had never dealt with that kind of volume. And there was no way he could say no to Omar.

So he recruited another local dealer, Hector Moreno, to help. And they started moving the kilos in semi-trucks across the international bridge. Pretty soon, they were moving a tonne of cocaine every month to Dallas, with a street value of $30 million. In return, they received up to $5 million every week from Chicago, Dallas and San Antonio, sent back in hidden compartments inside trucks and cars by their wholesale distributors in the United States. Once they had all the money inspected and wrapped, they'd stack it in ice chests and drive it over to Miguel's accountant.

Cuellar told the agents that he didn't know why he was designated by Miguel to handle the expenses for his racing business in the States. Maybe because he understood racing, or because his cell moved the most drugs and made the most money in the Piedras Negras plaza.

'So tell us how it works, break it down for us,' Pennington said, leaning forward in his chair with anticipation as Pérez translated his question. Like Lawson, he was excited that their case was finally coming together. They now had the evidence from Mexico they'd been working so hard to obtain for so many months.

Cuellar listened closely to Pérez's translation, then nodded. Every month, he said, Carlos Nayen would present him with a spreadsheet of the monthly expenses, then Cuellar would take it to Omar, who would go over it with Miguel. After Miguel authorised the expenses, his accountant, Cuno, would withdraw the money from Miguel's cocaine and marijuana accounts. Cuellar said he'd handled about $1.5 million in 2009 and an equivalent amount in 2010. Once Nayen got the cash, he worked with Yo, his accountant in Nuevo Laredo, who would use the US dollars to buy pesos at money exchange houses, then convert the pesos back into US dollars, giving the dirty money a clean rinse before they wired it to US banks and businesses. Or they would direct Yo Yo's cousin, Victor López, to hire mules to smuggle the US dollars back across the border, or have one of their wholesalers in Texas send the funds.

Lawson could feel it all falling into place. Everything that Cuellar had told them jibed with what they'd already gathered from documents and surveillance. All those months they'd waited, Lawson thought. If he had known how valuable Cuellar truly was, he'd have been even more angry about the DEA refusing them access.

There was still one question, though, that hadn't been asked. 'Why did you leave Piedras Negras?' Pérez shot an annoyed look at Lawson. She had planned on asking Cuellar herself, since it would lead directly to questions about Veronica's disappearance.

Cuellar's face grew even paler as Pérez translated the question. His problems, he said, had begun around the time of Ramiro Villarreal's death in March, when Miguel got a tip from the Mexican military that someone in his organisation was talking to the DEA. The previous year, Miguel had made a point of showing him what would happen to traitors. Cuellar remembered the men – some just teenagers – their faces so pale, even yellow with fear as they were forced to kneel before Miguel. He shot each one of them in the head, point-blank. When Miguel had pulled out his pistol, Cuellar had instinctively turned away. And Miguel had yelled at Omar, 'Tell him to turn around and look, to stop being a fag. He has to see it.'

Omar grabbed Cuellar and violently thrust him forwards, so he'd be forced to watch the massacre. When Miguel was done, Omar shot the men and boys again for good measure. Cuellar felt ill and began to walk away from the horror show. 'So are you against us, then?' Omar said, standing in front of him. The ones who had just been executed had deserted the Zetas, he said. Cuellar assured Omar he was a loyal employee. As he walked towards his car, two pick-up trucks filled with the men's bodies passed by.

As Miguel began interrogating his closest associates, Cuellar was tasked with buying several BlackBerrys for Miguel, Omar, Lazcano and his own crew, so they could toss their other phones. Miguel preferred BlackBerrys because he could use encrypted messaging. Cuellar put Hector Moreno in charge of distributing the new phones.

But a couple of days later, something strange happened. Cuellar was instructed to send all of his cocaine back to Miguel and Omar. There would be no more shipments, they said. Miguel also wanted a meeting with him. The signs were ominous. He was unsure of what to do. Finally, Hector Moreno came forward and confessed. He told Cuellar he'd given the phone numbers from the BlackBerrys to the DEA. Cuellar called an emergency meeting and advised his crew to leave the country at once and to take their families with them. Anyone remaining would be a target.

The repercussions from the Piedras Negras crew's defection were swift and brutal. Miguel and Omar marshalled a massive convoy of hundreds of *sicarios* to lay waste to any people or property related to Cuellar and his workers. One worker, José Luis Garza, had fled with his extended family, as Cuellar had advised, but after a few days, several of his relatives had decided to return. The Zetas killed every one of them and kidnapped his father. Miguel sent Garza a taunting text message: 'Not the DEA, ICE, the army or the navy of Mexico will ever catch me. If you turn yourself in, your father will live.'

But somehow, Garza's father had gotten word to his son: 'Don't even think about coming, because they will kill you.'

For weeks, the Zetas terrorised the small towns of Allende and Nava in the Cinco Manantiales region of the state of Coahuila, where some of Cuellar's workers and their families lived. They also attacked in Piedras Negras, kidnapping people, destroying homes and businesses with bulldozers and setting them on fire. Cuellar estimated that at least a hundred people had disappeared from Nava and Allende and another two hundred from Piedras Negras. Miguel and Omar had killed their neighbours, even their gardeners and their pets. As Cuellar described the massacres to the agents, he became angrier and angrier. They had killed Hector Moreno's mother-in-law and many of Cuellar's neighbours, who were only condemned because they lived next door to him. 'They are monsters,' he said. 'They killed innocent people.' Everything that Cuellar had built for himself – the coal mine he owned, the lucrative government contracts to build schools and sporting arenas in Coahuila – they were all gone. Miguel and Omar had burned down his mansions, stolen his ranches and horses. Miguel had even instructed Carlos Nayen to take Cuellar's horses in Texas. 'Everything I had, they took it away from me.'

Lawson had heard many stories about the Zetas' brutality in briefings and from other informants but hearing about the massacres from Cuellar and the scope of the Treviños' brutality and thirst for revenge gave him pause. They will come after you too, Cuellar warned the agents.

As Pérez translated for Cuellar, her mind kept playing over Veronica and her niece being picked up by a convoy of Miguel's men, and the pain and terror they must have endured. 'I need to ask you something,' Pérez said to Cuellar suddenly. He nodded, waiting. 'There was a woman, Veronica Cardenas, she knew your wife,' Pérez said, a sick feeling growing in her stomach.

A puzzled expression played across Cuellar's face, then he shook his head. 'I don't think I know her.'

'Maybe you don't but your wife did,' Pérez pressed him. 'She disappeared in Piedras last March with her niece. They were innocent.'

Cuellar looked down at the table. 'There were many innocent people,' he said softly. 'I'm sorry. I don't know anything about your friend.'

Pérez sat back in her chair, feeling defeated. She had convinced herself that Cuellar would provide her with the missing answers. 'I'll be right back,' she said, quickly getting up from the table. She went out to the hallway and propped herself up against the wall and took a deep breath.

Lawson came out into the hallway. 'You okay?' he said, looking concerned.

'Todo bien,' she said, not looking at him.

Lawson frowned as if he didn't believe her. 'Okay, we're going to wrap it up,' he said. 'You want to stay here?'

Pérez nodded. 'You think you can manage?'

'Sí, se puede,' Lawson said, smiling.

'Thanks, Scotty,' she said. 'I just need a moment.'

After the interview, Pérez was exhausted and had a headache. She went back to her hotel room to try to rest. For her, the interview had cut deeply, not only because of Veronica, but also because Piedras Negras was her father's hometown. He had always been proud of where he'd come from and now she knew that everything he'd loved was gone. If he were still alive, it would have broken his heart. As she lay back on her pillow and closed her eyes, the horrific scenes from the massacres that Cuellar had so vividly described played over and over in her mind.

The next morning, the three agents and Gardner met at the prosecutor's office again – this time with José Luis Vasquez Jr, a wholesale coke dealer in Dallas, who'd also turned himself in. It would emerge that Vasquez had also passed along the BlackBerry numbers to the DEA.

Since Vasquez was based in Texas, Lawson hoped he'd have first-hand testimony about cocaine money being sent directly to José. Listening to Vasquez, who didn't need a translator, tell his story was an eye-opening education about their multi-million-dollar business. Vasquez said his main point of contact in Piedras Negras was Hector Moreno, who had directed him at least eight times to send money for horse expenses, including a $150,000 delivery to José Treviño. Moreno had insisted that Vasquez send his most trusted courier and emphasised that 'it needed to be nothing but hundreds because it would be 40's brother.' To be extra cautious, Vasquez had sent his own father, who handed the shopping bag full of cash to José in a Walmart parking lot near Dallas.

Lawson traded a knowing look with Pérez and wrote the details of the money drop down in his notebook. Pérez was relieved not to have to translate. She was still recovering from the trauma of the day before. At least the information Vasquez had just shared with them was starting to improve her spirits. What Vasquez had to tell them next was even more enlightening, especially for Lawson, who had been at the All American when Mr. Piloto had won despite the long odds.

Vasquez said he was directed to send $110,000 to New Mexico. In Dallas, he stuffed the bribe money inside a pressure cooker and had a courier drive it to Carlos Nayen in Ruidoso. Apparently, Nayen had struck up an arrangement with the eleven gate starters, paying them $10,000 a piece on Miguel's instructions. When the starting gate flew open, each man, with the exception of Mr. Piloto's gate starter, had held back his horse just a fraction of a second. The timing was so quick – just a blink of an eye – it was nearly undetectable, even to the racing stewards who would analyse the footage later. In a race that could be over in twenty seconds, every fraction of a second made a difference. Miguel had always been unusually focused when it came to something he wanted. He had wanted Mr. Piloto to win the All American and he'd made sure it happened.

The debriefings went late into the evening over two days, as the agents and Gardner interviewed Cuellar and his men. The team were worn out from the long days but also elated. They now had the other side of the story from Mexico. Not only had Cuellar, Vasquez and the others told them how much drug money they received from Dallas, but they'd also discussed where the money went and how much of it they'd sent to Carlos Nayen and José. The men had given them invaluable first-hand information, which meant they had conclusive evidence that Miguel was laundering his drug money through his brother's racing business, Tremor Enterprises.

Cuellar's warning about Miguel reminded Pennington once again of the danger involved in prosecuting José and his men. He still hadn't forgiven himself for a Dallas police officer getting shot during one of his previous investigations. The officer had nearly died. In hindsight, there wasn't much he could have done to prevent it but he still felt responsible because he'd written the arrest warrant and sent the lieutenant out to knock on the door. He didn't want anyone dying under his watch. He also couldn't help but think about his own safety. He didn't go anywhere unarmed. Going after federal agents on US soil was a suicidal move that most cartels wouldn't even consider. But the Zetas had killed a US federal agent in Mexico already, so he imagined they were more than willing to cross that line.

THIRTY-NINE

WHEN LAWSON AND PÉREZ RETURNED TO LAREDO, VILLARREAL CALLED THEM into his office and asked for an update on the interviews in Plano. Lawson told him about their breakthrough with Poncho Cuellar and his cell from Piedras Negras. They'd made that crucial link between the drug money in Mexico and José and Tremor Enterprises. The men could testify at trial about their direct involvement in the conspiracy.

'Are they willing to testify?' Villarreal asked.

'I think so, as long as they can stay in the United States,' Pérez said.

Villarreal nodded. He was well acquainted with the delicate negotiations over co-operation in exchange for protection. In Laredo, they often had a difficult time getting anyone to testify against the Zetas in court. But if the trial were in Austin, they would have an easier time convincing them.

'I've got good news,' Villarreal said.

Lawson and Pérez sat up a little straighter in their chairs. It wasn't very often they heard those words come from Villarreal's lips.

'I'm putting you both on the case full time.'

'Hey, that's great,' Lawson said, glancing at Pérez, who smiled. 'The way I look at it, we've got ourselves a Big Mac,' Villarreal said, sitting back in his chair and relishing the moment. He was famous around the office for comparing their cases to fast-food orders from McDonald's. 'In Laredo, we do a lot of shakes and fries but we don't get enough Big Macs. I want you two focused entirely on this case from now on.'

'You got it, Boss,' Lawson said, grinning. It was funny, he thought. Villarreal had never officially given his endorsement to Pérez signing on as co-agent. They'd just kept on working the case together as they had done for months. He figured this was their boss's way of finally sanctioning the partnership and, not only that, he was allowing them to focus solely on this one investigation, which didn't happen often in a small border office inundated with work. They left Villarreal's office with a renewed sense of purpose. Pérez called it their 'Big Mac blessing'.

Almost two years had passed since he'd met Tyler Graham and started working the investigation. Now for the first time, it felt like everything was coming together – Pennington and his team were making progress on the financial end and Lawson and Pérez had a wealth of evidence from sources and the surveillance they'd been conducting over the past two years on José, Victor López, Carlos Nayen and the others. They were feeling hopeful. They should have known it wouldn't last.

FORTY

THE INVESTIGATION HAD FINALLY FALLEN INTO PLACE. VILLARREAL WAS GIVING
them the freedom to focus all of their energy and resources on
José Treviño and Tremor Enterprises. Lawson was feeling upbeat
as he entered the federal courthouse in downtown Laredo. It was
Valentine's Day 2012 and his love life was also on the upswing.
Spending time with Elena and her family, he'd begun to embrace
life on the border – the good food and the close-knit Mexican
American families. He was actually starting to like Laredo, much
to Pérez's amusement.

Leaving the courthouse, he ran into Ed O'Dwyer, an agent
with Immigration and Customs Enforcement who was also an
out-of-state transplant. They had gone out for beers several times
and Lawson had considered him a friend. But a few months
earlier, they'd had a disagreement when Lawson discovered that
O'Dwyer had been investigating Victor López and had had to
tell him to back off.

O'Dwyer, who worked the international bridges, had
questioned three Mexican women, each carrying $9,900 hidden
in plastic shopping bags, who had tipped him off to Victor

López. Afterwards, he started occasionally pulling López in for questioning on the bridge and building a case for bulk cash smuggling. López was José's main money courier and the FBI had already been watching him for several months. O'Dwyer sniffing around could jeopardise everything. So Lawson had gone to his office to explain that they were working something big with the IRS, which involved López, and had asked him to let it go. He tried to convince O'Dwyer to join them in their investigation but O'Dwyer's supervisor was against it. Lawson assumed O'Dwyer had dropped his pursuit of López after their meeting. So when he saw him leaving the courthouse, he was sympathetic. He knew how it felt to be muscled out of an investigation. 'What's new?' he asked good-naturedly.

O'Dwyer's face turned pale. 'We need to talk,' he said hesitantly. 'Why don't we get something to eat?'

They walked over to a hole-in-the-wall Mexican restaurant not far from the courthouse. Lawson felt a cold sweat coming on, even though it was a balmy morning. He didn't feel like eating. He had a bad feeling. O'Dwyer tried to make small talk as they sat down and ordered their food.

Finally, he got to the point. 'We're having Victor López stopped today in Oklahoma City.'

'Oh shit,' Lawson said. 'You're serious?'

O'Dwyer nodded. 'Yeah.'

Lawson felt like punching him in the face. If they pulled over Victor López in Oklahoma, José would immediately find out. The worst of it was that O'Dwyer didn't even know about José Treviño or who he was. Lawson had only told the ICE agent that he was working an OCDETF case, it had taken years, and López was an important part of it.

Lawson didn't know what to say. O'Dwyer explained that he'd never given up on López after their talk. Instead, he'd established a system to notify him whenever López boarded a flight. Lawson had to give him credit for his persistence. At this moment, O'Dwyer said, López was on a plane to Oklahoma City and would be returning to Laredo that same day. When he touched down at the Oklahoma City airport, O'Dwyer was going to have him followed by the local police and find out what he was up to. And on the way back, during his layover in the Dallas airport, he'd have López pulled aside for questioning. He was turning up the heat.

'I just didn't want to give up the target,' O'Dwyer said apologetically. As the waiter put down the plate of chicken tacos in front of him, Lawson pushed back his chair. He'd completely lost his appetite. He put some money on the table. It was out of his hands. There was nothing he could do about O'Dwyer and the traffic stop.

'Could you update me after you do the stop?' he asked.

'Yeah, no problem,' O'Dwyer said. 'I'll call you.'

Valentine's Day was getting off to a bad start. Now he'd have to share the news with Pérez and Pennington that their investigation could be blown by evening. He hoped the rest of the team could see a brighter side to what was about to unfold, because he couldn't.

Lawson had an anxious night. And when O'Dwyer got back to him the next morning, it was worse than he had imagined. López had briefly met José in the airport parking lot, then gone back to the terminal for his flight. Afterwards, an Oklahoma City traffic cop pulled over José's truck eight miles from the airport. The cops had no idea who he was – their target was López and they were just collecting evidence for O'Dwyer, trying to find out whom López was delivering the cash to. The Oklahoma cops, as well as undercover HSI agents, held José in the back of a squad car while they searched his truck with a drug-sniffing dog. José was travelling with a Mexican horse trainer and he told the agents they'd just come from the nearby Remington Park racetrack. He was helping the trainer get a licence to race in the States, he said.

José was carrying $5,000, which was a lot of cash but not a crime. The cops photographed him, dressed in an ordinary plaid shirt and stocking cap and wearing his glasses, in the back seat of the squad car holding the money. José was obliging but said little. If anything, he was too calm, the police said, not questioning why there were eight officers, some of them from HSI, milling around his truck after he'd been pulled over for a failure to signal when changing lanes, as the Oklahoma City cop had explained. He even consented to a search of his truck. After about forty-five minutes, they let him and the horse trainer drive away.

As O'Dwyer gave him the rundown on the traffic stop, Lawson tried to imagine José's next move. He may have been calm on the side of the road but he knew José would know now that the police were watching him. The traffic stop would have repercussions. Now they could only wait and see how it all played out.

FORTY-ONE

BOTH PENNINGTON AND PÉREZ HAD COUNSELLED LAWSON NOT TO WORRY ABOUT fallout from the traffic stop in Oklahoma – not until they saw José do something out of the ordinary. Graham said he hadn't detected anything unusual in any of his dealings with José or the others. And José appeared to be increasingly consumed by the running of his new farm in Oklahoma.

But as they moved into the spring of 2012, their luck continued to sour. The DEA agent who'd been taking notes in the back of the room during their debriefings with Poncho Cuellar and his crew had taken an interest in Carlos Nayen – especially when he'd heard that Miguel had been paying Nayen with kilos of cocaine. The industrious twenty-six-year-old was selling it in Dallas for a fat profit. Now Lawson had been tipped that the DEA planned to go after Nayen with an indictment for drug smuggling and arms trafficking. He was now very much on the DEA's radar. It wasn't enough to have ICE following Victor López; now the DEA wanted Carlos Nayen.

Pérez was also having problems trying to keep her best source, Parlay, from cracking up. They talked nearly every day and she spent much of her time consoling him. Parlay kept her informed on every move José's crew made at the racetracks. He told her about Nayen and José making a big push into California, hiring veteran trainer Paul Jones and a handful of other noted trainers who worked at the Los Alamitos track near Los Angeles. News was already circulating among the insular world of the backside that the Zetas were at Los Alamitos, paying for horses with duffel bags of cash. The grooms, hot walkers and other workers on the backside – some of whom had already fled the Zetas in Mexico – had thought they'd escaped the brutal cartel. Pérez tried to keep Parlay calm and focused on their mutual goal of arresting the men. But her source had already convinced himself that he was a marked man.

One morning, he finally snapped. Dishevelled and waving a gun around in front of a San Antonio police sub-station, he claimed the Zetas had commanded him to shoot up the station. After he was disarmed – miraculously, he hadn't been shot – he'd bragged to the cops that he worked for the FBI. Pérez got a call from one of the policemen, sceptical and almost sorry to be asking whether it was true, since the man was clearly unstable. He was surprised to learn from Pérez that it was.

Now the only way to get Parlay out of jail would be to deport him, since he was her informant. So Pérez went to San Antonio and drove Parlay back to Laredo. She couldn't hide her frustration during the two-hour drive back to the border. 'I could have paid you for your work after the trial was done,' she told him. 'But now I can't. You really screwed up.' He was apologetic as they drove, saying he was sorry he'd caused her so much trouble. With a heavy heart, she watched him disappear across the bridge into Nuevo Laredo.

WHEN IT SEEMED LIKE things couldn't get much worse, Lawson was hit with more bad news – this time in an email from Bill Johnston, a DEA agent who worked upstairs. On weekends, Johnston, who was originally from Philadelphia, sometimes went out to bars and clubs with Lawson and the other young agents in their building. Jeff Hathaway had been transferred to South America and Johnston had been trying to repair some of the frayed relations between Lawson and his agency by offering to help out with the investigation where he could.

In his email, Johnston said he'd overheard that the DEA in California were going to raid the Los Alamitos racetrack that morning. They'd got a tip that Omar Treviño would be there. Lawson sat back in his chair, shocked. Then he read the email again to make sure he hadn't missed anything. But the email was brief and to the point. He pushed his chair back, then got up and quickly walked over to Pérez's desk. He could feel his panic quickly turning to anger.

'The DEA is raiding Los Alamitos. We're fucking burned,' he told Pérez, pacing around her desk. He was too alarmed to sit down.

'What?' Pérez said, incredulous, turning around in her chair. 'When did you find out?'

'I just got an email from Bill upstairs. They're looking for Oma.'

'Oh shit,' Pérez said, letting it sink in. 'What else did he say?'

'That's it,' Lawson said, still pacing back and forth. 'I'm going to call Pennington.' He strode back to his desk, looking like he might punch someone or something. When he gave Pennington the news, he had a similar response – shock, then anger. His task force had been working the case for more than a year, poring over thousands of documents, carefully constructing a trail of evidence linking the drug money with the horses. If José and the others fled to Mexico, they would be out of their reach. It would all be for nothing.

After he got off the phone with Pennington, Lawson phoned Bill Johnston. 'What in the hell's going on in California?'

Johnston said that all the information he had, he'd put in his email. The DEA was so big and so compartmentalised, he knew very little about what other offices were working on, or even other agents in his own office.

'I'll be there in fifteen minutes,' Lawson said. 'See what else you can find out.' After hanging up the phone, he returned to Pérez's cubicle.

She was searching on her computer for any breaking news reports about the raid at the racetrack. 'It won't take long before it hits the news,' she said.

'This is bad,' Lawson said, pacing again. 'I'm going upstairs to find out what the hell is going on.'

'I'll check with my sources at the track and see if they've got anything,' Pérez said, picking up her mobile phone.

By the time Lawson got to Johnston's office on the sixth floor, Johnston had already called one of their agents in Mexico who was helping advise the agents on the ground in California, but he'd told Johnston he couldn't talk until things had settled. The raid was still going down at Los Alamitos. As Lawson paced the floor around his desk, he watched Johnston dial the DEA's Santa Ana office near the racetrack, where he seemed to have better luck. When he got off the phone, Johnston relayed the update to Lawson.

'They've detained some people,' he said. 'They're going to send me photos of them when it's all over.'

Lawson sat down in a chair next to Johnston's desk. What if they detained José? His head was beginning to throb. He could see their whole case unravelling before him.

Johnston gave him an apologetic look. 'As soon as I know something, I'll let you know.'

When Lawson exited the lift to his office, he instinctively grabbed for his mobile phone. He started to dial, then stopped suddenly. He looked at the call screen, which said 'Dad', and ended the call. It made him feel even more desolate. Since he'd returned to Laredo, the grief would wash over him like this – sometimes suddenly – catching him by surprise. He paused in the hallway and tried to recollect himself.

In the office, he could tell that Pérez had already informed Villarreal about the raid. Through the window, Lawson could see him pacing around his office.

'You told him?' Lawson said.

'Yeah,' she said. 'Not good. He wants an update as soon as we've got more.'

Pérez had more bad news, she said. She'd found out that the US Marshals had got the same tip that Omar Treviño had flown into Los Angeles on a private jet, along with his bodyguards, to inspect some horses at Los Alamitos. Both agencies were at the racetrack now, pulling people aside for questioning and detaining anyone who looked suspicious for further questioning.

Omar and his brother Miguel each had a $5 million bounty. Lawson knew that neither agency could pass up the chance to arrest Omar on American soil if they thought they had a credible tip. But he was sceptical about the whole set-up.

'Do you think Omar would ever risk coming here, with every law-enforcement agency under the sun looking for him?'

'I hate to say it but I think he's smarter than that,' Pérez said. 'What if they pick up José?' Lawson asked. There was nothing they could do but wait and see, which made it even worse.

'Then we're done,' Pérez said, frowning. *'Ni modo.'*

They went to Lawson's favourite place for lunch, with the

fried chicken and gravy, but neither of them had any appetite. They scarcely touched their plates of food as they waited for Johnston's email with the photos of the people the DEA had detained. Lawson kept checking his email on his phone.

'I got it,' Lawson said excitedly. It was Johnston's email. He downloaded the attachment on his phone. He knew it would be better to wait until they got back to the office so he could download it on his computer but they couldn't wait that long.

Pérez pulled her chair closer to Lawson so she could see the mug shots. 'Oh no,' she said. The first photo was of Carlos Nayen. 'I bet the DEA in Dallas won't be happy about this either.'

'What a mess,' Lawson said, shaking his head.

'Who's that other guy with the black hair?' Pérez asked, pointing to the other mug shot.

'That's Felipe Quintero,' Lawson said. 'He's a horse trainer they hired out in California.'

'Oh, right,' Pérez said. 'He was at the All American in Ruidoso.'

Lawson nodded in the affirmative. They were both cautiously relieved not to see José in the DEA's line-up. The text of the email from Johnston said that Lawson should come to his office right away because he had more details about the raid.

As soon as they got back, they went straight to Johnston's office. The DEA agent briefed them on what he'd found out from the agents in California. As the raid had progressed, with the agents spreading out across the racetrack, people had started leaving in droves. So the DEA had set up a checkpoint in the parking lot. Everyone else leaving the stables was in jeans and T-shirts but Nayen was wearing Ralph Lauren. He also seemed unusually withdrawn, not even glancing at the photo of Omar Treviño when a DEA agent asked if he recognised the fugitive they were searching for. Nayen also had a Mexican passport, so the agent had decided to detain him for further questioning, along with Felipe Quintero, who was driving. Once Nayen was in custody, the agents asked him repeatedly whether he knew Miguel or Omar Treviño. But Nayen had played ignorant, saying he'd never heard of them. After a couple of hours, they'd let him go. Omar, of course, had never materialised.

Much to their relief, none of the agents had encountered José either. With so much law-enforcement heat on the Treviños, Lawson knew they were incredibly lucky they had made it this far. They were running out of time. Too much had gone wrong: the DEA in Dallas hunting Carlos Nayen, ICE tailing Victor López, and now the Los Alamitos raid. He'd also heard that Francisco Colorado's ranch in Veracruz had been raided by the Mexican military.

They needed to move faster. The problem was that Doug Gardner didn't feel the same urgency. 'We need to be organised and ready,' he'd say whenever an anxious Lawson pushed him on the date they'd present the evidence before the grand jury to get the indictment. 'We need more time,' Gardner would say.

FORTY-TWO

MIGUOL TREVIÑO WAS ALWAYS SUSPICIOUS BUT THE RAID AT LOS ALAMIOS fuelled his paranoia of betrayal. After the raid, Carlos Nayen received a text instructing him to return to Mexico immediately. Nayen knew that, since he'd been detained and questioned by the DEA, Miguel would now consider him a liability. He took the battery out of his BlackBerry phone and stashed it in a drawer at his condo in California. There was no way he was going back.

With Nayen off the grid and hiding out, Felipe Quintero, the California horse trainer who had been detained along with Nayen, began receiving a barrage of emails in Spanish asking about 'El Chamaco', the Kid, which was how Miguel and his brothers sometimes referred to Nayen. 'What's going on? Why aren't you all answering? People in Mexico are concerned.'

Fernando Garcia, who had not been at Los Alamitos when the raid happened, returned to the stables. He received a text from Yo Yo instructing him to drop his phones and close his Facebook and other social-media accounts, which he obeyed. He continued training José's horses for the upcoming Ed Burke Million Futurity in June, the same race that Tremor Enterprises had won the year before with its million-dollar purse. A couple of weeks after the raid, he received a phone call from José asking him to go to Mexico to meet his brother. 'He wants to talk to you,' José said.

Garcia had met Miguel once before, the previous year, when he'd driven down to Mexico with Nayen. They'd discussed the future of his racing business and how the horses were doing in the States. Garcia had always wanted to stay on the cartel's perimeter. He knew that getting too close to Miguel or Omar was dangerous, and what would happen to people who knew too much. But Nayen had convinced him to go against his better judgment.

José had always made it known to Miguel that he preferred working with Garcia over Nayen, who was always scheming, always looking for ways to feed his ambition. Garcia knew his place. Now José was doing his best to try to convince him to meet with Miguel about a promotion. With some reluctance, Garcia agreed to go.

Shortly after his talk with José, he drove to Laredo, then walked over the bridge into Mexico to meet Yo Yo. They drove around Nuevo Laredo for hours in Yo Yo's car waiting for a call from Miguel. No call came, so they went to a restaurant to wait. After a few minutes, Yo Yo excused himself and went outside. He didn't come back. Garcia got spooked. What if gunmen were on their way? What if this was all just a ruse to get him to Nuevo Laredo so Miguel could kill him, as he had so many others? Garcia bolted for the door and hailed a taxi outside to take him to the bridge, where he quickly walked back to Laredo.

Moments after he arrived, he received a text on his BlackBerry. 'I'm the guy you met in Zacatecas. Just come back again. Everything's good. We're just going to talk.' Garcia knew it was Miguel because they had met the last time in Zacatecas. What should he do now? He hadn't even turned thirty and he was training some of the most coveted racehorses in the business. He was already making a name for himself as a trainer. If he didn't meet Miguel, the horses would be taken away from him. He decided he'd take the chance.

Garcia met up with Yo Yo again in Nuevo Laredo and, this time, they went to his apartment, where Garcia left his mobile phone – anyone whom Miguel and Omar summoned would be checked for electronic devices to make sure they weren't being tracked. Then he and Yo Yo drove around Nuevo Laredo waiting for the call. After a few hours, Yo Yo got a call from a driver who would come and pick them up. When the man arrived, Garcia and Yo Yo got into the backseat of the truck. By now, it was 2am and pitch-black outside when they reached the edge of Nuevo Laredo. They took a dirt road and kept driving until Garcia saw trucks parked up ahead and dozens of armed men illuminated in the truck's headlights. Something very bad was going to happen, he thought.

The truck stopped. One of Miguel's *sicarios* opened the passenger-side door. He asked the driver for a carton of cigarettes. Garcia was trying to remain calm. The driver handed over the cigarettes while Garcia and Yo Yo waited in the backseat for whatever might happen next. The gunman turned to them. 'My *compadre* will be right over to talk to you,' he said, then disappeared. They waited.

Miguel appeared out of the darkness and slipped into the passenger seat, closing the door. 'I want you to take Carlos's place,' he said to Garcia. 'I've talked to my brother and we've decided that Carlos is no longer going to be helping us.'

Garcia nodded. At this point it would be difficult to say no. Nobody said no to Miguel. From now on Garcia would be working with José and Yo Yo would help him with the payments like he had helped Nayen, Miguel said. He would also double Garcia's salary to $10,000 a month. Garcia agreed to the deal. Just as quickly as he had arrived, Miguel was gone. The driver backed out of the field and they bumped and rattled down the dirt road to the highway. His feeling of dread was turning into relief. He was alive. And now he would be helping manage Miguel's entire horse-racing operation in the States. He never could have imagined that he'd be in control of the most coveted bloodlines in racing, millions of dollars' worth of horses. It was more than he ever could have hoped for. He was living his dream. But the dream didn't come without a price.

When Garcia met Francisco Colorado later in Ruidoso, they talked about the horses that Garcia was training for him. Colorado had flown in on his private jet and Garcia had picked him up at the airport, then they'd gone to a restaurant to talk about the business. Garcia had helped a friend of Colorado's get a horse-ownership license and open a bank account for Bonanza Racing Stables, one of the front companies they'd created. Colorado didn't want any more of the horses in his name at the auctions. In Mexico, his contracts with Pemex were under scrutiny and so was his business; he didn't want to be arrested for money laundering. He seemed unusually contemplative as they sat down to eat. His wife and youngest son were in Houston now because it wasn't safe anymore for them in Veracruz. He knew that Nayen was hiding from Miguel in California. He had raised him like his own son. 'If you take over,' he warned Garcia, 'be careful.'

JOSÉ HAD GROWN INCREASINGLY suspicious since the traffic stop in Oklahoma City. He blamed Victor López. He called Miguel and let him know about the incident near the airport and that his courier, López, was bringing heat on them. 'Something needs to be done about Victor,' he told his brother.

In Nuevo Laredo, López had become worried. The police had stopped him at the Dallas airport after his brief meeting with José in Oklahoma City and asked him several questions about where he was going and what he did for a living. The last thing he wanted was Miguel thinking he was a snitch. And he had decided the best move was to tell Miguel about what had happened in Dallas.

What López didn't know was that he was already a dead man. Miguel had ordered his execution as soon as he hung up the phone with his brother. Yo Yo, López's own cousin, was put in charge of the hit. A team of *sicarios* was ordered to find López in Nuevo Laredo and make it look like he'd died in a botched carjacking, to throw off US law enforcement. Yo Yo felt he had no choice but to follow orders. He wanted to warn López to run but it was too risky. Miguel would only learn of his betrayal and then he'd be next.

FORTY-THREE

SINCE JANUARY 2010, PENNINGTON AND HIS TASK FORCE HAD BEEN LIVING OUT of their suitcases in Austin, working late into the evening each day in a conference room at the US attorney's office they'd designated as their war room. There was nothing high-tech about the arrangement, just a long narrow room at the end of a hallway, with more than a hundred cardboard file boxes stacked inside, so that it looked like a dense forest.

Among the columns sat the team members at their makeshift desks with their laptops. In the middle were Brian Schutt and Kim Williams, who were trying to match the names of horses to the pedigree and registration documents that had been filed for each horse with the American Quarter Horse Association. They'd received dozens of boxes from the AQHA in Amarillo from a subpoena several months earlier and they were working their way through the documents to identify which horses were being held under the various straw buyers for Miguel. Each horse was then entered into a long Excel spreadsheet on their computers.

Pennington and Billy Williams were still piecing together the bank documents for José and his various associates, including

Nayen, Garcia and López. They'd discovered that thirty-five mares that had been transferred to Zule Farms in Oklahoma, including Dashin Follies, were now listed under the name of Luis Aguirre. After the transfer of the horses, José's wife, Zulema, had written Aguirre a $122,000 cheque for the breeding mares, but it had bounced. Pennington had seen the name before in other documents. It appeared that Aguirre often held horses under his name for José and his brothers.

Lawson and Pérez worked with Graham and other sources to keep watch on the various members of José's crew. After the raid at Los Alamitos and the traffic stop in Oklahoma, they were on heightened alert for anything unusual. Much to their relief, Garcia and José carried on at the Los Alamitos racetrack as if the raid had never happened. They were preparing several of their horses for the upcoming trials in early June for the Ed Burke Million Futurity. Only Carlos Nayen had changed his routine. He spent most of his time at his condo near Los Alamitos with his wife and their new-born baby but never went to the racetrack anymore. Lawson couldn't help but think of Ramiro Villarreal.

THREE WEEKS PASSED and Lawson was starting to believe they'd dodged catastrophe, when he received a phone call from one of his sources at Los Alamitos that left him cold. His source said an investigative reporter named Ginger Thompson from the *New York Times* was asking around about José Treviño and Tremor Enterprises.

Unbeknown to Lawson and the team, Thompson had received a tip about Tremor Enterprises six months earlier and, by the time Lawson was alerted, she was close to publishing. A couple of hours later, Lawson got a call from another source at the track contacted by Thompson. Lawson was perplexed. The *New York Times* reporter seemed to be calling all of the key sources in their investigation.

If her story broke in the *New York Times*, it would be the end of their investigation, as José, Nayen and the others would be on the first plane to Mexico. They were in deep trouble. And this time, they were dealing with someone outside of law enforcement with a different agenda.

Lawson strode over to Pérez's cubicle. When she saw the look on his face, she frowned.

'I don't want any more bad news,' she said, shaking her head.

'You're not going to believe this,' he said.

Pérez raised an eyebrow, an expression of dread coming over her face. 'What is it?'

'There's a reporter from the *New York Times* sniffing around Los Alamitos,' Lawson said. 'She's talking to everyone. She knows all about José and Tremor Enterprises.'

'When is she going to publish?'

'I've got no idea,' Lawson said, pacing. He was starting to take all of the bad luck personally.

'*Chingao,*' Pérez said, sitting back in her chair. 'She can't publish that story. Not till we make the arrests.'

'I know,' Lawson said. 'Maybe we should talk to her?'

'Agents can't just talk to reporters,' Pérez said.

'Well, someone needs to,' Lawson said. He glanced over at Villarreal's office and could see through the window that his boss was at his desk, fully engrossed in a telephone conversation.

Pérez looked at him. 'He likes you better than me,' she said.

Lawson sighed. 'Let's go,' he said, heading towards the closed door of Villarreal's office.

The two agents made their case to Villarreal, who frowned as they laid out the devastating consequences that would occur if the *Times* reporter published her story. José would flee to Mexico, his crew would scatter and sources could be killed. They needed to make some kind of deal with the reporter to hold off on publishing her story, Lawson urged, at least until they could make the arrests. Villarreal sat back in his chair, mulling over the facts that the two agents had just laid before him. 'Let me talk to San Antonio,' he said finally.

As they left Villarreal's office, Lawson felt anxiety kick in. It was a feeling he always got when he knew he was trapped in the slow-moving gears of bureaucracy and there was nothing he could do about it. Villarreal was going to pass the problem up the chain of command to San Antonio and from there it would go to Washington. Where it would sit until it was too late.

'You had better tell Pennington,' Pérez said.

Steve Pennington took the news more calmly than he had with the raid. There was nothing he could do but keep working, he told himself. He was going to keep out of it and let the brass above his pay grade work it out among themselves. He'd keep poring through the financial documents with the same dogged determinedness as he did on every case. If there was one thing he had learned, it was that persistence and patience were usually rewarded.

As Lawson had feared, Washington debated what to do, then decided not to do anything – until the *Times* reporter contacted the DEA's press office in Washington for comment and told them she was going to run with the story. The DEA contacted the FBI about Thompson's impending story, which touched off a panic. The FBI contacted the reporter to try to negotiate a deal.

After a tense month of back-and-forth negotiations, Thompson agreed to hold her story until the day of the raid. In return, the FBI would give her the redacted search warrant from the investigation – an exclusive – that laid out the intricacies of the money-laundering operation. It was a win for the *New York Times* and a win for the FBI and IRS, which had just negotiated a few more precious weeks.

FORTY-FOUR

LAWSON WAS BEGINNING TO SEE THE BENEFIT OF A LOOMING PUBLICATION DATE IN the *New York Times* hanging over their heads. He and Pérez had been pushing Gardner since the Los Alamitos raid for an indictment but Gardner had wanted to wait until September. But with the *New York Times* reporter poised to publish her story on Tremor Enterprises, the prosecutor agreed they couldn't wait any longer. He set a date before the grand jury for 30 May 2012.

Pennington and Billy Williams drafted a document that summed up the entire investigation to be presented before the grand jury. The document, called a 'summary of facts', had to distil the nearly three-year investigation into fifty or so pages that would be digestible for the jurors in Austin.

Pennington, being the most experienced agent, took the lead in writing up the document, which Gardner would also use as a blueprint for his prosecution when they went to trial. Among the stacks of boxes, Williams and Pennington worked diligently to piece together the financial information, the legal framework and the many assets that would be seized, including Francisco

Colorado's two private planes, José's ranch and the hundreds of racehorses.

Each agent had his or her own task to accomplish in the war room. Lawson and Pérez were busy working on the arrest and search warrants they'd need. Schutt and Kim Williams sat at the long table putting together the extensive spreadsheets of horses owned by Tremor Enterprises and various straw buyers. So far, they had a tally of more than four hundred horses bought by Miguel Treviño in the United States.

For several weeks, supervisors at the FBI and the IRS along with Doug Gardner had been embroiled in a debate over whether it would be necessary to seize all of them. They considered taking only the cartel's most valuable horses – just fifty or so instead of hundreds. Some in Washington didn't want to seize any horses at all. But Pennington, Pérez and Lawson put up a vigorous defence. 'We can't leave these high-dollar assets in the hands of the cartel,' Pennington argued to his supervisors. 'It doesn't dismantle the ring. They'd just give the horses to relatives or take them to Mexico.'

The two agencies also quarrelled over which of them would be responsible for seizing the animals, then caring for them. It was an expensive and onerous task that neither wanted. The FBI brass argued that they were in the business of arresting criminals, not caring for dozens of high-strung, expensive racehorses. After some heated discussion in Washington, it was decided that the IRS would handle the seizure, which was what Doug Gardner had also wanted. It made the most sense, he argued, since the IRS was part of the US Department of the Treasury, with a large asset-forfeiture office. The management at IRS was more doubtful – they seized yachts and private planes, not livestock.

To assure Washington that the seizures could be done successfully, Pennington sought the expertise of Henry

Maldonado, an experienced IRS asset-forfeiture manager in San Antonio he'd worked with over the years. The plan would be to seize the forty most valuable horses the day of the raid and leave the rest under protective order. This meant facilities like Graham's Southwest Stallion Station and Paul Jones training facility at Los Alamitos would be required under court order to care for the horses until the IRS could get them sold at auction. Miguel's most valuable horse, Tempting Dash, would stay with Graham since the stallion was under quarantine and could only be moved with special permission from the state. In San Antonio, Maldonado got to work overseeing the most unusual and expensive seizure he'd ever undertaken for the IRS.

THE TEAM HAD BEEN putting in fourteen-hour days for the last several weeks in Austin, preparing the evidence for the grand jury and making plans for the raid, which would be a massive undertaking, rolling out simultaneously in Texas, New Mexico, Oklahoma and California. Lawson and Pérez worked non-stop through the week, then they'd return each Friday to Laredo for the weekend.

Pérez's three kids would already be asleep by the time she got home. She'd scarcely seen her family in months. The last time she'd been home, her husband had joked sarcastically, 'I'm going to have to get myself a girlfriend.'

'If you do, make sure she gives the kids a bath and helps them do their homework,' Pérez had shot back, testily. She knew her husband was frustrated by her frequent absences. But they'd been together long enough, knew each other well enough, that she felt their marriage would withstand the pressures of the investigation. Her husband was also from the border and he understood the case meant more to her than just a promotion.

Pérez also had something else weighing on her mind besides the impending indictment and raid. She was pregnant again. Other than Juan and her family, she'd only told Lawson, and no one else on the investigative team. The baby was just twelve weeks along and she didn't want her pregnancy to become common knowledge until she'd had her first sonogram. On a Monday morning in mid-May, she stayed behind in Laredo, and Lawson drove to Austin alone. Pérez went to the doctor's office without Juan. She'd told her husband there was no need to accompany her for just a routine check-up.

But as Pérez lay on the exam table and the doctor passed the ultrasound paddle over her stomach, she noticed him frown and his eyes narrow as he examined the outline of her baby on the monitor more closely.

'What is it?' Pérez said, suddenly feeling uneasy.

'Probably nothing,' he said. 'Sometimes with the positioning of the baby, it's difficult to get a heartbeat.'

Pérez had been through this before. But this time, the exam was taking longer than it should and she sensed her doctor was stalling for more time.

'Let's try this again,' he said, moving the ultrasound more slowly over her stomach.

'What's wrong?' she asked, trying not to panic.

'I'm sorry,' he said finally. 'The baby has no heartbeat.'

Pérez thought it must be a mistake. She had felt perfectly fine leading up to the exam. He must have interpreted the sonogram incorrectly. She glanced at the outline of her baby on the monitor – the baby wasn't moving – and then looked away, lying back on the exam table and staring at the colourless, beige ceiling. She knew he was right. There wasn't the familiar whooshing of her baby's heartbeat over the monitor, like there'd been with her other pregnancies. There was only silence.

With the realisation came anger, then sadness, and she barely heard the doctor as he made preparations for her to go to the hospital.

'Was it something I did?' she asked him, sitting up and rearranging her shirt. 'I've been under a lot of stress lately.'

'Sometimes these things just happen,' he said, his voice softening. 'It's not your fault.'

Pérez nodded. But it felt like her heart was plummeting through the floor. She walked blankly out of the doctor's office and to her car in the parking lot, where she called her husband. He immediately panicked and told her not to move until he got there. 'It's okay,' she told him. 'I'm okay.' But as she tried to console him, she started to cry. After she ended the call, she attempted to compose herself, then she called Lawson in Austin.

'Alma, what happened?' He could tell she was upset, despite her attempt to sound calm.

'The baby doesn't have a heartbeat,' she said, starting to cry again. Sitting in the driver's seat of her car in the parking lot, she watched as a smiling mother-to-be got out of her car and walked inside the ob-gyn's office.

'Oh God, I'm so sorry,' Lawson said. 'Can I do anything for you to help . . . anything at all?'

'No, I'll be all right,' she said. 'Just let everyone know, I'm going to have to take off a few days.'

'Of course,' Lawson said. 'Just take care of yourself, okay.'

'I will, don't worry,' Pérez said.

After their conversation, Lawson felt like he'd been kicked. He wasn't equipped to deal with such a crisis. He realised at this point in his life that he was probably closer to Pérez than anyone else, especially after his father had died. Every Monday morning, before the sun had even come up, Lawson would pull up to the curb of Pérez's house on the other side of town, in the newer middle-class sub-divisions, and they'd set out for the three-hour drive to Austin to join the others. On their drives to and from Austin, no topic of conversation was off the table. Sometimes they'd talk about religion. Pérez was Catholic and Lawson could see how she drew solace from her faith. The evangelical church where he'd been raised was often rigid and judgemental. And he'd begun to question its teachings, which had offered him little consolation after losing his dad. At the moment, he considered himself an agnostic. They also liked to talk about their goals for the future – Lawson's dream of a horse ranch in Tennessee and her desire for another child. She'd grown up with only her younger sister and had always wanted a larger, more boisterous family life. But she also wanted a career. She loved her job and loved the bureau. But it was a continuous struggle to balance the two.

During the course of the investigation, the two agents had spent just about every waking hour together, to the point where other members of their squad made jokes about it, asking Pérez if she liked Tennessee. To make sure there were no awkward feelings with Juan, Lawson made a point of getting together with him to play golf or to barbecue. He wanted Juan to be comfortable and know it was just work between him and Pérez, and nothing more. Lawson was lucky because Juan was supportive of Pérez and her career and seemed to take her long absences in stride.

Lawson's girlfriend, Elena, was less understanding. She increasingly complained often and bitterly that he was never home and that he spent all of his time with another woman – his partner, Alma Pérez. The few hours they did spend together often ended in arguments and jealous accusations that Lawson cared more about Pérez than her.

Two days after her doctor's appointment, Pérez went to the hospital for her D&C procedure. Villarreal had told her to take as much time off as she needed. When she got out of surgery, a large bouquet of flowers was waiting for her from Lawson and the team in Austin, which lifted her mood. Pérez was ready to bury whatever lingering sadness she had in her work. The next morning, she was back at the office.

Lawson called her on her mobile phone. 'How are you doing?'

Pérez was on her computer going over the arrest warrants they'd been working on. 'I'm good,' she said.

'Really?'

'Of course. I'd tell you if I wasn't.'

'Maybe you should slow down,'

'Scotty.'

'What?'

'Don't ever say that again.'

'I'm just saying . . .'

'I'll see you Monday morning,' Pérez said, not hiding the irritation in her voice. She'd worked to full term with three babies in the FBI without a problem. She ascribed her miscarriage to fate, no more and no less, and she didn't want any of her male colleagues judging her because of it, not even Lawson.

'I've missed you,' Lawson said, teasing.

'Yeah?' Pérez said, smiling now. 'Just don't be late to pick me up.'

EARLY ON A WEDNESDAY morning, 30 May, the grand jury convened at the federal courthouse in downtown Austin. Doug Gardner laid out the legal grounds for their case and Steve Pennington and Scott Lawson presented their findings to the sixteen men and women of the jury. They were seeking a federal felony charge for money laundering with a maximum penalty of twenty years in jail.

Lawson educated the jury on the Zetas and their violent history, while Pennington explained how various men – straw buyers who worked on behalf of Miguel Treviño and his brothers — bought the racehorses using bulk cash payments, wire transfers or structured deposits. Within a few hours, the grand jury handed down an indictment for fifteen members of the conspiracy, including Miguel Treviño and his two brothers. Also among the indicted were Carlos Nayen, Fernando Garcia, Francisco Colorado and Alfonso del Rayo.

A magistrate judge sealed the indictment so that José and his crew would not be tipped off to their impending arrests. The team settled on a date for the raid — 12 June, which gave them less than two weeks.

FORTY-FIVE

WITH EVERYTHING THAT HAD GONE WRONG, IT WAS A MIRACLE THEY'D MADE it to an indictment without José suddenly fleeing to Mexico and the protection of his brothers. Luckily, José seemed too preoccupied running his rapidly expanding empire to be suspicious. Increasingly, much of his time was also spent planning, along with his wife, Zulema, a lavish wedding for their twenty-one-year-old daughter, Alexandra, to a young Marine.

The family was sparing no expense and the large wedding would be held the first Saturday in June at the historic Adolphus Hotel in downtown Dallas. For Lawson, it was hard to believe that after nearly three years the raid was little more than a week away. But Lawson couldn't resist one more chance to collect evidence for their case. The wedding would be high-profile and everyone from the racing world would be there. He didn't think Omar or Miguel would take the risk of coming to Dallas but there was always the possibility of another member of the cartel making an appearance at the wedding. In case they did, they'd have a Dallas SWAT team on standby.

As the guests filtered into the hotel, Lawson stationed himself on a stool at the bar near the entrance of the ballroom. He worried he might be spotted by José or Nayen but he was the only agent, other than Pérez, who could quickly identify the players in the conspiracy. He wore his Glock hidden in an ankle holster under his business suit. As he nursed beers at the bar, he tried to look like a businessman unwinding after a long day. Lawson noticed Doc Graham come into the lobby, along with other respected members of the racing community, an indication of José's growing stature in the racing world. *Track* magazine, a well-known industry publication, was even covering the wedding, which was being touted as one of the highlights of the year. Tyler Graham had received an invitation but had had to decline. He was serving as best man at another wedding on the same day.

José and Zulema, standing in front of the banquet room with etched crystal doors, greeted the guests as they arrived. What they didn't know was that the room had been wired for video and audio. Upstairs, the FBI had a suite in the hotel equipped with video monitors and a tech team that would record everything that went on during the wedding. As Lawson sipped his beer, he wondered why Fernando Garcia hadn't shown. Neither had Carlos Nayen but this was less of a surprise since it appeared that Garcia was now running things for José. Lawson supposed that José was being careful and keeping anyone from the money-laundering crew away from his daughter's wedding.

Lawson milled around the lobby and bar pretending he was waiting for someone. Suddenly, two large tour buses pulled up to the front of the hotel and a seventeen-piece band unloaded brass instruments, guitars and drums. The men, in their matching velvet suits, drew stares as they filed through the lobby to the ballroom to set up for the entertainment after dinner. On the sides of the buses, it read 'Banda el Recodo'. Lawson texted a

Mexican source and found out that the band was from Sinaloa and was Miguel's favourite group. They typically charged $250,000 a performance, his source said. He supposed the drug lord had sent the band as a special gift for the newlyweds.

Lawson and another agent alternated hanging out at the bar. When he wasn't downstairs, he was upstairs watching the festivities over the live video feed. Other than a few racing-industry insiders like Doc Graham, he didn't recognise anyone of note. By the end of the evening, it was clear they weren't going to get anyone on their most-wanted list. José had not stayed under the radar all those years without being cautious. Lawson had taken a few photos in the lobby with his mobile phone to add to their file of evidence. But there was no need for a SWAT team. The only sign of José's brothers was in the ballads crooned by Banda el Recodo's two suave front men to the beaming bride in her long, white gown.

WITH THE WEDDING NOW out of the way, Pérez, Lawson and Pennington met with other agencies at the FBI's San Antonio headquarters to review the final details of the raid planned for the early-morning hours of Tuesday, 12 June. At the meeting were representatives from nine different FBI field offices, the IRS, the DEA and the US attorney's office. José's Oklahoma ranch was under round-the-clock surveillance by the FBI, and so were Nayen, Garcia and his other associates at racetracks in New Mexico, Texas and California. Since early April, they had been discussing every detail over video, phone and email. It would take an army of 1,200 agents and support staff to target 4 states in simultaneous raids. If any of José's associates were tipped off in advance, they'd flee to Mexico. The whole operation would have to be executed quickly and flawlessly before word reached any of their targets.

But there was one crucial thing that Pérez and Lawson still hadn't worked out. The investigation had dominated their lives for nearly three years and both looked forward to its culmination at José's ranch in Oklahoma. They relished the idea of meeting him face-to-face and snapping the handcuffs on his wrists before he was whisked away in an armoured SUV. But after the Tuesday meeting, Villarreal had asked them to stay behind for a moment to talk.

'Which one of you is going to work the command centre?' he asked. Pérez and Lawson were silent. They both knew that having someone at the command post in San Antonio to co-ordinate the sweeping raid and direct the agents across four states was crucial. No one knew the case better than they did. Only they and Steve Pennington knew exactly what evidence to look for during the raids and how the intricate web of straw buyers and limited-liability companies was connected.

They'd never had a serious argument, which was an accomplishment for two people who spent so much time together. But now there was a tense silence between them as they stood in the hallway facing Villarreal. Good cases fell apart because of ego, because of bad blood between partners that led to bad decisions. A rift between them could jeopardise everything they had worked for in the last two and a half years.

'So,' Villarreal said, this time with a note of impatience. 'Who will it be?'

FORTY-SIX

THE NIGHT BEFORE THE RAID, PÉREZ CHECKED INTO HER HOTEL ROOM IN San Antonio. She didn't expect to get much sleep. It was late in the evening and the temperature had barely gone down after a sweltering summer afternoon. The air conditioner in her room rattled on. Her mind kept relentlessly playing over the details of the raid in the morning. They would hit the homes and racetracks just as the sun was coming up. She debated whether there was any point in going to bed. She knew she wouldn't be able to sleep.

Just after midnight, her mobile phone rang. A panicked agent in New Mexico, responsible for keeping watch on Fernando Garcia, said the horse trainer wasn't at home. Lawson had been closely monitoring José Treviño's mobile phone, tracking his movements. They'd had a scare earlier in the afternoon when José had nearly missed his flight back to Oklahoma from Los Angeles, which would have meant disaster. But at the last moment, he'd made the flight. Besides several agents on the ground in four states, they had two planes conducting surveillance in New Mexico and California to make sure everyone was accounted for when the raid went down first thing in the morning. The news that Garcia was missing rattled Pérez. Had he been tipped off? She dialled Lawson in Oklahoma.

Lawson was pacing the sidewalk outside his hotel, too keyed up to sleep, when Pérez called. He'd arrived late in Oklahoma City, only to find 300 agents waiting for him at the National Guard Armoury downtown. He hadn't known that he would be briefing the roomful of agents, which immediately made him feel anxious. Throughout the morning and afternoon, FBI and IRS agents and police had been filtering into Oklahoma City, trying not to look conspicuous as they checked into blocks of hotel rooms for the night. The expansive armoury was the only place large enough for all of them to meet. Lawson had never stood in front of so many people. It helped having Pennington there next to him.

The two reminded the assembled agents that it was the Zetas who had killed Jaime Zapata, a federal agent with HSI, and nearly killed his partner, Victor Avila, in February. Lawson had friends in Laredo who had worked closely with both agents. During his first weeks in Laredo, he'd seen the pair in the hallway before they were transferred to Mexico. Now one of them was dead. The Zetas were the most brutal cartel in Mexico, Lawson warned. José was the elder brother of Miguel and Omar Treviño, two of the cartel's leaders, and the raid on family members in Lexington, including their elderly mother, could have deadly repercussions. The US Department of State had drafted an advisory, to be released after the raid, warning US travellers to Mexico of an 'enhanced potential for violence.'

On the outskirts of Oklahoma City, Henry Maldonado, the head of asset forfeitures for the IRS, had assembled his own army. He'd mobilised more than a dozen cowboys with horse trailers and told them to be ready at daybreak for his text. He didn't tell them where they were going or give them too many specifics on the job, only that they should be prepared for anything and would have plenty of security. Once Pennington and his task force took possession of the horses, the IRS would have to number and photograph each horse. They also had to identify the most valuable of the herd, which would be hauled away by the cowboys waiting with their trailers.

As Lawson walked circles on the sidewalk, he listened to Pérez, who sounded stressed as she explained that Garcia couldn't be located in Ruidoso. They planned on hitting his house at daybreak but the agents doing surveillance on his home said his car wasn't in the driveway.

'You think he suspects something?' Pérez asked.

'If he did, José would be out of here already. But he hasn't moved,' Lawson said.

'I'll keep you posted,' Pérez said.

'Alma?'

'Yeah,' she said, stifling a yawn.

'I wish you were here,' Lawson said.

'Me too,' she said. 'But I'm glad you're there. It was yours from the beginning and you should be there.'

'Thanks,' Lawson said. He didn't know what else to say. 'Good night,' he said and hung up the phone. Pérez cared as much about the case as he did, if not more. A good agent always wanted to be there at the take-down because that's when things could get sloppy, important pieces of evidence overlooked. No one knew the case better or was more invested than the case agent. He would see things that even the evidence team, who were trained professionals, would miss. It was just human nature. When you'd poured nearly three years of your life into something, you tended to pay attention to even the smallest details. They had sacrificed time with their families. Lawson's girlfriend was close to breaking up with him, and Pérez had missed out on her kids' birthdays, Little League games and pre-school performances. It wouldn't all be for nothing if they arrested José and his brothers. But to do that, everything had to flow smoothly during the raid. There couldn't be any mistakes.

In San Antonio, it was Pérez's job to co-ordinate the 1,200 agents and personnel involved in the simultaneous raids in Texas, California, New Mexico and Oklahoma. They would be hitting Ruidoso Downs and Los Alamitos and the residences of Garcia, Nayen, Huitron and José's ranch in Lexington. Of the 1,200 personnel, 300 would be at the raid in Lexington and the rest would be spread out at the other locations. Pérez would be tracking and entering every new piece of evidence in a secure database, co-ordinating search warrants and running down new leads alongside a team of representatives from the DEA and IRS, and with Doug Gardner from the US attorney's office.

Even though they had indicted Miguel and Omar, the two were still out of the FBI's reach in Mexico. But Pérez and Lawson hoped not for long. Their main priority, besides arresting José in Lexington, was to locate all of his mobile phones. When Lawson entered José's house, he'd have a phone technician with him from one of their evidence teams. Rarely did one come across a drug kingpin's number but the agents knew that José spoke with his brothers regularly. Once they had Miguel's number, they could track him to his exact location. But it would have to be fast; as soon as word of the raids spread, he and Omar would drop their phones. The agents had only a matter of minutes. A strike team of Mexican soldiers was already waiting on standby. This time, Miguel wouldn't get away.

Lawson went back to his hotel room. He was restless and ready to hit José's farm. In less than four hours, they would assemble at the armoury again and then set out for the hour-long drive to

Lexington. Lawson thought about his dad and what he would think about what his son, the FBI agent, was about to do. He would have been proud in his typically understated way. 'You'll do all right,' he'd say. More than a year had passed since his dad had died, and Lawson still couldn't bring himself to delete his number from his mobile phone. As he lay on the bed staring up at the ceiling, he wished he could call him one last time.

IT WAS STILL DARK outside when the convoy left for Lexington. Anyone awake would have thought that Oklahoma was under siege. But the agents had not wanted to take any chances. They were also sending a message of overwhelming force. SWAT police in marked vehicles led the long convoy of unmarked federal vehicles and two mine-resistant, ambush-protected troop carriers. At the rear of the convoy were more SWAT-team members in marked police vehicles. Lawson and Pennington rode towards the front of the convoy. As they left the outskirts of Oklahoma City, Pérez sent Lawson a text from the command centre in San Antonio. 'Here we go. I wouldn't have traded you as a partner for anything.'

It made him feel better that he was about to finally confront José – a moment they had both anticipated and imagined for so long – and Pérez wouldn't hold it against him. She'd never held grudges, which he appreciated. In another text, Pérez also let him know that Garcia had finally shown up at his home. All of their targets were in place now.

The SWAT team drove up the long gravel driveway to José's ranch. Lawson and Pennington waited in their vehicle in the driveway until the SWAT gave them the all-clear. Overhead, a surveillance plane circled the property to make sure there were no surprise ambushes or escapes. The plane had barely made it to Lexington; upon take-off, the pilot had radioed that he might not be able to land. He'd struck a deer as he taxied down the runway and damaged his landing gear but had decided to go through with the mission anyway.

'This is the FBI. Come out with your hands up!' one of the SWAT officers shouted through a megaphone as the other officers surrounded the ranch house. The hundred-acre ranch had several buildings, including five barns and an office, but Lawson wanted to hit José's house first before he could destroy the mobile phones and other evidence. José came out of the house followed by his wife, Zulema, and three of his children – José Jr, who was no longer a teenager, and two younger children. José and Zulema had their hands in the air and looked confused. The sun was just beginning to rise and they were still in their pyjamas and dishevelled from the abrupt awakening. José's mother was staying in a mobile home behind the ranch house. A SWAT-team member escorted the elderly matriarch to the front of the property along with the rest of the family. Lawson, Pennington and the other federal agents were given the all-clear to enter the ranch after the SWAT searched the barns and homes on the property. José and his wife were handcuffed. Lawson immediately went in with one of the evidence teams to search for the mobile phones. He knew he had very little time.

As they searched José's room, Lawson got a text from Pérez that the other raids were going as planned. In California, the FBI and DEA had arrested Nayen at his upscale condo near Los Alamitos. One of the FBI agents noted that his BlackBerry had no battery in it, which would slow down the recovery of any useful phone numbers. Lawson doubted there was anything there anyway. After the Los Alamitos raid, Miguel, Omar and the whole crew had immediately dropped their phones.

The rest of the Waco Treasury Task Force had split into two

teams tasked with the seizures and arrests at Ruidoso Downs and Los Alamitos. In California, Brian Schutt arrested horse trainer Felipe Quintero, and Steve Junker, with the help of Kim and Billy Williams, picked up Fernando Garcia in New Mexico. Outside Austin, Chevo Huitron was handcuffed by local FBI agents and driven to a nearby courthouse to be arraigned.

But it was still too soon to feel any sense of triumph. Lawson needed to find José's mobile phones and time was running out. Lawson and the phone technician dug through drawers and closets, while Pennington went out to search the office in the barn. Finally, Lawson's persistence was rewarded. In a drawer filled with socks and underwear, he discovered a BlackBerry and several thick rolls of cash. It was all crisp, clean hundred-dollar bills – the kind that Miguel preferred. The phone technician powered up the BlackBerry and searched the contacts. There was just one phone number and he could tell by the long prefix that it was Mexican. Lawson felt his adrenaline racing with the find. Because the phone was hidden, had just one number and was a BlackBerry, Miguel's usual method of communication, all the signs were encouraging. They would need to move quickly to triangulate the cartel leader's GPS co-ordinates before Miguel tossed his phone. Lawson quickly texted the number to Pérez at the command centre so it could be relayed to the analysts and their strike team in Mexico.

As they searched the ranch, the *New York Times* story on José Treviño and Tremor Enterprises was already reaching tens of thousands of readers. Ginger Thompson, the reporter, had her exclusive, which made for a blockbuster story that was soon picked up by other media outlets around the world, especially in Mexico, where an in-depth investigation into the Treviños would have been unthinkable because of government collusion and corruption.

After the evidence team had combed through José's office in the barn, Lawson and Pennington wanted to give it one more sweep. Lawson needed to get to a nearby FBI office, where he would finally meet with José face-to-face, but first he wanted another pass at the evidence. Lawson rifled through the filing cabinets looking for anything useful. He pulled out a cheque from Tremor Enterprises made out to Francisco Colorado for $400,000 that had never been cashed. 'That's gold,' Pennington said. Lawson tucked the cheque away in an evidence bag and gave it to the team.

Altogether, the evidence team had hauled away a hundred boxes filled with horse records, financial documents and other evidence. They also seized several computers that José used for his business. Finally satisfied, Lawson drove to the FBI office in Norman, halfway between Lexington and Oklahoma City, where José and Zulema had been transported. He'd been trying to imagine this meeting for years. When he got to the office, they had José sitting in an interrogation room waiting for him. José had been allowed to change into a pair of jeans and a work shirt. He still acted like they had nothing on him and that it had all been a mistake. Lawson sat down across from him with task-force officer Ernie Elizondo, who spoke Spanish, in case there was a language barrier, but he knew José's English was good, so he proceeded.

'I want you to just listen before I read you your Miranda rights,' Lawson said. 'We've been working on this a long time, it's not something we just started two or three months ago. If there's anything you can say to shed light on the situation and help yourself, I would appreciate it.'

José nodded. 'I understand my rights,' he said.

Lawson read him his rights, then passed the consent form over to José, who refused to sign it. 'All my life I've worked hard

. . .' José said. 'I'm an American and I respect the uniform of law enforcement.' But law enforcement had made his life hell, he said, because of his brothers Miguel and Omar. 'I can pick my friends and associates but I have no control over picking my family,' he told Lawson. He said he didn't keep in contact with his brothers anyway.

'What about your horse farm? Aren't the horses owned by Miguel?' Lawson asked.

José shook his head. 'I've worked very hard to become successful,' he said. It was all because of Tempting Dash, which he'd bought for a cheap price, and had won him a lot of money. Everything he had today was founded on his initial winnings from the champion horse. 'It's unfair for you to connect my success to my brother.'

Lawson hoped he could rile up José enough that he'd let something slip about Miguel that they could use to locate him. He'd given José a chance, told him that this wasn't just some light-weight investigation, so he might have a come-to-Jesus moment and offer up some information that could help their case. But that wasn't José's style.

'Why would Ramiro Villarreal sell you Tempting Dash for almost nothing after the horse had been so successful?'

'I don't know why Ramiro sold him so cheap,' José said. He told Lawson he had no idea that Villarreal had worked for his brother Miguel. Nor did he know that Tempting Dash had raced in Mexico, either.

Now he was really starting to insult Lawson's intelligence. 'What about Carlos Nayen?'

'He's a client of mine,' José said.

'We know that Carlos works for Miguel.'

'You should talk to Carlos and Miguel about that.'

Lawson could see he wasn't going to get anywhere. He'd

offered up a taste of what he had but José wasn't going to budge. It was time for him to show José just how deep he was in it this time and that he wasn't going to walk away like he had before. 'We know that Miguel sends the drug proceeds to Carlos Nayen so he can pay the expenses for your operation.' He pulled a copy of a spreadsheet out of his pocket and put it down on the table. 'You took this to a meeting with Miguel and Carlos in Mexico.'

'That would be the business of Carlos and Miguel. It's none of my business,' said José, hardly glancing at the paper.

'We have proof you took it to them personally,' Lawson said. He could tell he had got to José this time by his blank expression. José was trying to think of what to do or say next.

'I don't have anything more to say,' José finally said with a defiant look, and sat back in his chair. The interview was over. Lawson stood up from the table and folded up the copy of the spreadsheet. He knew the next time he talked to José it would be through his lawyer. He hoped they'd have better luck in Mexico.

FORTY-SEVEN

IN OKLAHOMA, LAWSON WAITED FOR NEWS FROM THE FBI'S OFFICE IN MEXICO CITY. He kept texting Pérez but she told him she'd heard nothing. It was unclear how the FBI at the US embassy in Mexico City assembled their strike teams but he'd heard they were using a different set of analysts and a new, recently vetted team of Mexican soldiers.

By lunchtime, there was still no answer from Mexico City. An anxious Lawson knew that by now Miguel and Omar would have been fully briefed on the raid and dropped their phones and abandoned their safe houses for new ones. The window of opportunity had closed. They weren't going to get the cartel leaders, who had slipped through the net again. It was a stinging disappointment. They were as close as they could get to Miguel's inner circle but they'd come away empty-handed.

In Mexico, everything appeared to be chaos but, in reality, the violent incursions and assassinations often had a purpose behind them. US law enforcement could only push and wait but Miguel and Omar would not be caught until the complex world of Mexican politics deemed it was time to give them up.

Lawson felt that same frustration and futility as the day he'd stood at the edge of the Rio Grande and realised that the Garcia brothers' killer would go free in Nuevo Laredo. He could only take comfort in the fact that the gunman's freedom hadn't lasted long. He'd succumbed to the war's rough justice a few months later – decapitated by a *sicario* from the Gulf Cartel – another body in a growing sea of bodies. Just like the Garcia brothers' killer, Miguel and Omar's day of reckoning would also come. Maybe not today, Lawson thought, but soon.

WHILE PENNINGTON WORKED WITH Lawson in Oklahoma, the rest of the Waco Treasury Task Force toiled in New Mexico and California. Their main goal was to identify all of the horses that belonged to Miguel Treviño, which could take several days. Each horse had its own unique number tattooed on the inside of its lower lip, which had to be checked against a stack of records from the American Quarter Horse Association and various auction houses, so they could be sure they were seizing the right horses.

Billy Williams, Steve Junker and Kim Williams had spent two sleepless days in Ruidoso since the raid on Tuesday, hurrying to seize all of Miguel's horses before he sent someone to reclaim them. Kim Williams was the only one who felt comfortable 'lipping the horses', which meant jamming her fingers inside a horse's mouth to find the identifying tattoo. One of the more valuable racehorses, Coronita Cartel, had already nipped Junker's arm, which was enough for Billy to give the animals a wide berth.

It was difficult and dirty work, made even worse by a looming forest fire moving rapidly towards Ruidoso. The billowing clouds of grey smoke looked ominous on the horizon. After the track, they had moved on to a training facility south of Ruidoso to seize a few more horses they had discovered that belonged to José. The air smelled of smoke, and ash blew in the breeze. They tried to work quickly. The FBI agents and police who had been despatched to help them with the raid had already left town. Just when they thought they were nearly done, Billy got a call from a source at Ruidoso Downs that stopped him cold – the Zetas were on their way.

The task force had left six valuable racehorses at the track under the protective custody of a trainer. But now Billy was informed their trainer had taken off to California as soon as he realized whom the horses belonged to – federal court order be damned. Now, according to Billy's source at the track, some cartel men were on their way to pick up the horses. The three agents were exhausted and covered in muck from the horse stables. And now, even worse, they were the only thing left standing between Miguel and his horses. Billy broke the bad news to Junker and Kim.

'Shit, we're going to need back-up,' she said.

'We'll have to go to the locals,' Junker said, frowning. There was no way they could mobilise any federal agents in such a short time. The closest FBI office was in El Paso, three hours away, and there was a raging forest fire between them. Their only hope was the already overwhelmed Ruidoso police department. If they could get a couple of squad cars to patrol the track, it might make the Zetas think they had plenty of back-up and think twice about rolling up with a horse trailer.

'If it's one Suburban of gunmen, it's a fair fight but, if it's two or more, we're going to be the best damn witnesses from a distance that we can be,' Junker said, cracking a smile. The three piled into Junker's black Cadillac Escalade and headed north again towards Ruidoso. Kim Williams, in the passenger seat, cradled an AR-15. The police had already shut down the main road in and out of town. And there was a police roadblock up ahead. Junker could see the cop's eyes growing wider as they rolled up. The look on his face said, *What the hell is this?* No doubt he'd been briefed on the federal raid that had gone down at the racetrack and now here was a SUV pulling up to his roadblock with three heavily armed people inside of it. Junker quickly flashed his badge before the cop got any more ideas. 'We're part of the task force over at the racetrack,' he explained. 'Think you could send a couple of squad cars over there to help us out? Word is we're going to have some visitors and we need back-up.'

The cop laughed. 'We're evacuating the town. You've got to be kidding.' The fire had already burned through more than two hundred homes. They could see a DC-10 circling overhead in the distance, dousing the burning pine forests with crimson clouds of fire retardant to try to stop the fire from advancing any further towards the centre of town.

Luckily, the racetrack was on the other side of Ruidoso. The fire still had a way to travel before it would reach the horses. 'We'll have to take our chances,' Junker said. The cop shrugged and let them through the roadblock. It was eerie driving down the empty road as ash rained from the sky and flittered across their windscreen. The homes and businesses were empty and abandoned. Almost everyone had already been evacuated. It was only a matter of time before they were stopped at another roadblock and they'd have to start all over again with their long, convoluted story, which would only be met with derision from the overworked locals. Junker pulled over to the side of the road and jumped out. Kim gave Billy a puzzled look as Junker started rummaging through the back of his SUV. He came back with an old red strobe light that plugged into the cigarette lighter.

'Wow,' Kim said, grinning. 'Has that been back there since the nineties?'

'Old school,' Billy nodded, with a note of approval.

Junker plugged in the strobe light and placed it on the dashboard. With the red light flashing in the Escalade, the cop at the next roadblock waved them through and they finally arrived at the entrance to Ruidoso Downs. They were now working off nothing but adrenaline and black coffee as they scanned the perimeter of the track for any sign of Miguel's henchmen. 'We need to get the horses out of here fast,' said Kim. The other two agreed. They couldn't take a gamble on the Zetas being deterred by the roadblocks. Billy called the track's manager, who loaned them a horse trailer. It would be up to Kim to get the six spooked horses to co-operate. After several failed attempts and a lot of cursing, she guided them into the trailer, which they'd hooked to the Escalade.

As they turned down the only narrow mountain road that was still open out of Ruidoso, Junker couldn't help but keep glancing in his rear-view mirror. Behind them the mountains were cloaked in smoke and fire but, much to his relief, the road was empty and there was no sign of Miguel's men in pursuit.

BRIAN SCHUTT HAD HIS own worries in California. On the morning of the raid, he'd arrived at the Los Alamitos racetrack, along with California agents from the FBI and IRS, only to be told by the guard at the gate to the backside that José's horses weren't there. 'Like hell they aren't,' Schutt said, pushing past the guard. Through their sources, he knew José had at least twenty horses at Los Alamitos being trained at various stables. Schutt phoned the track's office to tersely remind them they had several armed federal agents waiting at their gate. Less than ten minutes later, a flustered stable foreman arrived with a list of every stable registered on the backside.

'I don't know what the deal is with these guys but something's up,' the foreman muttered, quickly leading Schutt and the other agents to Bonanza Racing Stables. In the long row of stalls, Schutt found several of José's horses, including the three that had just qualified for the Ed Burke Million Futurity. Of the three contenders, only one was registered under Tremor Enterprises and the other two were under Bonanza, which was run by Fernando Garcia. With nine horses in the race – three of them José's – the odds were heavily in his favour that he'd win the million-dollar purse for a second year in a row.

Schutt wondered whether they shouldn't let the horses go forward with the race anyway, now that they were the property of the US Treasury. He had a handful of cowboys with horse trailers standing by. But they were becoming increasingly nervous and anxious to leave, having just discovered the true owner of the horses. Some were in the process of trying to cover up the names of their transport services with cardboard and duct tape. Schutt knew he needed to work fast. The parking lot was starting to fill with hot walkers, groomers and trainers, all rushing to leave before they were stopped and questioned. He called Doug Gardner at the command centre in San Antonio to ask what he should do about the three horses. One of them, a sleek bay stallion named Mr. Ease Cartel, had come close to breaking the track's speed record during his qualifying round. Appraising the horse in his stall, Schutt couldn't help but be in awe of its muscular strength and speed. For him, it was like standing next to a Ferrari or a Lamborghini.

Gardner answered the phone. 'Hey, Brian. How are things?'

'All good on my end,' Schutt said. 'But I need to ask you something. I've got these three qualifiers here for the Futurity. It's in less than two weeks. Should I pull them from the race?'

'I'll send it up the chain of command, then get back to you,' Gardner told him.

While Schutt waited for an answer, the agents fanned out through the rows of stalls looking for more of José's horses. Like Kim in Ruidoso, Schutt was left to lip the horses and look for the tattooed number that matched their records, to make sure the cowboys didn't load up the wrong horses. After about fifteen minutes, his mobile phone rang. 'Yes, seize them,' Gardner said.

Much later, Pennington, Schutt and the rest of the task force would come to regret the decision to pull the horses from the race. The contenders would have made hundreds of thousands of dollars for the Treasury Department just by participating, and the odds of Mr. Ease Cartel winning the million-dollar purse had been favourable. The horses would have been worth much more after the Futurity. But none of them had known enough about racing at the time to realise their mistake.

Schutt had the horses quickly loaded into the trailers. Altogether they identified twenty-four horses. An elderly Mexican man leading one of the horses out of the stables said *'gracias'* quietly as he passed Schutt, so that only he would hear. He thought he saw relief in the man's eyes.

AS SOON AS THEY RETURNED to Larado, Lawson and Pérez focused on capturing their fugitives in Mexico before Miguel and Omar killed them or they paid someone off for protection. Francisco Colorado was still at large and so was Alfonso del Rayo. But Lawson had a feeling that del Rayo wasn't so much a player as he was a captive in Miguel's conspiracy. He called Tyler Graham and asked him for del Rayo's phone number. He was going to take a chance on his hunch and try to make a deal with del Rayo to turn himself in. Lawson took comfort in the knowledge that Colorado already had a target on his back in Mexico. His only chance of survival was to lie low in the United States. He'd have to eventually turn himself in if he wanted to stay alive.

The news that Miguel Treviño's brother had been arrested in the United States was the top story in Mexico, especially in Veracruz, where the indictment of Francisco Colorado, along with the allegation that he'd served as a conduit between ex-governor Fidel Herrera and the Zetas, became a leading topic of discussion.

Alfonso del Rayo had been living in limbo, too afraid to speak to any authority about his kidnapping. Nayen, after his arrest, had called from California demanding that del Rayo send him more money for a lawyer. He also asked for the keys to his home in San Antonio. His wife and son needed a place to live while he was in jail, he said. Del Rayo gave the keys to Nayen's wife. He worried that, with Nayen in jail, the Zetas would come after him and his family. He had no choice but to try to keep Nayen happy or else be kidnapped again, or worse. It seemed there was no way out of a nightmare that was only growing darker.

Just when del Rayo thought his situation couldn't get much worse, he received a phone call that gave him such a shock, he momentarily forgot his English. It was an FBI agent from the United States, calling to tell him he'd been indicted.

'¿Qué?' del Rayo asked, not sure that he'd understood the caller. 'How can this be possible?'

The agent, who said his name was Scott Lawson, explained that for months they'd been listening to his phone calls and the FBI knew he'd bought a horse for Miguel Treviño in Oklahoma.

But del Rayo had never even heard of Miguel Treviño. He only knew Carlos Nayen and Fernando Garcia, he explained to the agent. He told Lawson how he'd been kidnapped and that Nayen, along with an employee from the governor's office, had told him he needed to buy the horse in Oklahoma or his family would be killed. The Zetas had been extorting him ever since.

'If this is true,' Lawson said, 'then you need to come right away to the United States and prove it, and clear your name.'

Del Rayo was silent on the other end as he tried to work out what to do. If he went to the United States and testified in court and told the authorities everything he knew, the Zetas would kill him.

'Work with us on this,' Lawson urged. 'Bring your wife and kids with you. My partner and I will meet you at the airport. We won't put you in handcuffs in front of your family.'

'Okay,' del Rayo said finally. 'But give me two weeks to put things in order.' As he hung up the phone, the ramifications of what he'd just agreed to hit him. He and his family would have to leave everything they loved. Mexico was no longer safe. It would only be temporary, he told himself. Someday, they'd return.

THE MORNING OF HIS arrest, José Treviño had been preparing to make the final $200,000 payment on his Oklahoma ranch. His elderly neighbour, who had sold him sixty acres, had taken to sleeping with a shotgun under his bed. He told Lawson that, in his estimation, José had far too many horses on his property and took unusual security measures to guard his ranch. Late at night, men with flashlights often patrolled the property, a dangerous practice because horses were herd animals that easily took fright and, in a panic, they could bolt, hurting themselves or other horses around them. But by then, the old man was familiar with the rumours about José and his brothers in Mexico, which was why he had sold the property against his own better judgement – he didn't want any trouble. But now, with José gone, he felt some measure of relief. The months of anxiety were finally coming to a close.

With the seizure of the ranch and the horses, Miguel's legacy was coming undone. José and his wife were in custody and federal agents guarded the property and the nearly three hundred horses still on the ranch that now belonged to the Treasury Department.

José's winning streak had finally run out. The 12 June raid at Los Alamitos had revealed his plot to win the Ed Burke Million Futurity for a second time. With his three horses now in the custody of the US government, and scratched from the Futurity line-up, there would be no more trophies and million-dollar purses for José Treviño.

FORTY-EIGHT

BY ALL ACCOUNTS, THE RAID HAD BEEN A SUCCESS. JOSÉ AND THE OTHER SUSPECTS had been arrested without a shot fired. Even the FBI's surveillance plane with the damaged landing gear had been able to finally touch down in Oklahoma City without any injuries, just a few dings on the fuselage and a shaken crew.

But any triumph that Lawson and Pérez felt was dulled by the realisation that Miguel and Omar were still roaming free in Mexico. At least, Pennington said, they could take pride in the knowledge that they had ended the brothers' plans north of the Rio Grande.

José, who had pleaded not guilty, was placed in solitary confinement at a county lock-up near Austin. Federal judge Sam Sparks had denied bail since José was considered a flight risk. Sparks, a former trial attorney, had served the Western District of Texas for more than two decades. The seventy-three-year-old judge was considered conservative but not ideological, and deliberative when it came time for sentencing. He had already released José's wife, Zulema, and eldest daughter, Alexandra, on bond.

Besides Miguel and Omar, Sergio 'Saltillo' Guerrero, Luis Aguirre and Victor López were also still at large in Mexico. Not long after the raid, they would learn of Victor López's suspicious death in Nuevo Laredo and cross him off their fugitives' list. As they had hoped, Francisco Colorado turned himself in to the FBI in Houston three days after the raid. He had little choice since he couldn't go back to Mexico. He was a marked man in the eyes of Miguel, just like Carlos Nayen.

In yet another entanglement with the DEA, the agency had indicted Nayen in Texas's Eastern District on charges of drug smuggling and arms trafficking, a month before the FBI and IRS could file theirs in the Western District, which would now complicate the proceedings in Austin. Nayen had pleaded guilty to the charges and refused to testify at trial.

The two young horse trainers, Felipe Quintero and Adan Farias, along with Raúl Ramirez, one of the young bidders at the auctions, had struck plea agreements. And the two horse trainers had agreed to testify for the prosecution.

The rest of the defendants – Francisco Colorado, Eusevio Huitron and Fernando Garcia – would go on trial with José Treviño.

Judge Sparks set the trial for October 2012 at the federal courthouse in Austin, which gave the team just four months to prepare. The case was the biggest the US attorney's office in Austin had worked in more than a decade. Gardner knew he'd need the help of another federal prosecutor in his office, so he enlisted Michelle Fernald. The two had worked together on several trials over the last two decades and their very different personalities complemented one another in the courtroom. Fernald had a flair for dramatic delivery that contrasted well with Gardner's deliberate, no-nonsense style.

For the team, the task before them of condensing, in less than four months, a nearly three-year investigation into a coherent presentation before a jury was cause for panic. They had at least four hundred boxes of evidence seized during the raid crammed into the conference room at the US attorney's office. The stacks were so high that they obscured the windows and the view of the Capitol and downtown Austin. The outside world largely went unnoticed anyway, with the venetian blinds always closed, so that the agents could scrutinise one document after another on an overhead projector to help build their body of evidence.

They'd been working overtime since before the raid in June and were now feeling the pressure of the looming trial date. Every morning before the sun came up, Schutt and Kim Williams would hit the trail at Lady Bird Lake for a run to try to decompress. Pennington had no such outlet, after blowing out his knee while running a half-marathon with the two in the spring. He blamed his injury on a dream he'd had. The night before the marathon, he'd dreamed he was at the race watching Schutt, Junker and Kim Williams run but he was high above them looking down. As they ran further away from him, he realised he was dead. When he'd woken up, the dream had stayed with him, even spooked him a little. He wasn't that old, he told himself, and he wasn't retired yet.

That morning, when he arrived at the marathon starting line, he was determined to outrun anyone who got in front of him. But as he'd charged downhill, something in the back of his knee had popped and he'd felt a surge of white-hot pain shoot up his leg. After the race, the pain had settled into a nagging discomfort, which he'd ignored for months until his wife had forced him to see a doctor. The prognosis was not good: he'd torn a ligament and would need surgery. It couldn't have come at a worse moment, he thought. He'd be hobbling around on crutches with Miguel and Omar still at large.

For Pérez, it was becoming increasingly difficult to leave her kids every Monday morning and not see them again until the weekend. One morning as she was getting ready to leave for Austin, her eldest son, who was seven, asked why she was never home. 'Don't you love us?' he asked. He'd recently watched a TV show about the police and had a vague awareness that his mum did something similar. Pérez tried to explain to him that she was a federal agent but he was disappointed she didn't even wear a uniform like on television.

'I'm a policewoman, I just don't dress like one,' she said. 'And sometimes I have to put bad people in jail. And there are bad people everywhere and sometimes I have to go far away to arrest them.'

He looked up at her, blinking, trying to make sense of it. 'Well, can't you just get another job?' he said.

'But I love what I do,' Pérez told him.

'Oh,' he said, looking disappointed. 'Okay.'

Afterwards, when she and Lawson pulled away from the curb for the drive to Austin, guilt washed over her. At least her husband understood what the job meant to her. He knew her well enough to know that any ultimatum to make her quit would only backfire. When Lydia decided she'd had enough of taking care of their kids, Pérez might have to give up the violent-crimes squad. Then she didn't know what she'd do. The guilt subsided as they hit Interstate 35 and she and Lawson began to discuss their next task for the trial but it always lived in the back of her mind. Still, she knew she had to see the case through. She was doing her small part to help her parents' homeland. She sometimes wondered if it was already too late.

Lawson's girlfriend, Elena, had finally broken up with him when he'd gone back to Laredo after the Oklahoma raid. He had seen the rupture coming for months and, now that they were finally done, he admitted to Pérez that he felt nothing but relief.

In preparing for the trial, their primary job was keeping an eye on their sources and lining up co-operating witnesses to testify. Graham's cool demeanour was finally starting to crack under the stress of living a double life for so long. He kept asking Lawson when it would be over. But all Lawson could promise him was that they were getting closer to trial. Once again, he was impressed by Graham's nerve when he agreed to take the stand as a witness. He knew that the FBI would have to keep a close security detail around him, since his life could be in danger. Many others in the horse industry had been too scared to even consider testifying. One well-known horse trainer at Los Alamitos who had worked with José hired bodyguards after he found out who José's brothers were. He was so terrified at the thought of testifying that Gardner had determined he'd never hold up on the witness stand.

TWO WEEKS AFTER LAWSON spoke on the phone with del Rayo, the wealthy real-estate developer arrived at the San Antonio airport from Mexico City with his wife and two children. Pérez and Lawson met the family in the baggage-claim area. The agents wore business suits, their gold FBI badges and their pistols hidden under their coats.

'¿*Cómo están?*' Pérez greeted them, trying to put the family at ease. '¿*Cómo fue el viaje?*'

The family had brought a mountain of luggage. It was clear that del Rayo knew they wouldn't be going home anytime soon. His wife looked wary and the children grabbed at their father's arm instinctively.

'Not bad,' del Rayo answered in English. He raised the suitcase he was carrying. 'All of my medical records, financial documents are in here,' he said as they walked through the terminal towards the exit. 'I want to clear my name.'

As Lawson had promised, he didn't put handcuffs on del Rayo in front of his family, even though the businessman was still under indictment. They walked to the curb outside the airport terminal and del Rayo, with his suitcase of evidence, got into the back of their unmarked car. Del Rayo tried to smile and wave so his children wouldn't be scared at seeing their father being taken away by two strangers. But they were already near tears as the car pulled away from the curb.

They drove directly to the federal courthouse in Austin, where del Rayo was arraigned before a judge, then bonded out. After that, they met with Doug Gardner in his office for a debriefing so that del Rayo could make his case for innocence.

FORTY-NINE

STEVE PENNINGTON AND BILLY WILLIAMS WERE BEGINNING TO REALISE THAT they needed help with Francisco Colorado's ADT Petroservicios and with tracing the funds that had flowed through José Treviño's various US bank accounts.

Through co-operating witnesses, they'd learned that Miguel treated ADT Petroservicios like his own personal bank, depositing money into the business and then using it to wire money to the United States. But their weakness was still the lack of documents to prove it beyond a reasonable doubt to a jury. They'd both requested bank documents for ADT from Mexico but had never got a response. Gardner and Fernald would need to show the jury that the millions Colorado had spent on horses had come from Miguel's cocaine trafficking. They also had to prove that people in the industry, like the horse trainer, Chevo Huitron, had taken money from José and Carlos Nayen knowing it was dirty. But this was turning out be an even tougher challenge than they had anticipated.

Michelle Fernald suggested her husband, Michael, might be able to help with the financial analysis. Thirty-eight years old,

Michael Fernald was a criminal investigator with the IRS based in Austin, who still had the short military cut from his days in the army, where he had worked in intelligence. Fernald had been hearing about the Treviño investigation for months and he was intrigued by the scale and complexity of the money-laundering conspiracy.

Fernald was an expert in wire fraud and a CPA, unlike Pennington or Billy Williams. His background was in white-collar crime. Pennington knew Fernald and respected his opinion. The younger agent had helped Pennington out in the past with search warrants but he'd never worked full-time on a drug-cartel case. Pennington phoned Fernald and asked whether he'd be willing to join them. He assured Fernald that he wouldn't need to worry about the drug-trafficking side of it – that was his specialty. What he needed was an in-depth financial analysis on Colorado and José's businesses, the kind Fernald would do in one of his white-collar investigations.

Fernald readily agreed to help. And when Pennington pitched him to the rest of the team, they were quickly in agreement that it was a good idea.

The next morning, Fernald arrived early and cleared a spot at one of the folding tables in the crowded conference room. Brian Schutt and Kim Williams were already there. There were now eight investigators working through the evidence. Each cardboard box had been colour-coded to denote the city or state where the evidence had been seized. There were receipts, veterinarian bills, even pieces of scratch paper with names and phone numbers and doodles drawn across them, because someone on the evidence team during the raid had thought the notes might be important. Now they had to sort through all of it and figure out if it was. Each scrap of paper would be made into an electronic document. The whiteboards on the walls around them were scrawled with various names, flow charts and other notes in black marker pen that had struck someone as important.

Throughout the day, Pennington or another agent would shout out the names of horses to Kim Williams and Schutt seated at a table in the middle of the room with their laptops. They would check to see if the horse was already on their growing Excel spreadsheet and dutifully add it to the list if not. By now, Pennington and his task force had been working the investigation so long, they had it down cold. But Fernald had less than four weeks to understand everything there was to know about the finances of Francisco Colorado and José Treviño. He opened up his laptop and started reading.

TWO WEEKS WENT BY quickly and Michael Fernald was feeling the intense pressure of trying to come up with a financial analysis of a complex money-laundering conspiracy in so little time. Every day, he combed through stacks of documents until he was blurry-eyed from lack of sleep. He hoped to get some financial documents from ADT Petroservicios during reciprocal discovery. He'd also submitted another MLAT request for financial documents from Mexico – this time through the US State Department. He'd made it a broad request and included the Pemex contracts with ADT Petroservicios. It was his first time working a case with a Mexican business. Typically, he would send his court-ordered subpoenas to banks and corporations and they would provide him with the financial documents within a few weeks or face stiff penalties, even jail time. But he had no such authority in Mexico. He could only request the documents and wait. He knew that Billy Williams and Pennington had got nowhere with their first request. In any investigation, an agent waited for that lucky break, set his hopes on it, but Fernald knew his time was running out.

Five days before the October trial, and seeing that neither side was anywhere near ready, Judge Sparks made a decision. With more than thirty thousand pages of documents from the prosecution, competing trial schedules on the part of the defendants' lawyers and ongoing negotiations over the hundreds of horses in IRS custody, both sides had begged the court for more time. Judge Sparks relented and set a new trial date for 15 April 2013.

The judge's ruling brought much-needed relief for the team. They now had six more months. This meant Michael Fernald had a more realistic chance of getting the information he needed to dig deeper. Lawson's friend, DEA special agent Bill Johnston, had also joined them in a further effort to make amends between the two agencies. Doug Gardner had learned from another prosecutor about some wiretaps between Ramiro Villarreal and Miguel and Omar that the DEA office in Houston held. The recordings the DEA had would help them build their link between Miguel's money and the horses. Johnston told Gardner he would do his best to get the wiretap recordings. Gardner also tasked the young DEA agent with doing email search warrants. Johnston would start with Fernando Garcia's email and work from there.

The one downside to extending the trial date was figuring out what to do with the horses for several more months. Some of them were already getting sick and dying from illnesses due to overcrowding at José's ranch. The IRS had seized 485 horses, many of them still in Lexington under a protective order. At least eleven had already died. José's eldest son, José Jr, had been left in charge of them with a handful of workers. But Junior, who had been born and raised in Dallas, hated the ranching life. He couldn't wait to get out from under the burden of the horses and back to the city. He had already asked the IRS whether he could sell sixty of the less valuable broodmares so there would be fewer animals for him to maintain.

The costs of caring for the horses were also mounting for the federal agency. The day of the raid, the IRS's hired cowboys had hauled away forty-nine of José's most valuable racehorses and were now paying for their care at various stables. The agency had already spent close to a million dollars in just four months. And it didn't help that the press had been tipped off to the sick and dying horses at the Lexington ranch, which generated more bad press for Pennington's thin-skinned bosses in Washington. Horse-racing experts also warned Billy Williams and Pennington that the dozens of yearlings on José's ranch would need to be saddle-broken and trained in the next couple of months if they had any hope for a racing career. They told their bosses that the horses would need to be auctioned off, and soon.

But José's lawyer moved to block the sale of the horses, arguing before the judge that his client had a 'sentimental attachment' to them. After close to a week of sparring in court, José finally agreed to the auction but on one condition: that the government not sell his five most prized horses, which included Mr. Piloto, Separate Fire – which had won the Ed Burke Million Futurity at Los Alamitos – and Tempting Dash. Michelle Fernald and Doug Gardner agreed to the deal. It was also agreed that the proceeds from the auction be held in escrow by the IRS until after the trial. If José were found not guilty, the money would be his.

FIFTY

MIGUEL TREVIÑO HAD LOST THE RANCH IN OKLAHOMA AND HIS BROTHER WAS in jail but, four months after the raid, he'd finally reached the pinnacle of his power. In October 2012, Heriberto Lazcano, the leader of the Zetas, had been gunned down by soldiers in the small town of Progreso, Coahuila, eighty miles south of Nuevo Laredo.

The death of the Executioner made Miguel the sole leader of the Zetas and Omar his second in command. The brothers now controlled half of Mexico. But Miguel's brutal ascension had fostered more enemies than allies. The cartel, now the second largest in the country after the Sinaloa Cartel, was beginning to fracture. After Lazcano's death, a banner was hung in Nuevo Laredo denouncing Miguel as a traitor who had tipped off the military to Lazcano's location and helped authorities capture Mamito and 'El Taliban', another Zeta leader, so he could gain greater power. Some viewed Miguel's siphoning of Zeta funds into the horse ranch and the buying of flashy racehorses in America as reckless and indulgent. The banner, hung in Miguel's hometown, announced that the new splinter group of the Zetas, called Los Legionarios, would kill Miguel and his followers. 'An eye for an eye,' the banner said.

Now the brothers would not only have to fight the Sinaloa Cartel and elements of the Mexican military, they would also have to battle defectors from within their own organisation.

ON THE FIRST DAY of November 2012, Heritage Place held the most unusual and most talked-about auction in its history. Thousands showed up, hoping to buy from some of racing's finest bloodlines put up for auction by the US Department of the Treasury. Having read about José Treviño and the Zetas, many of the auctiongoers were also there just to gawk at the more than three hundred horses up for sale, with names like Big Daddy Cartel, Break Out the Bullets, and Cartel Syndicate.

Pérez had dusted off her cowboy boots for the auction and Lawson wore his customary boots and jeans. Both of them wore concealed holsters under their jackets. As the auctioneer rattled off the bids, the two agents scanned the crowd for anything or anyone that looked suspicious. Pennington and his task force circulated through the stables and around the sales arena. Steve Junker had come along too, since he had pledged to help Pennington with surveillance and security whenever they needed him.

The agents hadn't received any direct threats since the auction had been announced but, with Miguel Treviño now the leader of the Zetas, they knew he could give the order at any time to have them or their sources killed in retribution. Or he might set up a new web of straw buyers to repurchase his most valuable horses at the auction. To prevent this from happening, Pennington and his team would do an extensive background check on each buyer before the sale would be approved.

As Lawson moved in closer to the sales ring, he noticed a

heavy-set Mexican man filming bidders with an iPad and he nudged Pérez, then motioned with his chin to draw her attention.

She glanced over at the large man with the iPad, then nodded at Lawson, letting him know she thought he looked suspicious too.

They moved away from the crowd. 'What do you think?' Lawson asked her.

'He could work for Miguel,' Pérez said, speaking softly so that no one else could overhear them. 'He'd want to know who was bidding on his horses. There could be other cartels here trying to buy them. And he could get his revenge later.'

Lawson sent a text to Pennington and the task force so they'd know to look out for the heavy-set man with the iPad. When Junker got the text and read the description, he realised he was standing right behind him. With his mobile phone, he pretended to snap a photo of the horse being led around the sales ring and got a photo of their suspect in profile. 'You mean this guy?' he wrote back to them in a text with the photo.

Lawson forwarded the photo to a Mexican source to see whether he could identify him as someone who worked for Miguel. The source texted a few minutes later: 'It looks like one of Miguel's *sicarios*, a guy they call "El H,"' he wrote.

'Shit,' Lawson said under his breath and showed the text to Pérez. Now they were both becoming more alarmed. Reporters had turned out to cover the auction and there were thousands of spectators milling around the massive auction house and walking up and down the long rows of stalls to check out the Zetas' horses. Numerous vendors from jewellery makers to livestock insurance companies had set up booths to cater to the throng of spectators. Heritage Place was the size of a small village. If there was a shootout among the cartels, or a kidnapping, it would be a front-page disaster.

'Are you sure?' Lawson wrote back.

'No,' the informant wrote.

'He's not sure,' Lawson said with annoyance to Pérez, who was keeping an eye on the man while Lawson tried to confirm whether he worked for Miguel or not. Lawson sent the photo to two other sources but no one could agree if it was 'El H' or not.

'Well,' he texted to the rest of the team. 'He may be a *sicario* but I can't confirm it.'

'Helpful,' Pennington wrote back.

Lawson and Pérez kept watch over their maybe-or-maybe-not *sicario*, who was taking great interest, along with many others, as the bidding started for a horse called Dash of Sweet Heat. The filly – like Tempting Dash – was the progeny of First Down Dash, one of Miguel's favourite bloodlines.

The filly's previous owner, Julianna Hawn Holt, a co-owner of the San Antonio Spurs, had sold Dash of Sweet Heat at an auction-topping sum of $650,000 the year before in Ruidoso, to Carlos Nayen. A dedicated horsewoman and a mainstay in quarter-horse racing, Holt had been shocked to learn she'd sold her horse to the Zetas. After the raid hit the news, she'd contacted the IRS, offering to buy the filly back. But she was told she'd have to bid for it at auction just like everyone else.

A trusted envoy of Holt's stood near the sales ring with express instructions to buy Dash of Sweet Heat no matter the price. The bidding was fierce and Lawson and Pérez found it hard to identify the bidders in the crowd. The man with the iPad kept filming but never raised his hand to bid. They'd already heard about Holt's quest to get her filly back and expected it would go for a meteoric price. Eventually, Holt's representative prevailed, paying $1 million for a horse Holt had sold the year before for far less. By the end of the three-day auction, the IRS had netted $9 million.

It was a relief to have the auction over with. Even better, there had been no violence, despite the sighting of the alleged *sicario*. With most of José's horses sold off, now the agents could put all of their energy into preparing for the upcoming trial in April.

Steve Pennington could no longer put off his knee surgery. Afterwards, he was ordered by his doctor to stay home and convalesce. Sidelined at home, Pennington had taken to pacing around his yard with his cane when he should have been in bed recuperating. In his view, it was the worst kind of timing, considering he'd just arrested the brother of a drug kingpin and then sold off his prized horses. All he wanted to do was to get back to work in Austin.

FIFTY-ONE

THE FIRST MORNING OF THE TRIAL, 15 APRIL 2013, WAS A WARM AND HUMID spring day in Austin. The newly opened federal courthouse, with its white limestone, steel and glass façade, encompassed half a city block. With its sharp corners and high walls, the eight-storey courthouse looked like an imposing modernist castle ringed by Homeland Security agents hefting high-calibre rifles.

For weeks, stories about Tremor Enterprises and José Treviño had received heavy coverage in the media, much of it centred on the Zetas and the brutality of José's brothers in Mexico. As people filtered into the courthouse, TV reporters set up for their live shots outside, while photographers stationed themselves near the bottom of the stairs to snap photos of the defendants and their family members as they arrived.

Within a one-block radius around the courthouse, Department of Homeland Security SUVs blocked the intersections and the DHS officers responsible for the security outside the courthouse rerouted traffic away from the building. A few days earlier, they'd learned from the city's development office that someone had tried to purchase a copy of the blueprints of the courthouse but a wary clerk had sent the requester away empty-handed. The suspicious incident only heightened the tension among the security team.

The police and the sheriff's department were tasked with the round-the-clock surveillance outside the homes of Michelle Fernald, Doug Gardner and Judge Sam Sparks. Steve Junker was assigned to be Gardner's bodyguard and escort him each day to the courthouse and back home. IRS special agent Bob Rutherford would guard Michelle Fernald.

The two prosecutors had arrived early at the courthouse to prepare for the long day of picking a jury. Both carried bulletproof vests in their cars, which they couldn't bring themselves to put on. It was hard to imagine even the Zetas being brazen enough to open fire on two federal prosecutors in laid-back Austin. But the courthouse's head of security reminded them that the cartel's gunmen had already killed one federal agent in Mexico. Miguel and Omar Treviño were known for their brutal acts, and they couldn't take any chances. As Junker, in a bulletproof vest, scanned the horizon for anything suspicious before Gardner exited the car the first morning of the trial, he couldn't help but think the vests would be useless if the cartel employed a sniper.

The inside of the courthouse was as imposing as its façade – the echoing white marble hallways made many of the potential jurors lower their voices to a whisper. As Judge Sparks watched the biggest courtroom they had fill to capacity, he couldn't hide his annoyance as people stood in the doorway trying to get in. The source of his anger wasn't the people waiting outside but the architects and the bureaucrats in Washington. This would undoubtedly be one of the biggest trials Austin had seen in years. Sparks had chosen the first-floor courtroom for the *voir dire* because it was the only one that could fit in the pool of potential jurors, the media and the defendants' families. But it was still too small. He'd argued for larger courtrooms in the new courthouse but his request had fallen on deaf ears. The judge ordered the bailiffs to set up an overflow room, with a video and audio feed, to accommodate the family members and reporters still waiting in the hallway.

José Treviño's family had arrived early. His mother, petite and with her long grey hair in a single braid, sat stoically in the middle of the second row, flanked by two of her daughters. She had been the only family member in the courtroom in 1995 when her eldest son, Juan Francisco, had been dealt a twenty-year sentence in Dallas. Now she watched as her third-eldest son, dressed in a dark-blue suit, sat down at the crowded defendants' table next to Francisco Colorado, Francisco Garcia, Chevo Huitron and Chevo's brother, Jesse, who was indicted as an accomplice a few weeks after the raid. If convicted, José faced up to twenty years in prison. And since money laundering was a federal charge, there was little chance he'd be granted an early release.

The first day would be devoted to picking the jury. The lawyers, their paralegals and the defendants sat crowded around the long rectangular defence table. Nearly half of the dozen lawyers sitting around the table were on Francisco Colorado's legal team, including his attorney from Mexico and the well-known Houston trial attorney, Mike DeGeurin, deeply tanned and silver-haired, who would lead Colorado's defence. José sat next to his lawyer, David Finn, a high-profile Dallas defence attorney and former federal prosecutor. Next to Finn sat Christie Williams, an experienced defence attorney from Austin whom Finn had brought on as his co-counsel.

On the opposite side of the courtroom, at another long, rectangular conference table, sat the prosecutors: Doug Gardner, Michelle Fernald and Daniel Castillo, who was in charge of asset forfeiture for their office. Steve Pennington and Scott Lawson, dressed in suits and ties, sat across from them at the table facing José and the defendants. Lawson was nervous. This would be the most complex trial he'd ever participated in. He'd given nearly three years of his life to taking down José Treviño and Tremor Enterprises. And he couldn't help but worry about the constellation of high-profile defence lawyers gathered at the table across from him. It would be up to Finn, DeGeurin and the rest to poke holes in their case and plant doubt in the minds of the jury about the guilt of their clients. They would fight for an acquittal or, at the very least, the lightest sentence possible. He thought of the Garcia family and all of the other victims of the Zetas' bloodshed in Mexico. For Lawson, it was about more than just dirty money and racehorses; it was about showing men like Miguel that no one was untouchable.

In the gallery, Alma Pérez sat on one of the hard, wooden benches behind José's mother and sisters, who whispered to one another in Spanish. Pérez noticed that the sisters had brought pens and notepads. The Treviño sisters taking notes would undoubtedly unnerve some of their witnesses on the stand, especially the Mexicans. Pérez imagined they'd report everything they heard back to their brothers. But Judge Sparks couldn't forbid people from taking notes during the trial. Several reporters also sat around Pérez with their pens poised and notebooks ready.

Gardner and Fernald planned to call at least sixty witnesses to the stand. They felt they had enough evidence to prove their case overwhelmingly. But for prosecutors, there was always that fear in the back of their mind that there was something they had missed. As far as the evidence was concerned, there was never enough.

From a pool of at least one hundred potential jurors, it took most of the day to pick sixteen. Twelve would sit in the jury box and the remaining four would serve as alternates in case any of the jurors dropped out because of illness or other reasons. The long day had nearly come to a close when Lawson was jolted by the unexpected. José's lawyer beckoned Tyler Graham's grandfather into the courtroom to be sworn in as a potential witness.

Finn walked to the lectern at the centre of the courtroom. 'He's been kind enough to wait for me to get him before Your Honour. He has been subpoenaed. His name is Dr Charles Graham. If you wouldn't mind swearing him in, then I could put him on telephone standby and he can get on about his business, if that's all right,' said Finn.

Graham, ramrod straight and without his signature cowboy hat, strode down the centre aisle of the courtroom with all eyes on him. He stood in front of the judge's bench, then held up his right hand and swore the oath before the clerk.

Gardner and Fernald had held off on posting their witness list until the last possible moment. There were too many protected witnesses from Mexico who could be scared off, or even killed, by Miguel and Omar. Three men had already died in the course of their investigation. They didn't want to lose another witness in the middle of the trial.

But by now, Finn obviously knew the prosecution would be calling Doc's grandson, Tyler, as their witness. What Finn didn't know was the substance of his testimony, or that he'd been a key source for the FBI throughout their investigation. Doc Graham surely must have had an idea of what his grandson was wrapped up in but he'd been subpoenaed by Finn to appear in court as a witness for José. If he didn't present himself at court, he'd be in contempt and they could issue a warrant for his arrest.

Lawson figured that Finn's strategy was to show how much the Graham family had enriched themselves from their involvement with José. That way he could chip away at Tyler's credibility. But what Finn didn't know yet was that Graham had kept doing business with the Treviños because Lawson and the FBI had asked him to. Lawson supposed that Finn would change his mind about calling Doc Graham to the witness stand once he heard what his grandson, Tyler, had to say about his client.

After Tyler's granddad was sworn in, they adjourned for the day. The real fireworks would begin in the morning. Lawson watched as Doc Graham strode out of the courtroom. He followed quickly through the crowd to try to catch him in the hallway before he left. They had never met and Lawson was curious to meet the man who had shaped so much of his grandson's hard-nosed outlook on business and life.

'Dr Graham!' Lawson called, his words echoing down the white marble hallway. The old man stopped and turned around. 'Dr Graham, I'm Scott,' Lawson said, walking fast to catch up to him. Graham looked at him for a moment, coldly, assessing the stranger before him.

Then his expression changed and he smiled. 'Goddamn,' he said as he realised who Lawson was. 'I don't know what the hell you done but my grandson has a lot of respect for you.' His hand was like a vice on Lawson's as they shook hands. Then Doc Graham turned towards the door and was gone.

ON THE SECOND DAY of trial, photographers rushed to snap photos of Fernando Garcia and the Huitron brothers as they jogged up the stairs of the courthouse, trying to outpace them. Unlike the others, José and Francisco Colorado had been denied bond, so the bailiff brought them into the courtroom from a cell in the back where they held the detainees. The trial would begin at 8.30 am sharp. Judge Sparks didn't tolerate tardiness.

The prosecution would go first, laying out the government's case against José Treviño and his co-conspirators. Doug Gardner, tall and lean and with dark circles under his eyes from long hours of preparing for trial, stood up to address the courtroom and the jury.

'This case is really pretty simple. Los Zetas are a drug cartel. They make their money by drugs, extortion, kidnapping, murder, bribery. They've taken that money, they're sending it to the US to buy racing quarter horses. The two leaders of the drug cartel are Miguel Treviño and Omar Treviño, known as "Cuarenta", "40", and "Cuarenta Dos", "42". They're doing that through their brother over here, José Treviño.' Gardner turned towards José sitting at the defendants' table. 'In thirty months, they've amassed roughly $16 million worth of expenses related to horses. It's that simple. Drug money coming forth to the US to be invested in what is a legitimate business here in the United States. That's money laundering.'

Francisco Colorado, in a designer suit and red silk tie, listened intently to the simultaneous Spanish translation through his headphones. With his sharp nose, shock of grey hair and deep-set eyes, he resembled a predatory bird closely following Gardner's movements around the courtroom. José stared at the jury. He didn't need headphones because he spoke English well enough. He examined the jurors' faces one by one, with an expression of disbelief, as if he couldn't quite believe that these twelve strangers would decide his fate. From time to time, he jotted something down on a notepad in front of him on the table.

Gardner paced in front of the prosecution table. 'The judge said this is a conspiracy case,' he said, his eyes glancing over the jury to make sure he had their full attention. '. . . Really, in this case, we have two charges: we have conspiracy and we have the money laundering. It's all wrapped into one.'

The prosecutors knew that one of their toughest challenges would be making the links on the conspiracy charge for the jury. They had to prove without a reasonable doubt that José and everyone who worked with him knew that the money for the horses came from cocaine. Gardner resorted to the mundane example of a Walmart, which every juror would be familiar with, to explain how a conspiracy worked.

'You have a number of people and they're looking to make money. How do they make money? They sell goods. So you have the CEO, he's in charge. You have the chief financial officer with the money. You have the store managers, the checkout clerks, the people stocking the shelves, the people driving the trucks, the people taking the money to the bank, the financial people, the accountants. Walmart is a conspiracy. It's a legitimate conspiracy.' But instead of cheap imported goods, the Zetas sold cocaine and marijuana, and Miguel Treviño was the cartel's acting CEO. This was the picture Gardner was trying to paint. Unlike Walmart, there was nothing legitimate about Zetas Inc., which dealt in drugs, extortion and murder. And José, Nayen, Garcia and the others, the government alleged, had taken pains to conceal the source of the millions they'd spent on racehorses and the ranch in Lexington. One way they had done this was through the structuring of funds, by making bank deposits under $10,000 on numerous occasions, to avoid filling out reports to the IRS designed to prevent money laundering. Another way was filtering the drug money through businesses in Mexico that would then wire funds to the United States.

Scott Lawson sat across from Michelle Fernald at the prosecution table, watching Gardner pace the floor. It was the second day and he was already feeling antsy, wishing he were back on the street. He knew he'd probably be one of the last to testify. He and Pennington would be called up the final week to wrap up their case for the jury, make sure they recapped all of the key pieces of evidence before the jurors went off to deliberate.

Gardner had predicted the trial could last three weeks or more. Before trial, Pérez had told him he was lucky – at least he didn't have to sit on the hard, wooden benches in the gallery. She wasn't testifying but she'd been working intensively behind the scenes to prepare their Spanish-speaking witnesses for trial – most of them former members of the Zetas. Billy Williams would serve as an expert witness, like Brian Schutt and Michael Fernald, so the three had been advised to stay out of the courtroom until after they'd testified. Kim Williams had been called back to Irving to work on another case.

With so many defendants in the indictment, another challenge for the prosecutors was getting the jurors to remember who each co-conspirator was in the expansive money-laundering scheme. A large screen descended from the wall behind the defendants' table. The jury seemed to rally, welcoming the visual display. Gardner projected one photo after another, first of Miguel, then his brother Omar. The two, he said, had decided to put their brother José into the horse-racing business.

'Tempting Dash wins a race in Dallas. He is transferred between the qualifier and the finals . . . from Ramiro Villarreal to Jose Treviño. And Tempting Dash wins and José Treviño wins four-hundred-and-some thousand dollars based on a fixed race that he begins to build his horse empire with.'

Gardner clicked to the next slide, a photo of Nayen that Lawson had taken at the Ruidoso auction. 'You're going to hear about Carlos Nayen. He's the money man. After Ramiro Villarreal gets killed . . . Carlos Nayen takes his place. He's texting with 40 and 42 for directions. He's the man responsible for co-ordinating the purchase of horses at auctions . . . the payments of the horses at breeding facilities and payments for horses to sustain them in boarding facilities.'

Another photo, this time of Francisco Colorado, appeared on

the overhead screen. 'Also known as "Pancho", you're going to hear evidence that he has an oil-field services company, called ADT Petroservicios. You're going to hear testimony that the company is built on a lie. All of the money he received for that company came from the Zetas' drug money. He's funnelling money based on his legitimate-looking business, both in Mexico and to the United States, for the purchase and sustainment of American quarter horses.' The flesh-and-blood Colorado sitting below the screen shook his head, a look of incredulity on his face, as if everything Gardner had said was an unimaginable lie.

'Next slide, please,' Gardner called. 'Defendant Fernando Garcia . . . Carlos Nayen's right-hand man. When I talk about structured payments, you are going to see at least one day where Fernando Garcia received $90,000, all in $9,000 increments on a single day, and quickly moved them out of his account.'

Gardner cycled through several more photos, including the two horse trainers from California, Felipe Quintero and Adan Farias, whom Carlos Nayen had hired to train horses for them at Los Alamitos.

The next slide showed Eusevio Huitron, Tyler's friend Chevo, the horse trainer who had worked with Tempting Dash and who had introduced José Treviño to the young racing scion, leading him down the path to FBI informant and later witness in federal court. 'You're going to hear evidence that he has met with 40, he trains 40's horses. In between him and his brother, they received over the last two years approximately $500,000 in cash structured into their accounts here in Austin, Texas. Next slide, please. Jesús Maldonado Huitron . . . He is listed along with his brother as the account holder for the Wells Fargo account in which the half a million dollars was washed through.'

At the end of his slide show, Gardner paused for a moment to allow the jury to digest all of the information before he wrapped up his opening statement. He wasn't a fan of the down-home homilies and folksiness that many Texas lawyers trotted out to the jury for a bit of theatricality. He'd save that for the defence lawyers. Gardner was a life-long military man. He favoured a straightforward delivery. The facts were the facts. 'When I come back here at the end of this trial, I'm going to ask you one thing. I'm going to ask you to convict these five defendants and find them guilty of conspiracy to money launder. Thank you.' Gardner gathered up his papers from the lectern and took his seat at the prosecution table.

Now it was the turn of the defence. José's lead attorney, David Finn, sprang up from the table and strode towards the lectern. With his perfectly coiffed dark-brown hair and tailored suit, Finn was going to bring some of the drama that Gardner had eschewed in his opening statement.

'There's more to this story, a whole lot more,' Finn said. 'You're going to hear that my client, who's forty-six years old, US citizen, no criminal history, is related to two bad guys. Two brothers that are in Mexico.'

Finn looked at the jurors knowingly, shaking his head, as if they shared a secret. 'How badly do they want them? Well, the US government has a $5 million bounty on his brother. The Mexican government has a $3 million bounty. There's eight million reasons why my client is sitting in this courtroom right now. His brothers are not here. His brothers are not on trial. My client is on trial.'

Finn was tackling one of their biggest challenges first, and that would be painting his client, José, as humble and law abiding – someone altogether different from his brothers and their brutal, billion-dollar drug business. With the heavy media coverage of the raid and the Zetas' mayhem in Mexico, it would be no easy task.

'José works hard. You're going to hear, over and over, from every single witness, that José is an incredibly hardworking guy . . . You're going to hear he's not some drug-dealing guy going to topless joints. He lived in a little house with his wife and their four children, just outside of Dallas, little ranch house worth about $40,000, maybe. Drives beat-up cars, beat-up trucks. You're not going to hear about Porsches and Lamborghinis, you know, all kinds of cash, because that's not José.'

The money that had built José's racing empire in Oklahoma had all started with one racehorse called Tempting Dash, Finn said. '. . . José's passion other than his family, his passion is his horses . . . And you are going to hear from all sorts of horse people that José knew his stuff . . . This isn't some front. This is a legitimate, real business with real horses, real assets, built on the sweat of my client and his wife. That's what you're going to hear. The big break that José got, he and his wife saved up money and bought this horse that you're going to hear a whole lot about, Tempting Dash. Good horse. José got a good deal on it . . . This horse could run and this horse did run and did win. Quite a bit of money, as Mr. Gardner said. Did José go out and just fritter the money away on wine, women and song? No. What did he do? He invested it.' Finn drew closer to the jury box and looked at the men and the women in the jury again, as if they shared a secret that no one else in the courtroom was privy to. 'They buy another horse. And you're going to hear about a lot of horses. Let me tell you something: a bunch of these horses were bought for, like, four hundred bucks, five hundred bucks, eight hundred bucks. And a whole bunch of these horses, especially the ones up in Oklahoma, didn't even belong to José. He was taking care of them. He was trying to breed them. He did not own them. And you're going to hear all about that from a lot of different people.'

He was trying to build sympathy for his client in the minds of the jurors, planting that seed of doubt, hoping it would flourish. Wanting them to believe that José, a hardworking bricklayer who had lucked out on buying a champion horse for cheap, was now being unfairly persecuted for his brothers' crimes.

'This is all about the brothers. They couldn't get the brothers, boy, they wanted the $8 million bounty. So who are we going to get? Let's get the low-hanging fruit. Let's get José, the brother, who's busting his tail raising his family, paying his taxes, no criminal history, ever . . . Oh, by the way, you know, all these ill-gotten gains that José supposedly made, well, he paid taxes. Boy, that sounds like a criminal, doesn't it? No criminal history. Just going to wake up one day and say, "Hey, I'm going to launder money for the Zetas." Baloney.'

Finn's face took on an expression of disgust at even the mere thought of his client being unfairly accused. He made eye contact again with the jurors. 'I'm going to ask y'all to keep your eye on the ball because the government's going to be talking Zeta, mayhem, beheadings, cartels, oh my – the sky's falling. That ain't why we're here. Don't be prejudiced by the shock and, ah, Zeta, Zeta, Zeta, mayhem, murders, beheadings. And unlike the judge's crystal ball, where you look through it and everything is upside down, when you look at this evidence, the end of the day, everything is going to be right-side-up. And you are going to say, "Man, I don't know."' Finn shook his head from side to side, as if he were a juror struggling under the burden of doubt. '"I just don't know. They didn't prove it."'

Having planted that seed, Finn moved on to his next target: the informants who would testify against José in the coming days. Some of them had worked for Miguel and Omar. 'You know, I was expecting to hear maybe a confession, maybe DNA, maybe fingerprints, maybe guns, maybe money, something other than a bunch of paid confidential informants who have every reason to say whatever the government wants. And the judge will instruct you, ladies and gentlemen of the jury, right before you deliberate, you are to weigh the credibility of this informant or snitch testimony with great care. Why? It's inherently unreliable. Why? They want something. They want a reduced sentence. They want their case dismissed, which, oh, by the way, they've done. They want to stay in the US They're getting paid and they're not telling their probation department they're getting paid. They're not paying taxes on what they're being paid. They're liars. And the government is going to ask you to hang your hat on a bunch of confidential informants, which, frankly, we found out their names yesterday when you did. Yesterday.'

Gardner stood up, not hiding his annoyance. 'Excuse me, Your Honour, I'm going to object to this point. We disclosed all those names to the defendants' attorneys on Friday. That's a misstatement of facts.'

A look of contriteness washed over Finn's face. 'Okay. Excuse me, Your Honour, let me rephrase. Friday before a Monday trial. And I am from Dallas and I'm driving down here, and I don't know who the heck I'm going to be cross-examining. Boy, confidential informants. And this – you're going to love this,' he said with a conspiratorial tone. 'One of the government's witnesses is a guy named Tyler Graham, okay? You heard us talking yesterday about . . . Dr Graham, who is a big vet . . . Owns a bunch of horses in the area, et cetera, et cetera. Initially, this Dr Graham kind of took José under his wing and kind of mentored him and helped him build his business. But José got to be so dadgum good at his business that he became a threat to Dr Graham, and Dr Graham more or less ran him out of town. That's why José, you'll hear about this, why he went to

Oklahoma to get away from Dr Graham, because Dr Graham was getting PO'ed at him, okay?'

Then Finn tried to drive another spike into the notion of Tyler Graham being a reliable witness for the prosecution. 'So, anyway, Dr Graham has a grandson, Tyler Graham, one of the government's witnesses. They're going to call Tyler Graham, "Hey, Mr Graham, what do you know about José Treviño Morales?" And he's going to say whatever he's going to say. And I'm going to ask him, "Hey, buddy, you know what structuring is?" "What do you mean?" "I got your records that show a whole boatload of nine thousand, nine thousand, nine thousand, nine thousand, nine thousand, nine thousand deposits made by you in cash." Remember Mr Gardner just told you, that's structuring. Their own witness is guilty of structuring and he's up to his eyeballs in this. But you don't see him in the courtroom anywhere. Tyler Graham? Tyler? Him . . .' Finn called out, laying it on thick now for the jury.

'Okay. That's enough,' Judge Sparks said. '. . . Let's stay with the opening statement.'

'He's a white guy,' Finn said, nodding knowingly, trying to plant another seed of doubt, so that the jurors would start to wonder why everyone who was indicted was Mexican. What about Tyler Graham or Paul Jones, the well-known horse trainer at Los Alamitos?'

'Your Honour, I'm going to object to that.' Gardner shot up from his seat. 'That is uncalled for.'

'I sustain the objection,' Sparks said with irritation. 'Make your opening statement. All people in this courtroom, including the defendants, have equal rights, no matter what their race or background is. And I strike those remarks. Now, proceed.'

'When Tyler Graham comes to court, you can size him up,' Finn said, eyeing the jury once again as if they were the only ones in the room. 'The judge will give you, and the government just told you, what proof beyond a reasonable doubt is . . . If you think the government proved the case, the state proved the case, you convict; if not, you vote not guilty . . . It's going to be an interesting trial. Thank you,' Finn said, then walked solemnly back to his seat at the defendants' table.

Now that the opening statements were over, the prosecution would go first. Gardner and Fernald would devote the first days of the trial to educating the jury about the Zetas and the kind of power and money that José's brothers possessed in Mexico.

Lawson watched José's face to see if his expression would change as Gardner called Poncho Cuellar to testify. A US Marshal escorted Cuellar, wearing a prison uniform, into the courtroom. José's face retained the same blank expression, Lawson noticed, masking any hint of recognition as Cuellar sat down at the witness stand. The former smuggler for the Zetas had been a major breakthrough for their case, providing them with a complete picture of how Miguel's operation worked, from the cocaine going north to the money coming south, then being redistributed to his brother and their network of straw buyers. And now Lawson hoped Cuellar would connect all the dots for the jury.

Gardner moved in closer to the witness stand to address Cuellar. 'Do you know why 40 and 42 have never been arrested in Mexico?' he asked.

'Yes.' Cuellar nodded. 'All right. Why is that?'

'Because they had bought off all the police in Mexico, the army, and people in high places in Mexico. Everything,' Cuellar said.

In the gallery, one of José's sisters took notes, watching Cuellar closely. By testifying, no doubt, Cuellar hoped to reduce his twenty-year sentence for drug smuggling and become a protected witness. The US government would give him a new identity. In Mexico, he was already dead.

'And were you aware of 40 and 42 or Mamito buying horses in the United States?' Gardner asked.

'Yes, sir.'

'And where would you buy those horses?'

'In Oklahoma and Ruidoso . . . First at auctions and then we went directly to the owners.'

'And are you familiar with an individual named Ramiro Villarreal?'

'Yes, sir.'

'And how do you know him?'

'He's the one that bought Tempting Dash and Mr. Piloto, lots of horses, a lot of mares that were really fast in Mexico. He was recognised as buying really good racehorses in Mexico.'

'And who would he buy these horses for?'

'For Omar and Miguel and for other people. That was his business.'

'And speaking of business, how were these horses paid for in the United States?'

'They were bought through people that didn't – weren't being investigated by the IRS who were very solvent and could not be questioned about where the money was coming from.'

'And what type of people were these?'

'People that had big businesses like Pancho Colorado and Alejandro Barradas.'

'. . . How would the businessmen, after they first took the horses, get reimbursed by the cartel?'

'They were paid in Mexico . . . [by] Miguel, or through Cuno or Metro or whoever was in charge in Veracruz.'

'Do you know what happened to Ramiro Villarreal?'

'He was killed.'

'And who killed him?'

'Omar. Sorry, Miguel . . . They realised that he was co-operating with the US authorities.'

'Are you familiar with an individual by the name of Alejandro Barradas?'

'Yes, sir.'

'And what happened to Mr Alejandro Barradas?'

'He was killed, thanks to Carlos Nayen going and telling Miguel that Alejandro Barradas didn't want mares in his name [anymore] . . . and so he was killed.'

Gardner now turned his line of questioning towards José and his involvement in his brothers' conspiracy. 'Did Cuarenta ever tell you about the role of his brother José Treviño in the horse business?'

'Yes, sir.'

'And what did he tell you?'

José's other attorney, Christie Williams, stood up abruptly. 'Objection. Hearsay. Confrontation clause.' She was unleashing an arsenal of legal objections to Cuellar's testimony on her client and hoping one of them would stick.

Judge Sparks apprised Williams for a moment. 'I sustain the objection to the question asked.'

Gardner tried to recast the question. 'Did Miguel Treviño ever tell you he involved his brother José Treviño in the horse business?'

'Same objection,' Williams said.

'Well, that I'm going to overrule,' Sparks said.

Omar had spoken to him about his brother José, Cuellar explained, and how he worked hard and wanted nothing to do with their drug business. 'I met him, I learned that was true that he wanted nothing to do with the drugs.' But then Ramiro Villarreal bought Tempting Dash for Miguel and soon the horse was registered to José, making him rich.

After several more questions, Cuellar was escorted out of the courtroom. The prosecutors had one more important witness they wanted to bring before the jury that day. Lawson watched as José Luis Vasquez Jr was led to the stand. Their debriefing of Vasquez in Plano had been an education for Lawson in the vast wealth that could be made from selling drugs in the States – the biggest drug market in the world. Slight of build and ordinary-looking, Vasquez had started off at age fourteen selling dime bags of coke in the streets of South Dallas. By the time he was thirty-two, he was a multi-millionaire and the Zetas' biggest cocaine distributor in Dallas. It was Vasquez, along with Hector Moreno, who had passed along the cartel leaders' phone numbers to the DEA, touching off Miguel's murderous purge of Cuellar's workers. After Miguel and Omar unleashed their vengeance on Piedras Negras, Vasquez had figured a jail cell in the United States wasn't so bad. Now he was testifying with the hope of reducing a thirteen-year prison sentence handed down by a federal judge in Dallas.

Vasquez explained to the jury how he usually distributed 1,000 kilos of coke a month and held 2,000 more for other dealers in the region. 'Once I had it in my possession, I was like a warehouse for them . . .'

'Would you supply the transportation for the cocaine?' Gardner asked.

'Yes,' Vasquez said.

'And can you let the ladies and gentlemen of the jury know some of the cities in which the cocaine was distributed?'

'Well, we were working everywhere in Dallas, Fort Worth, Arlington, Grand Prairie, St Louis, Missouri . . .'

'. . . How was the money transported from Dallas once you received it to Mexico?'

'We were sending it in a lot of trucks in the gas tanks. We

would put three vacuum-sealed bags and take off the bed of the truck and open up where the fuel pump goes and put it in through there, inside the gas tank.'

Now that their witness had described how the drugs were received and the money hidden and transported back to Mexico, Gardner directed his line of questioning towards the drug money and the horses. 'Were you ever directed to deliver drug proceeds for the payment of horse expenses in the Dallas, Texas area?'

'Yes, sir.'

'Okay. And how many times?'

'Maybe about eight or ten times.'

Gardner asked him to describe the time he'd sent money to José Treviño, who was waiting in a Walmart parking lot near Dallas. Because it was Miguel's brother, Vasquez had sent his own father to deliver the money.

'Hector Moreno told me it was going to be for 40's brother, that it needed to be nothing but hundreds because it would be 40's brother.'

'. . . And you said earlier that you made some deliveries to Carlos Nayen in the Dallas area . . . How many deliveries do you think you made to Mr Nayen in Dallas?'

'I want to say about at least four, four or five times.' The delivery destinations had included Lone Star Park, Retama Park in San Antonio and various hotels in the Dallas area, Vasquez said.

Vasquez then described to the jury how he'd sent some of Miguel's cocaine profits from Dallas to Ruidoso to bribe the gate starters at the 2010 All American Futurity. 'Hector told me . . . he needed $110,000 to be in New Mexico before a race. I think they had a horse that was called Mr. Piloto was going to race over there.'

'Mr Vasquez, in total, could you give the jury an idea of how much money you were directed to spend for horse expenses during the time you were distributing in Dallas?'

'Maybe about $900,000.'

'Was all that money derived from the sale of cocaine?'

'Yeah. That was the only money I had for them. It was all from selling cocaine.'

'And how were you reimbursed, or were you reimbursed that money?'

'Like I said earlier, I would get a thousand kilos of cocaine a month. So I always had their funds because I would send back maybe three or four million [dollars] a week. So if they needed something there in that week, it would come out of whatever I was going to be sending. So it was never my money. It was always their money.'

Gardner left off with his testimony there, so that the jury could consider the vast amounts of money the Zetas were making. Vasquez was just one of the cartel's many wholesale distributors. It was clear that Miguel and Omar could afford to spend as much as they liked on their passions. All they had to do was give the order.

Now it was the defence's turn to cross-examine Vasquez. Lawson could see that his testimony had had its impact on the jurors, who had raptly followed the testimony. Here was one of the Zetas' own dealers talking about how he'd delivered cash to José Treviño in a parking lot outside Dallas. Now José's defence attorney would try his best to discredit Vasquez's damaging testimony. But time was not on Finn's side. It was nearly 6 pm and soon Judge Sparks would adjourn the court for the day.

Finn stood up and, with a furrowed brow, walked solemnly toward the centre of the courtroom to begin his questioning of the former drug dealer.

'You were looking at something like three hundred months in the pen until you started co-operating, correct?'

'I believe so. I'm not aware how much months I was going to get.'

'You're telling this jury you don't know what your exposure was on that federal case. Is that your testimony?' Finn said, incredulous.

'You're asking me how much did I know before I started co-operating,' Vasquez said, blinking. 'I didn't know when I started co-operating, I didn't know how much time I was going to get.'

'And you got your sentence cut basically in half because the government filed a five-K motion for downward departure, correct?'

'Yes, sir.'

Finn pointed towards Gardner sitting at the prosecution's table. 'And you're really hoping big time that this gentleman right here, Doug Gardner, the prosecutor in this case, at the end of this trial will pick up the phone and call the AUSA in Plano, Ernest Gonzalez, and say, "Hey, Ernest, this guy really came through for us, let's cut his sentence even more," or at least ask the judge to cut it even more. That's what you want to have happen, correct?'

'I know that they're going to ask – they can ask the judge and it's up to the judge to decide on it. Yes, sir.'

'Okay. Maybe you didn't understand my question,' Finn said more forcefully. 'That's what you're hoping will happen, yes or no?'

'Well, when I started . . .'

'I'm sorry . . .'

'Now, wait a minute,' Judge Sparks interjected. 'He's letting you ask the question. You let him answer.'

'Fair enough,' Finn said, shaking his head.

'When I first turned myself in, I signed a proffer agreement with the government stating that I was going to help the government in full, not to withhold no information. So I've told, in full, information against my father, against my own family. So I know that they told me, if I get caught in any kind of lies, that anything that I say would get wiped out immediately. So from day one, I knew that, when I signed the paper, I was already – whatever the government requested of me, if I knew anything, to tell the truth.'

'So whatever the government requested, if you could, you're going to come through for them, right?'

'Yes, sir.' Vasquez nodded.

'. . . Tell the members of the jury what other kind of criminal activity you've been up to lately.'

'Your Honour.' Gardner sprang up from his chair. 'We object to that with respect to improper impeachment.'

'Your Honour, I've got a good . . .' Finn sputtered.

'Well, no,' Judge Sparks said, waving a hand. 'Just wait . . . I'll listen to the lawyers for five minutes and let y'all go home,' he said, directing his gaze toward the jury. The judge had heard enough and it was late in the day. Everyone in the courtroom stood up, then waited and watched as the twelve men and women got up and filed out through a back door in the courtroom.

Once they were gone, Judge Sparks turned his gaze back to Finn, who was now on the hook. He didn't want to reveal his line of questioning to Gardner and Fernald without the jury present. 'I think it's unfair to me to give them a preview because, then, over the break this evening, they can try to, quote, get their story straight. But I'll do it in any way you want,' Finn said.

'Judge, I can't talk to that witness, so there's no cross-examination,' Gardner protested.

'I know that and he knows that too,' said Judge Sparks. After a few more minutes of verbal sparring among the three, he adjourned the courtroom for the day. Finn would be ready for Vasquez in the morning.

THE NEXT MORNING, THE JURORS were seated and, as Vasquez sat down again at the witness stand, Finn appeared before him, coiled and ready to strike.

'. . . Tell the members of the jury, if you don't mind, how you're so familiar with assault weapons . . . You've admitted that you sold AR–15s, AK–47s, .308s, and anything bigger. You could get whatever you wanted, maybe even a machine gun if you wanted, and those were sold by you, transported to Mexico, is that correct?'

'Yes, sir.' Vasquez nodded.

'Tell the members of the jury about the chimney.'

Vasquez hesitated. 'Well, I had money inside my mother's chimney.'

'Couple of bucks?' Finn said, smiling.

'Five hundred thousand dollars.'

'Five hundred thousand dollars . . . in your mother's chimney?' Finn said, making sure it sank in with the jury. By the time he was through, he was going to make the twelve jurors think Vasquez was such a lowlife that no one could trust a word he said. 'Tell the members of the jury about when you were arrested. How did that go down?'

'. . . I turned myself in at the border in El Paso.'

'. . . You were worried that the *federales* in the US were going to go after your wife and then your mum because they found out she had half a million squirrelled away in her chimney, is that right?'

'Yes, sir,' Vasquez said, blinking. Finn paused for a moment, letting it sink in so the jury could consider what kind of son left his mother facing federal charges while he went on the lam in Mexico.

Gardner stood up with a redirect for the witness. He wanted the jury to know that the government was fully aware of Vasquez's criminal past, but that didn't mean their witness wasn't telling the truth. 'Mr. Vasquez . . . who was the organisation you were sending the guns to?'

'To Los Zetas . . . they were in a war with the Gulf Cartel and other cartels.'

'So, I know it's an obvious question. But what purpose did they need the guns in connection with their war with the Gulf Cartel?'

'To defend themselves. They were fighting for territory. They were killing each other.'

'And this money in the chimney, did you let law enforcement know you had money in the chimney?'

'My wife let the agents know and they asked me and I confirmed it. Told them where it was at.'

'And law enforcement recovered that $500,000 in the chimney?'

'Yes, sir.'

'Pass the witness, Your Honour.' Gardner sat back down.

Finn unsuccessfully hammered away at Vasquez for another round until the judge finally put a stop to it. The drug dealer was excused and a US Marshal took him through a side door to the holding cell in the courthouse.

After Vasquez and Cuellar, Gardner and Fernald were still not done giving the jury a crash course in the Zetas' domination of Mexico and the international drug trade. But this time, their next witness wouldn't be one of the cartel's dealers, but one of the men who truly understood how the Zetas' drug empire worked – one of the cartel's accountants.

Pale and bespectacled, José Carlos Hinojosa, known as 'Charly', wasn't a defector from the Piedras Negras plaza like Poncho Cuellar and his crew. Hinojosa had turned himself in to the US authorities in 2008 to save his own life. And while he couldn't attest to the more recent actions of Miguel and Omar Treviño, he'd once served as the accountant for Efraín Teodoro Torres, or Z-14, one of the cartel's former military founders, who had helped the paramilitary organisation become a shadow government in Veracruz. Hinojosa, a former attorney in a federal prosecutor's office, had helped his boss, Z-14, put their candidate in the governor's mansion in Veracruz and control every level of government down to the local police squads who patrolled the streets. Now he would testify about how powerful businessmen in Veracruz, like Francisco Colorado, had been crucial in helping bring the Zetas to power.

Michelle Fernald stood up from the prosecution table and stepped towards the witness stand. Fernald liked to move around the courtroom, unlike Gardner, and with her short blonde hair and stylish skirt and heels, she was an energetic counterpoint to Gardner's more unadorned style.

'Do you know who Francisco Colorado Cessa is?' asked Fernald.

'Yes.' Hinojosa nodded.

'And did he go by a nickname?'

'We knew it was "Pancho" Colorado.'

'Can you identify him for us?'

'I see him from here,' said Hinojosa, staring at Colorado.

'Okay. Can you point toward him?'

Hinojosa raised his hand and pointed at Colorado sitting at the defendant's table. 'Yes, he's seated at that table over there and he's in a grey suit.' As Hinojosa pointed, Francisco Colorado made a sour face like he had never seen Hinojosa before in his life.

It was in 2004, Hinojosa testified, that he met Pancho

Colorado, the wealthy cattle rancher and businessman from Tuxpan, Veracruz.

'Tell me about ADT Petroservicios. We've heard a little bit about it. But tell me what type of company it was,' asked Fernald.

Hinojosa nodded. 'It was a company to build highways, to do Pemex projects, to do drilling, to do clean-up, things like that, anything that the government Pemex hired them to do.' Hinojosa explained that it was his boss, Z-14, who had given Colorado the millions to grow the company, in which Z-14 was a partner. They had also funnelled millions to Fidel Herrera's gubernatorial campaign – the candidate for the PRI – so that, when Herrera won, he'd be sure to steer valuable government contracts to ADT Petroservicios. Hinojosa had made note of it all in his accounting ledger for Z-14. 'For the governor's campaign, what I had entered was $12 million. For the purchase of the machinery, it was $6 million; for the purchase of some horses, $180,000. That's what I remember, more or less.'

'When was Efraín Torres killed?'

'March of 2007.'

'Was Pancho Colorado Cessa able to sell ADT Petroservicios and do what he wanted with it?'

'At that moment, I don't believe he could have sold it because he was really in debt to Zeta 14 when Zeta 14 was killed.'

Fernald paced in front of the jury box, making eye contact with the jurors, to make sure that what Hinojosa was saying was connecting with them. Her parents had been teachers and she often thought of the courtroom as her classroom. 'He was in a lot of debt. So I need to know, who took over the position of Efraín Torres, "Zeta 14", after he was killed?'

'Forty,' Hinojosa said.

'And who did Francisco Colorado Cessa report to after Efraín Torres was killed?'

'With Forty.'

'And how do you know that?' Fernald asked.

'Because when Zeta 14 was killed, I was pulled into a meeting. They called a meeting about everybody – for everybody that worked there – and there was an accounting . . . It was to find out what had happened and to get everybody who had worked with him, with Zeta 14, together and to see if we could continue working; and to find out everything that there was, everything that they had, all the debts, find out everything about the state of Veracruz.'

'Who is "they"? Who called the meeting?'

'Lazcano and Forty.'

'Were you present at this meeting?'

'Yes.'

'Did you directly report to Forty about Efraín Torres's property and money? . . . And when you reported to him, did you, in fact, tell him about Francisco Colorado Cessa?'

'Yes . . . I gave him the full list of everybody who owed money. It wasn't just Pancho. It was a lot of people. But then I explained to him that what I had listed there as the debt was I did not have the last report and that Zeta 14 had told me that he owed much more than what's showed.'

'Do you know whether or not the debt was ever settled with Francisco Colorado Cessa and Forty over Efraín's affairs?'

'Yes. Well, yeah, because I had the list, and he said, "All the people that owe you, you go get – collect that money – and the ones that don't, you tell the ones there at the border to have them picked up." And then, about a month to a month and a half later, he called me and said to take Pancho off the list because he had already worked it out with Francisco Colorado.'

'Who called you and told you to take him off of the debt list?'

'Forty.'

Colorado's lead defence attorney, Mike DeGeurin, was already standing at the defence table, anxious to cross-examine the witness. He could scarcely wait for Fernald to vacate the lectern as he strode towards the centre of the courtroom. He was going to try to distance his client from the taint of being in business with Z-14, as Hinojosa had just testified.

DeGeurin looked down at his legal pad then made direct eye contact with Hinojosa. '. . . Let's just say that he was slowly paying him back, I don't know. For sake of argument for the government's argument, he's slowly paying him back, this loan from a bad guy, maybe he knew that the bank had – or that Mr Torres had – gotten some bad moneys along the way, and he borrowed the money and he's paying him back. Then Mr Torres dies in 2007. In 2008, this man [Hinojosa] goes to jail. And the government is saying that that money that was loaned back then, it was owed to the man that's dead, is ill-gotten gains, that they're paying later out of a company that's very successful.'

DeGeurin shook his silver mane and frowned, then looked up at the judge. 'It would almost be like saying if Mr Kennedy – old man Kennedy bootlegged whiskey and that, later on, the children took money from the grandfather's inheritance and made their own businesses, you'd follow it. There's got to be a line somewhere. What I'm saying is, Judge, I think there's too far a gap between a loan that he talks about, $6 million loan, and a $1 million, $2 million wires from ADT in 2010 or '11 and '12. You cannot point to the specific activity and the money that is illegal.'

Judge Sparks stared at DeGeurin, looking slightly incredulous. 'You're taking the position in this case, Mr DeGeurin, that Mr Colorado didn't use Zeta funds?'

'That's correct.'

'To buy horses.'

'That's right,' DeGeurin said. '. . . Yes. I'm not quite sure what he's going to say when he wrote down in his machine, as he puts it, that $180,000 was given to Mr Colorado to buy horses. Mr Colorado was buying horses for much more than that. He was paying a lot more. One horse or two horses cost more than that. So I'm not really quite sure about that $180,000. But the other's so far removed, Judge, that it should not be allowed.'

'Well, you denied that he used Zeta money to buy horses,' said Sparks dryly.

'Yeah.' DeGeurin nodded. 'He did not use Zeta money . . . did not knowingly use any Zeta money because the money that he used was money that was paid to his company. And he owned contracts, legitimate contracts with Pemex, and you saw the list of some of those contracts. He was being paid in excess of $70 million a year from the oil company . . .'

Lawson watched the noted defence attorney make his case. Oratorically, DeGeurin was walking in circles. Maybe he was trying to confuse the jurors, if nothing else. Now he launched into his second attack – this time arguing like Finn had that the government's witness was nothing more than a jailhouse snitch whose word wasn't worth the paper it was printed on.

Hinojosa hadn't exactly been the model prisoner. In South Texas, he'd bribed the warden to allow prison visits from his wife and girlfriend on alternating days. Then he paid off the guards so they wouldn't tell his wife about the girlfriend. He'd also bribed them for a mobile phone, which he'd used to try to negotiate the release of his brother and father, who had been kidnapped in Mexico by the Zetas after he'd run to Texas. Since his arrest in 2008, he'd offered anything he knew to several prosecutors in an effort to reduce his long stretch in federal prison.

DeGeurin sized up Hinojosa with a befuddled look. '. . . What's bugging me is that, through all those years of meeting with the multiple agents, talking about all these people, it wasn't until after the newspapers came out—'

Now it was Fernald's turn to object. 'Your Honour, again, objection . . . Is there a question aside?'

'Eventually,' Sparks said with a note of sarcasm. 'Just ask questions, counsel.'

'Yes, later, after multiple meetings, the first time you mentioned anything about Francisco Colorado was after the newspapers said Mr Colorado has been indicted and accused of a crime. That's when you first talked about or said you had information about Mr Colorado. Is that true?' asked DeGeurin, his eyes narrowing on Hinojosa.

'I don't remember when the first — that was the first time. But since the time I was arrested, they've known everything, everything about who I worked for. And that, once he was arrested . . . they asked me for information about him.'

'Now being 2012?'

'Don't remember, but it seems like it. Yes.'

'. . . You continued to commit crimes that had the potential of corrupting our justice system while you were incarcerated, didn't you? . . . And that included not only the $100,000 you offered to get out of jail. Did we talk about that earlier?'

'No.' Hinojosa shook his head.

'Okay. You did offer $100,000 to get out of jail, right?'

'One of the bonds people . . . told me that, for $100,000, he could get me out of jail. He'd get me out of jail as long as I didn't come back to the United States and that I shouldn't ask about how he got the $100,000. And since he had gotten other people out, I put my trust in him.'

Hinojosa was starting to sweat and growing paler as DeGeurin hammered him with questions. The defence attorney turned and grabbed a piece of paper from a file folder on the defence table, then approached the witness stand, waving the paper for a bit of a flourish. 'I have gone to the trouble to try to put together the number of times that you spoke with agents and prosecutors to try to reduce your sentence,' DeGeurin said.

Fernald quickly stood up. 'Your Honour, I object. Either he's going to testify, take the oath and get on the witness stand or he can ask a question,' she said, exasperated.

'Well . . .' said Judge Sparks.

'It's a predicate,' interjected DeGeurin quickly.

'He's showing a piece of paper to the witness,' said Sparks. 'I'll allow him to tell his description of the paper . . . But let's don't testify. Just describe what the exhibit or paper is.'

DeGeurin went ahead with his bit of theatre. At least the jurors were fully awake now and watching to see what he'd do next. 'Would you quarrel with the statement that you met with [government agents] at least twenty-eight times to give them information to see if it would be useful to lower your sentence?'

Hinojosa barely glanced at the paper that DeGeurin put down before him. 'I do not remember how many times but there were many times that I met with government agents . . . I've been locked up for fifty-five months . . . I don't remember if it was five, ten, fifteen. I could tell you it was many times.'

DeGeurin kept chiselling away at Hinojosa's credibility until Judge Sparks finally adjourned for the day at 6 pm. The jurors looked as exhausted as the witness as they filed out of the courtroom.

THE FIRST PART OF the week had been devoted to educating the jurors about drug cartels, guns and money. The latter half would focus on the quarter-horse industry. On the fourth day of the trial, Doug Gardner called Dr Shalyn Bliss as a witness. A young, attractive woman with long, wavy dark hair tentatively sat down in the witness box and swore the oath. Bliss explained to the jury how she was just starting off in her veterinary practice when she was hired in January 2012 by José Treviño to oversee his horse-breeding program in Lexington. Bliss said her former boss was hardworking, and chivalrous towards her when she was pregnant and working long hours on the farm. But he also seemed unusually paranoid. He didn't want owners' names attached to any of the horses' files and he forbade pharmaceutical reps and anyone else he didn't know from visiting her at the farm, which she thought was unusual at the time.

'In the course of your employment with the defendant José Treviño, did you have a discussion with him on how he obtained his funds to purchase this ranch and those horses?' Gardner asked.

Bliss nodded, looking nervous. '. . . He told me that he was a mason and had built up a construction company, and that the business had been kind of rough the last few years and that he had decided to sell his companies and invest in the ranch,' she said.

'And did he provide you the names of those construction companies?'

'No.' Bliss shook her head.

When she first started working at the ranch, Bliss explained, José had around three dozen horses but, in a few short months, there were as many as four hundred and the ranch was becoming dangerously overcrowded. The horses could die from infectious disease or trample one another.

'Do you recall if he had all of his horses on the ranch?' asked Gardner.

'No. Not all of the horses were on the ranch. There were mares at other breeding farms being bred there. And I also was aware that he had some horses in training at various tracks around the country.'

'Once you began talking to Mr Treviño, was he very open and honest with you about the fact that he didn't know much about breeding?'

'In the beginning, I don't know that we had that frank of a discussion about it. He told me he had a lot of mares and owned the two stallions that were in Texas. And then, once we started going on things, then, yeah, we talked a lot about that he had never ran an operation like this and that he didn't – there were a lot of things he didn't know . . .'

José watched Dr Bliss on the stand as she carefully answered Gardner's questions. His face was a mask that Lawson couldn't read. José didn't wear a fat gold Rolex or drive a Ferrari. He could see how Bliss would not have expected anything when she first started working on the Lexington ranch. It must have been a shock when she learned her new boss was the American front for a Mexican cartel.

FIFTY-TWO

ON MONDAY MORNING, THE SECOND WEEK OF TRIAL, ALMA PÉREZ TOOK HER seat in the gallery directly in front of the prosecutors' table, where she made eye contact with Lawson and he smiled back. Reporters were still milling around outside in the hallway looking for people to interview. Pérez was glad to see that no one had approached the man with the dark, slicked-back hair in an elegant business suit, who stared out the window, a mobile phone pressed to his ear. She knew that today the reporters would not be disappointed with their star witness.

Judge Sparks called the courtroom to order. And as the reporters, José's mother and sisters, and other family members of the defendants settled in their seats in the packed gallery, Doug Gardner stood up to call their first witness to the stand.

'The government calls Mr Alfonso del Rayo Mora.'

Del Rayo walked down the aisle and through the small swinging door to the front of the courtroom and the judge's bench. All eyes were on the man in the expensive suit as the clerk administered him the oath.

Lawson felt relief as del Rayo took a seat on the witness stand

and a bailiff brought him a glass of water. He'd been worried that he might be killed before he could ever testify in Austin. Del Rayo had been advised to call Pérez or Lawson immediately if he received a threat or saw anything suspicious outside his home. He'd also been assigned a security detail to escort him to the courthouse in Austin and back to San Antonio.

After Lawson and Pérez and the prosecutors had met with del Rayo in Austin and examined his evidence and heard his story, they'd been convinced that he wasn't a willing participant in the money-laundering conspiracy and removed him from the indictment. Instead he'd been a victim and was lucky to be alive. Del Rayo had managed the almost impossible – he had survived a Zetas kidnapping. And now he was brave enough to testify, even if it meant he might never be able to return to Mexico with his family. Throughout the weeks leading up to the trial, del Rayo's resolve to testify had never wavered. Lawson knew that his testimony would be one of the most riveting of the trial.

Sensing that something newsworthy was about to happen, the reporters sitting around Pérez already had their notebooks out and pens poised. As del Rayo began to tell his story of how he'd been picked up by the Zetas in Veracruz and beaten and tortured for nine days, the courtroom became so quiet that Pérez could hear someone coughing outside in the hallway. The reporters were furiously writing down del Rayo's every word, trying not to miss a single sentence. One of José's sisters was also busily writing.

'When they . . . kidnapped you, did they inflict any injuries upon you?' asked Gardner, wanting del Rayo to paint a fuller picture for the jurors of what the Zetas had done to him.

Gardner displayed some slides on the large screen hanging behind the defendants' table of a battered del Rayo. These were photos that he had brought with him in his suitcase, along with his medical records, when he'd met Lawson and Pérez at the airport in San Antonio.

'Yeah. They beat me up. They beat me up pretty bad. I thought I was going to be killed,' said del Rayo. He had remained stoic during the beginning of the testimony but, as Gardner clicked through the various photos of his battered face and hands, he began to choke up and tears came to his eyes as he described his ordeal for the jury.

'Did you feel you had the option of saying no to Carlos Nayen?' asked Gardner.

'No . . . I started receiving calls . . . with death threats about, if I didn't get that money, I will get killed or my family.'

Gardner showed a series of del Rayo's bank cheques on the screen made out to Graham's Southwest Stallion Station. 'Could you explain to the jury what these are for?'

'. . . I had a lot of trouble transferring the money from Mexico to the States for obvious reasons, you know, that was a lot of money. And it took some time to get the wire through . . . So there was money left to pay this company. I had to come over myself and give the cheques to Tyler Graham . . .'

At the defence table, José's lawyers had decided not to wade into a cross-examination of del Rayo. It could only open up other lines of questioning from the prosecution, which wasn't going to help their client after what the jurors had just seen and heard. The tension in the courtroom was palpable. Del Rayo's testimony had hit a nerve with the jurors, Lawson could tell. No doubt they were starting to fully comprehend the devastation the cartel had wrought on ordinary citizens in Mexico who were just like them, trying to raise their families and go on about their lives. But in Veracruz, it had become impossible. And now here was del Rayo, a man without a country, who only wanted to go home.

Judge Sparks excused del Rayo from the witness stand. He walked slowly up the aisle as everyone stared, and a guard held the door open for him. Some of the reporters quickly grabbed their notepads and followed, hoping to get an interview. But del Rayo, surrounded by his security detail, didn't linger in the hallway for any questions. He was gone before they could even ask.

IN THEIR PRESENTATION BEFORE the jury, Gardner and Fernald had laid the groundwork for Miguel and Omar's brutal ascent through the Zetas' criminal empire. Alfonso del Rayo was living proof of Miguel's power over Veracruz and the Zetas' role as a shadow government in states like Veracruz, Tamaulipas and Coahuila. They'd also called members of the quarter-horse racing world to the witness stand to illustrate how loosely regulated racing was and how easily cash changed hands with minimal paperwork. Money and greed fuelled the industry. This had been one of Lawson's most troubling findings during the investigation. It was a sad realisation that the horses were often used up quickly and sacrificed for the sake of winning. The trainers injecting them with everything from a concoction called 'purple pain' to steroids like clenbuterol or zilpaterol to get the injured animal to race, even if the horse died afterwards.

This was a cruel, high-stakes world that men like Francisco Colorado understood. And he had been a crucial player in Miguel's money-laundering scheme, but the evidence they needed – the bank statements and business ledgers from ADT Petroservicios – had been impossible for Pennington's task force to obtain. Michael Fernald had also struck out with his request through Mexico City, just like Pennington and Billy Williams before him.

But as Pennington had hoped, Fernald hadn't given up there. An expert in unravelling white-collar fraud, the young IRS agent had finally made a breakthrough. Fernald discovered that Colorado had an account in Miami with the global Swiss bank UBS. Fernald subpoenaed UBS. From those documents, he discovered that the businessman had applied for an $18 million loan from UBS, which meant he'd been required to provide financial statements about his cash flow and his profits and losses at ADT Petroservicios. This was exactly the type of financial evidence the team had been trying to track down for months.

As Doug Gardner called Fernald to the witness stand, Pennington felt a sense of satisfaction. Fernald's testimony and the charts he would be presenting to the jury would clearly show that, while Colorado was a wealthy man, his company couldn't afford to be pouring millions of dollars into racehorses. He had to be getting his money somewhere else – just like José Treviño, who had suddenly become a millionaire. Fernald had also combed through José's Bank of America accounts and would lay out for the jury the evidence behind his sudden and mysterious spike in wealth.

First, Fernald broke down his findings on the business run by Francisco Colorado. Ninety-nine per cent of ADT's revenue came from its contracts with Mexico's government-owned oil company, Pemex. Yet the company had had its contracts with Pemex suspended twice in the last five years because of allegations of fraud and overcharging for services. Meanwhile, Colorado had kept spending millions and applying for large loans like the one with UBS. Colorado lived out of his ADT account, mixing his business and lavish personal expenses, which included private jets, four-star hotels and expensive racehorses.

As Fernald testified from the witness stand, Gardner displayed on the wall near the defence table an illustrated chart that

Fernald had helped create with a timeline of ADT's income and expenses. The chart started at the beginning, with the formation of the company in 2001 and the $18 million invested by Z-14 before he was killed in 2007. Also included was the $2.2 million Colorado had spent in 2010 at the horse auction in Ruidoso. The money had been wired from ADT to his US bank account at Compass Bank.

In a span of three years, Colorado had spent $10.1 million on horses and horse-related expenses, explained Fernald to the jurors. What he had concluded from his financial analysis and what the evidence showed was that Colorado didn't have the cash flow in ADT to be buying so many expensive racehorses. 'He couldn't operate and pay the expenses of the company and buy and pay for $10.1 million worth of horses,' Fernald said. '. . . Mr Colorado had to get money from somewhere else.'

Fernald had taken an equally close look at José's bank accounts at Bank of America, three of them personal and the other two business accounts related to Tremor Enterprises and his Lexington stud farm. Fernald had taken great time and care to distil all of the numbers into a chart for the jurors. Most people were visual learners and he had found over the years that, in complex money-laundering cases, discussing a long string of numbers was only going to put half the jury to sleep. A good visual could go a long way. And what his chart showed was that José Treviño, a bricklayer, had become a millionaire overnight, with a 9,518 per cent increase in income once he'd acquired Tempting Dash. Fernald had also discovered that nowhere in José's finances was there any record of him paying the $25,000 he claimed to have paid for Tempting Dash, just the $445,000 in prize money deposited to the Tremor Enterprises account after Tempting Dash's win at the Texas Classic Futurity.

As Lawson had hoped, the $400,000 cheque he'd found at

José's ranch during the raid had turned out be a crucial piece of evidence. The cheque made out to Colorado from Tremor Enterprises, for a horse called First Fly Down, had never been received or cashed by Colorado, though he certainly could have used the money, according to Fernald's chart. And Fernald had also made another interesting discovery about First Fly Down. When the horse died, José had collected $400,000 in insurance proceeds on it, which he'd deposited into his Tremor Enterprises account. So he'd supposedly paid $400,000 for a horse but the cheque was never cashed. Then he'd turned around and collected on its life-insurance policy.

After Fernald had fully explained his findings, Gardner ceded the floor to the defence. This time, it would be José's other attorney, Christie Williams, who would cross-examine the witness. She argued that the $25,000 José had used to buy Tempting Dash had come from small sums of money he had saved over a very long period of time, which he'd never deposited at the bank. This was why Fernald could find no record of it, she said.

Gardner was already standing up at the prosecution table. He couldn't resist a follow-up to William's claim. He wanted to underscore with the jury that the narrative about where José had come up with the $25,000 to buy Tempting Dash kept changing, and it was clear from looking at his bank statements that he'd never had as much as $25,000 in his account at one time before he'd suddenly become a millionaire in 2010.

'. . . Special Agent Fernald, under Ms Williams's theory, José Treviño would have had to withdraw cash and stuff it under his mattress to get that $25,000?' asked Gardner in a sarcastic tone.

'That's I think the fourth source of funds that I've heard during the course of the investigation where the money was derived,' Fernald said.

'And what are the other three?'

'I understand that he sold his construction company and that's where he got the money to pay. I know that he supposedly received an inheritance. There was a tip from his brother-in-law. And now it's cashing cheques.'

'. . . Special Agent, I just want to make sure Ms Williams just offered a fifth theory of how they got their $25,000 for Tempting Dash, correct?' said Gardner, with a slight smile.

'Correct. I lost count,' Fernald said.

FIFTY-THREE

AS THE TRIAL MOVED INTO ITS THIRD AND FINAL WEEK, LAWSON AND PENNINGTON still hadn't been summoned to the witness stand. It had been a long two weeks of sitting in the courtroom, which could be tense and monotonous at the same time. The prosecution hoped that, with the sheer amount of testimony and evidence they were presenting before the twelve jurors, they would be convinced beyond a reasonable doubt that José, Colorado and the others on trial were guilty. It would be up to Lawson and Pennington to recap all of the government's evidence in the last days. But it was not their turn yet. Gardner and Fernald had two more crucial witnesses.

As family members and other spectators filed into the courthouse to go through the security screening early Monday morning, they couldn't help but notice that security around the courthouse had been intensified. A line of Department of Homeland Security SUVs with flashing red lights blocked the road behind the courthouse while a special witness in an armoured SUV was transported to the back of the building.

Guards with grim faces, holding assault rifles, paced around the perimeter of the courthouse. As Judge Sparks called the courtroom to order, reporters sitting in the gallery took turns trying to guess who the mystery witness might be. Whoever he was, he was considered extremely dangerous, judging by the demeanour of the guards.

Alma Pérez, sitting next to the reporters, knew they would soon have their headline for the day. She had been tasked with interviewing and translating for the witness, who was being guarded under a layer of security that was usually reserved only for terrorists and other enemies of the state. What she remembered most about him were his eyes – black and lifeless like a shark's. They were the eyes of a killer.

Gardner stood up from the table to call forth the witness. 'Your Honour, the government calls Jesús Rejón Aguilar.'

A murmur of recognition rippled through the gallery. Rejón was better known as Mamito, or Z-7, and a member of the Zetas at his level – one of the founding military leaders – had never testified publicly in a US courtroom. Kingpins of his stature almost always pleaded guilty rather than testify, or testified under seal in a closed courtroom. Transporting Mamito to Texas from a jail cell in Washington, D.C. had not been easy. Nor had it been easy for Gardner to convince the DEA to loan their key witness to him for their trial.

But Mamito had been as close to Miguel and Omar as anyone within the cartel. Securing his testimony as a witness had been a coup for Gardner and Fernald. It would be the first time a founding member of the Zetas spoke publicly about how the secretive and brutal organisation was run. It was almost as good as having Miguel Treviño himself on the stand.

An armed bailiff escorted Mamito, in a loose white T-shirt and grey prison sweats, to the witness stand, where he sat down with an air of resignation. His hair had been shaved in prison.

His dull and lifeless eyes scanned the courtroom as if he expected his enemies to be waiting for him there in ambush. He had been arrested two years earlier in Mexico City and then extradited to the United States, where he faced ten-to-life for drug trafficking. He'd also been implicated in the death of HSI federal agent Jaime Zapata, since he'd been *comandante* of the region where Zapata had been murdered. After his capture, Mamito had made it no secret that he blamed Miguel Treviño for his predicament.

Now he was going to testify against Miguel's brother. Mamito explained that he had been a corporal in Mexico's Special Forces working in counter-narcotics when he joined the Zetas in 1999 to serve as a bodyguard and executioner for El Mata Amigos, Osiel Cárdenas Guillén, leader of the Gulf Cartel.

'Did you also provide bribes to the Mexican military?' asked Gardner.

Mamito nodded. 'I did.'

'And what would the Mexican military do in exchange for those bribes?'

'Helped us fight the opposing group to our cartel.'

Gardner played some of the phone calls the DEA had recorded in 2009 from the wiretap on Ramiro Villarreal's mobile phone. Lawson wished he had known about these wiretaps at the beginning of their investigation. Luckily, his friend Bill Johnston had been able to get the recordings from his fellow DEA agents in Houston. When Gardner, Lawson and Pérez had flown to D.C. to meet with Mamito, he had identified the voices in the wiretaps and given them the context of each phone call. In many of the calls, he had been sitting right next to Omar and Miguel as they chatted with Ramiro about the horses, fixing races and doping. So there were additional details he could add. Lawson noticed that the jurors appeared fascinated as they listened to the recorded conversations with the knowledge that one of the men was already dead and the other, Omar Treviño, was in Mexico helping his brother run the brutal cartel.

'Why did Forty want to kill Ramiro Villarreal?'

'Because he knew a lot about the horse business and Forty had a lot invested . . . and Ramiro knew it all . . . If he was arrested, he could testify. He knew all the names of the horses . . . He could bring down his whole business.'

'What did Forty tell you about why he wanted to put Tempting Dash into his clean brother's name?'

'He wanted to put it in his brother's name because the horse was going to run in Dash for Cash and, if he won . . . his value would increase and they would be able to get the money, and the money would stay within the family.'

At the prosecution table, Lawson was seated almost directly in front of the witness but he tried to avoid looking at him. He remembered when he and Pérez had debriefed the drug lord and Lawson had met his cold stare. He had wanted to show Mamito that he wasn't intimidated as Pérez translated for them. Mamito had told them he was a devoted practitioner of *Santería*, which called forth spirits who demanded a blood sacrifice. 'I can hurt you without even touching you,' he'd said, a slight smile on his face, and Lawson had looked away. He thought he'd glimpsed real evil in those eyes, and Mamito was considered a gentleman compared to Miguel. Both he and Pérez had found their meeting with the drug lord deeply disturbing.

After Gardner was finished, it was the defence's turn to cross-examine the former cartel leader. Christie Williams would be the first at trying to portray Mamito as an unreliable witness to the jury. Mamito, only in his mid-thirties, was contemplating a lifetime in prison and he hoped, like the other former cartel members, to have his long prison sentence reduced in exchange for his testimony. When he was done serving time in the States, he faced additional jail time in Mexico on organised-crime charges.

Williams started by attacking his military service and defection. 'So you're sixteen years old and you join the military and you're trained as a sniper, and you're supposed to be protecting the citizens of your country, right?'

Gardner stood up quickly from his seat at the prosecution table. 'Your Honour, I'm going to object to this as argumentative.'

'Well, let's just proceed,' said Judge Sparks, nodding at Williams to go ahead.

'Were you trained to protect the citizens of Mexico as a member of the Mexican military?'

'That's right.' Mamito nodded.

'And after that, you became corrupt . . . You turned your back on the citizens of Mexico and you became a hit man, right?'

'That's right,' he said, showing no emotion.

'So now you get arrested in Mexico after you've killed people, correct?'

'I am arrested for organised crime.'

'But you've also killed people?'

'Correct.'

'And kidnapped people . . . and tortured people.'

'Correct,' Mamito said again, his eyes flat and dull. Any spark of humanity within him had been buried a long time ago like the bodies he'd left in his wake.

Next, it was DeGeurin's turn to cross-examine the witness on behalf of his client, Francisco Colorado. DeGeurin stepped to the centre of the courtroom to address the former *sicario* from the lectern. 'Is it true that you, yourself . . . made about $50 million in your Zeta business?'

Mamito nodded. 'That's correct.'

'And of that $50 million that you made, where is it today?'

'It's part of the war . . . Some of it was taken from the businesses I had. Some of it from the cocaine . . . and some of it I kept.'

'. . . After all is said and done, how much did you keep?'

'. . . Maybe two million, three million.'

'And where is that two or three million now?'

'Put away in a safe.'

'And did you tell the government about where you put that money away?'

'Yes.' He nodded.

'Do you mind telling me where it is?'

'I don't have a reason to tell you where that money is,' Mamito said matter-of-factly.

'Let's stay with the questions,' Sparks said dryly.

After several more minutes of verbal sparring, DeGeurin passed the witness to Chevo Huitron's lawyer, Richard Esper, who wanted to make it clear that Mamito had never met Chevo or seen him in the company of Miguel or Omar Treviño as the prosecution had alleged. Mamito testified that he had only heard from the Treviños that Chevo was a good horse trainer but had never seen him in their company.

'They never told you that they suspected him of being involved in illegal activity, did they?'

'That's right.' Mamito nodded.

It was a nice stroke for Esper and he couldn't suppress the hint of a smile as he went back to the defence table to take his seat next to his client. After the entire morning and much of the afternoon, the former Zetas leader was excused and led back to the holding cell for detainees within the depths of the courthouse.

AS DOUG GARDNER PREPARED to call their next witness, Lawson shifted in his seat and could feel himself growing nervous. He had rehearsed Tyler Graham for hours, so he would be prepared for anything the defence lobbed his way. By now, they knew that Graham had been key in the FBI's investigation and that much of their case was riding on him. Lawson knew they would throw every trick they had at him and try to get him riled so he'd say something that made him look less credible in the eyes of the jurors. Lawson told himself there was no point in being nervous. They'd never get a rise out of the unflappable Tyler Graham.

Lawson hadn't seen Doc Graham since they'd shaken hands in the hallway the first day of trial. Finn had wisely decided not to bring the elder Graham back to the courthouse to testify. The jurors and the rest of the courtroom were now going to find out why. They were going to learn that his twenty-eight-year-old grandson had been co-operating with the FBI for more than two years and had been crucial in taking down José Treviño and Tremor Enterprises. Graham, wearing a tan suit and freshly shaven, sat down at the witness stand and raised his right hand to be sworn in by the clerk. Lawson could see that he didn't look nervous at all.

'. . . Where's Tempting Dash today?' Gardner asked.

'He's in Elgin right now at the Southwest Stallion Station.'

'And is there any particular reason he's still at Southwest Stallion Station?'

'Yes, sir. We're still currently breeding him – it's breeding season right now. This is our third year of standing for a full breeding season.'

'. . . And are you operating that horse on a contract with the United States government?'

'Yes, sir.' Graham nodded. He was answering the questions in a calm and measured way, as Lawson had advised him.

'. . . And how did you come to be aware of Tempting Dash as a horse for the purpose of your breeding operation?' Gardner asked.

'. . . He came across to run up here in the fall futurities at Lone Star Park. And I knew Eusevio Huitron, who trained him, and he had told me, you know, about him coming across and that, you know, it looked like a prospect. I mean, we talked about the horses that came across the border often.'

Graham explained to Gardner how he'd met José Treviño at the racetrack outside of Dallas, then eventually persuaded him to send the champion Tempting Dash to be bred at his farm in Elgin. After that, José had asked him to bid on some horses at Heritage Place and his $875,000 bid for Dashin Follies had drawn more than just the attention of the auctiongoers and the media.

'At some point, were you contacted by Special Agent Scott Lawson over here?" Gardner pointed towards Lawson, sitting at the prosecution table next to Pennington.

Lawson shifted in his chair and tried not to acknowledge that the whole courtroom was now staring at him.

'Yes, sir,' said Graham, nodding.

'And what was your understanding of your agreement with Special Agent Lawson and the government?'

'My agreement was that we just — they were informed on the, you know, operations of the horse business that we had to do with Mr Treviño and Carlos and the group.' Eventually, Graham said, he'd also agreed to allow the FBI to listen in and record all of his phone calls too.

After Gardner led Graham through the long story of his involvement with José, Nayen and the others, he felt content that he'd laid out the full extent of Graham's involvement in the case to the jury. He handed Graham over to the defence for cross-examination. They were going to do their best to make the government's key informant look as guilty as the defendants. Christie Williams was first up to the lectern.

'Now, when a mare would come to be bred to Tempting

Dash, that caused you to make a lot of money, correct? . . . You got to charge for the horse care, for boarding, for breeding. For all the veterinary services that you already had someone on salary to do that, right?'

'Yes,' Graham said.

Williams made several more jabs at how much Graham gained profit-wise from working with José and his associates. But now the defence was starting to run out of time with Graham. Questioning the former Zetas leader, Mamito, had taken most of the morning and afternoon. It was 6 pm and they were just getting started. Judge Sparks adjourned the courtroom for the day and asked that Graham be ready first thing in the morning.

WHEN GRAHAM SAT DOWN at the witness stand the next morning, the gallery was filled to its maximum capacity. Pérez noticed that one of the Treviño sisters had her notebook and pen out again and was watching Graham intently. This time, another attorney from the crowded defence table, Guy Womack, who was representing Fernando Garcia, would subject Graham to a battery of questions about his role in the FBI's investigation.

'. . . Okay. So you try to recruit the very best stallions because it will bring the most money and prestige to your stud farm?'

'It's more about business than prestige with us, but yes.' Graham nodded.

'All right. Okay. You said the FBI registered you as a form of informant; is that right?'

'They never used the word "informant".'

'What did they call it?'

'Co-operating citizen. I don't know that they ever really gave me a title.'

'Okay. But you fill out forms for them every ninety days or less?'

'Yes, sir.' Graham nodded.

'And basically, the form you're signing says that you promised to work for the FBI at their direction and not to do anything that would be illegal unless they tell you to do it?'

'I don't believe I was working for the FBI. They weren't paying me,' Graham said evenly. Womack was trying to unnerve him but Graham wasn't going to let the attorney throw him off his carefully marked course.

'Okay. Well, how did you become one of their sources? Did you go to them and apply for a job as a source?'

'No, sir. I did not.'

'. . . They came to you, they said they thought you might have done something illegal?'

'I don't remember them indicating that. No, sir.'

'You were afraid that you might be in trouble, correct?'

'I don't see any reason I would have been in trouble,' Graham said calmly.

'. . . How did it become that you were a registered informant?'

'Once again, I don't ever remember them saying registered informant.'

'Okay. Whatever you call yourself, do you have like a junior G-man badge or something you can wear that says FBI?'

Womack was getting flustered now because he wasn't getting anywhere with Graham.

Gardner stood up to protest. 'Your Honour. Relevance,' he said, with a note of exasperation in his voice. Womack was just badgering Graham now out of frustration.

'I'll sustain the objection,' Judge Sparks said.

Womack hammered away at Graham for several more minutes before passing him to another defence attorney. They went at him like prizefighters in the ring, jabbing and weaving and trying to throw him off his feet for more than an hour. But throughout it all, Graham remained calm. His composure under stress never failed to impress Lawson. Mercifully, Graham was finally released before the lunchtime break and escorted out by the security detail the FBI had assigned to keep watch over him. Like del Rayo, Graham was quickly whisked out of the courthouse before the reporters or anyone else could intercept him.

FIFTY-FOUR

STEVE PENNINGTON HAD SPENT THE LAST THREE WEEKS SITTING IN A CHAIR at the prosecutor's table waiting to be called to the witness stand. He'd never been someone who was good at staying still. Like Lawson, he preferred to be out on the street working, not sitting behind a desk. So it was a relief to him when Doug Gardner finally called his name to testify. The jurors and the courtroom had got a three-week seminar in drug cartels and horse racing. It was a lot to digest, and now the prosecutors wanted to make sure that Lawson and Pennington wrapped up their case and put a bow on it, to erase any doubt in the jurors' minds that José and the other defendants might be less than guilty beyond a reasonable doubt.

Pennington had been on the witness stand too many times to count over his long career. Still, as he took a seat on the raised dais, it never failed to get his blood pumping and make him break out in a sweat once all eyes were upon him.

'Could you explain the concept of commingling to the jury?' Gardner asked. Commingling was an important part of the prosecution's argument that they wanted the jurors to fully grasp.

A key complaint against the Huitron brothers and Francisco Colorado was that they had mixed the 'dirty' cocaine proceeds from Miguel and Omar with the 'clean', legitimate money in their businesses.

Earlier in the trial, Gardner had likened it to 'spiking the punch bowl.'

'Yes.' Pennington nodded. 'Anytime that you have funds, say, from an illegal source and you put those with an ongoing business or funds that are from a clean source, once you mix those funds together, then you have commingled the funds, and you can't distinguish between clean and dirty.'

What Gardner also wanted to do was convince the jury that the defendants knew exactly where the dirty money had come from, which would make them active participants rather than passive, unknowing players in the conspiracy.

'. . . Special Agent, I want to turn your attention to some of the horse sales . . . Could we first start with the September 2010 Ruidoso sale? . . . For the jury's recollection, how many horses were purchased?'

'Twenty-three horses,' said Pennington.

'And what was the purchase price?'

'Little over $2.2 million.'

'And who filled out the cheque for that?'

'It was signed by Francisco Colorado Cessa.'

'And based on the records obtained from Southwest Stallion Station and Paul Jones, were you able to trace those horses as they left the auction house?'

'. . . Yes. We reviewed the documents . . . and found out that twenty of the twenty-three were boarded and were trained at Paul Jones and Southwest Stallion under the account of Carlos Nayen.'

Gardner took Pennington back to the horse First Fly Down and the $400,000 cheque he and Lawson had found in Lexington made out from José's Tremor Enterprises to Francisco Colorado. Pennington described to the jury how the cheque had never been cashed by Colorado, and that the horse was being trained by Paul Jones at Los Alamitos for Tremor Enterprises. The horse had died suddenly, explained Pennington, and afterwards José had collected on a $400,000 insurance policy taken out on the racehorse.

Another six of the twenty-three horses that Colorado had bought in Ruidoso were at José's Lexington ranch. Pennington and his task force had found that the horses were listed under various owners' names, including Victor López, who had been dead for several months. Two more of the horses were found in Ruidoso by Pennington's task force. One was listed under Tremor Enterprises and the other under Desiree Princess Ranch, an LLC started by Fernando Garcia. Six others were transferred to other members of the organisation and another six remained in Colorado's name but their whereabouts were unknown, explained Pennington.

Gardner pivoted to another big auction, this time in Oklahoma at Heritage Place in November 2011. '. . . In addition to selling four horses, did the organisation purchase a number of horses?'

'Yeah, including the four that were, quote, "sold", twelve total were purchased with funds from Francisco Colorado through Arian Jaff.'

'Is that the Quick Loans?' Gardner asked, citing the name of Jaff's company.

'Yes, sir. Quick Loans, Arian Jaff.'

Now Gardner wanted Pennington to explain how he was different from the normal IRS employee that probably every one of the jurors was familiar with – the tax auditor sitting in a grey office whom everyone dreaded.

'. . . What does an IRS auditor do?'

'An IRS auditor is going to look at the first level of receipts to determine whether or not what you have on your tax return you have a receipt for.'

'So what does an IRS criminal investigator do in contrast to that?'

'We're going to look below that level of receipts to try to determine where the source of the funds came from, and whether or not the expenses you've reported are legitimate.'

What Pennington and his task force had found, he testified, were mostly structured deposits and bank wires from Mexico going into various US bank accounts and auction houses. José, Nayen and the others moved the horses from one LLC to another and the money from one bank account to another in an elaborate shell game to hide the true mastermind behind the scheme, Miguel Treviño.

'Now, part of the government's indictment alleges the international movement of funds . . . Could you explain to the jury what international movement of funds were discovered in this case . . . ?' asked Gardner.

'Yes, sir. We had bulk currency from the sale of narcotics being physically shipped from the United States in bulk-cash smuggling into Mexico. And then we have a number of wire transfers going back in from various different banks in Mexico such as Banco Monex, Banco Regional de Monterrey, Basic Enterprises, ADT Petroservicios. We had some from Grupo Aduanero from Sabanco. Those wires originated in Mexico and the money is wired into banks in the United States for the purchase of quarter horses.'

'. . . Now, the government has also alleged the interstate movement of funds.'

Pennington nodded. 'You had currency deposited into various

banks in Laredo, Texas, and then you had the money from those accounts in California, Arizona and other states.'

'And what banks were they using?'

'IBC Bank, Wells Fargo, we have UBS and Bank of America.'

'. . . And what was the total amount expended on horses in this investigation.'

'Over $25 million.'

Now Gardner asked Pennington how many horses José Treviño had bought with his own money for Tremor Enterprises, or his companies 66 Land or Zule Farms.

'One,' Pennington said. In nearly three years, José had only paid for one horse out of his accounts at Bank of America.

Gardner looked down at his notes on the lectern, letting this sink in with the jury for a moment. 'And what was the amount of that horse?'

'Five thousand, five hundred dollars, I believe.'

'. . . How many horses total did Colorado Cessa purchase?'

'I believe that was a hundred and twenty-one.'

Of those, Gardner now asked, how many were still in Colorado's name at the time of the raid?

'He had – I believe it was still forty-one listed under his name . . .'

'And when you break down the forty-one,' said Gardner, 'what did you discover with respect to the location of those horses?'

'A number of those horses were cared for at places like Southwest Stallion Station, Paul Jones under the Carlos Nayen account. And some of those horses were seized by IRS either at Lexington, Oklahoma, or California or New Mexico.'

'And the horses you discovered being stabled under various places, how were those expenses paid for?'

'They were paid for by currency through Carlos Nayen, Victor López, and by the funds from Alfonso del Rayo Mora.'

Pennington had been on the witness stand for more than an hour. The judge called the court to recess for a fifteen-minute afternoon break. When the trial reconvened, it was time for the defence to have a go at Pennington. The defence attorneys took turns questioning the IRS agent, trying to mitigate their clients' involvement in the conspiracy and build doubt in the minds of the jurors.

Pennington had testified that Eusevio 'Chevo' Huitron and his brother Jesse had received more than $500,000 into their Wells Fargo account for horse expenses, much of it structured deposits from Victor López and others in Laredo. Jesse Huitron's lawyer, Brent Mayr, argued that his client had no idea that the funds had been structured because his daughter, Jessica, kept the accounts. Nor did he make any of the structured deposits himself or have any idea of the illicit nature of the money he was receiving.

Of all the defendants, Jesse's case for being indicted was the weakest and his lawyer knew it. Jesse hadn't been included in the original indictment, not until he'd inadvertently testified under oath to his involvement in his brother's racing business, unwittingly making his own case for being indicted. Now Pennington watched Mayr work to grow a seed of doubt in the jurors' minds about his client's guilt. After nearly an hour and a half of peppering Pennington with minutiae over each structured deposit that was made, Mayr was starting to wear not just on him, but on the judge and jury as well. It was nearly 5 pm and Pennington had been on the witness stand for most of the day.

'If I may, I'm only going to cover three more of the transactions. Then I will be done,' said Mayr, rifling through his notes.

'Have it all you want,' said Judge Sparks, who was losing patience. 'You're just burying everyone in the concrete. Your entire last hour and five minutes could have been done in three questions . . . If you would be watching the jury as I am, you would see you're not doing any good. Three questions would have cleared it.'

'Okay,' said Mayr, making an apologetic face.

'I don't know what they're going to do but they're sure not happy,' Judge Sparks said, frowning. After a short recess, Mayr finished his questioning. He had been quiet for much of the trial and this was his chance to drive home the innocence of his client, Jesse Huitron, which he had done with perhaps too much zeal. Only the jury's verdict would tell. Pennington was finally excused and Judge Sparks adjourned the courtroom for the day.

THE NEXT MORNING, AS they assembled in the courtroom, Lawson could feel himself starting to sweat. Gardner and Fernald had called fifty-nine witnesses so far in the trial and Lawson would be the very last one. He'd been sitting in the courtroom for nearly three weeks, silently watching and waiting for his turn. Now Doug Gardner called him to the stand to be sworn in for his testimony. Lawson quickly made eye contact with Pérez, who was sitting towards the front of the gallery, and she smiled and nodded.

Earlier in the morning, she'd had an awkward run-in in the bathroom with one of José's sisters, who had tried to make small talk with her as she stood at the sink washing her hands. Pérez had smiled politely then quickly walked out, not saying a word. Some of the reporters had tried to approach José's mother and sisters for interviews in the hallway during the break but the family had refused all requests. Pérez wasn't going to give José's sister anything to write down in her little notebook either.

It would be Lawson's job to reinforce all of Pennington's testimony with more evidence – all of the surveillance photos, the recorded phone conversations and documents that he, Pérez and the rest of the team had collected throughout the nearly three-year investigation. Lawson spoke of Tyler Graham and the information he provided as being key to unravelling the conspiracy.

'In the two years you were working with Mr Graham, did any piece of information that he gave you prove to be untrue?' asked Gardner.

'No.'

'And how did you confirm the information that Mr Graham gave you?'

'His information was confirmed by a variety of means: subpoenaed bank documents, surveillance conducted after information he gave us, debriefs of other witnesses, and debriefs with other law-enforcement officers.'

Gardner clicked through the photos that Lawson and Raúl Perdomo had taken at the auction and afterwards at the All American Futurity. A giant image of Carlos Nayen at the auction in his pink shirt was projected on the screen behind the defence table. Gardner stopped at a photo of Nayen texting on his BlackBerry.

'Do you know who he was texting?'

'Through other informants, it was Miguel Treviño,' Lawson said.

One of José's lawyers, Christie Williams, leaped to her feet. 'Objection, Your Honour. Hearsay.'

Gardner rephrased his question. 'Do you know personally who he was texting with?'

'No.'

Gardner took Lawson through several more surveillances he had conducted along with Pérez and other agents. There was the money drop with Victor López in front of La Posada Hotel in downtown Laredo and photos of López leaving the duffel bag in the truck belonging to their undercover agent. The jurors seemed to welcome the visuals after the financial minutiae they'd been asked to digest during Pennington's testimony. Finally, Gardner came to the day of the raid at José's farm and the BlackBerry Lawson had uncovered hidden in a drawer in José's room. It had been their ticket to capturing Miguel – the Holy Grail of their investigation – but it hadn't played out the way he'd planned.

'Did you power up that phone?' Gardner asked.

'I did.'

'And do you recall the specific contacts that you saw?'

'There were no contacts on the phone but it had a Mexican phone number.'

'Just one in the address book?'

'Yeah.' Lawson nodded.

Gardner pivoted away from the line of questioning. They weren't going to get into what happened afterwards. It wasn't going to help their case. He had passed that Mexican number along and done his part but Miguel and Omar were still running free, committing mass murder and smuggling tractor-trailers full of cocaine across the Rio Grande. But Lawson couldn't dwell on that now.

AFTER LAWSON TOOK HIS SEAT again at the prosecution table, the government rested its case. The courtroom now belonged to the defence. Each of the attorneys, including Christie Williams on behalf of José Treviño, made a motion that the court enter a judgement of acquittal. The government hadn't shown sufficient evidence or proved that any of their clients were knowingly participating in a conspiracy to launder dirty money through the American-quarter horse industry. One by one, they made the same argument. It was a last-ditch move in their arsenal and it didn't hurt to deploy it, even if they knew there would be little chance of it being successful.

'The motions are overruled,' said Judge Sparks after a few minutes of debate. 'Bring in the jury.'

The attorneys at the defence table passed on calling any witnesses to the stand, with the exception of Richard Esper, who represented Chevo Huitron. When Esper called Shae Cox, one of Chevo's former employees, it explained why. Esper was opening up uncharted territory for the prosecution to explore, which had the potential to harm his client. After Esper was done throwing softball questions at their sole witness, Gardner eagerly approached the lectern for the cross-exam. 'Now, you also stated that Chevo Huitron . . . is an excellent trainer?'

'Yes.' Cox nodded.

'And you also stated that he was extremely honest?' asked Gardner.

'Yes.'

'Do you also recall your response to the question, did you ever see him do things that were illegal or underhanded?' Gardner asked, setting up the witness for what was about to come.

'Do I recall the question? Yes,' she said tentatively.

'Do you recall that?' Gardner asked again.

'Yes, I do.'

'Were you aware that, on August twenty-sixth of 2011, Chevo Huitron was suspended and fined—'

'Objection, Your Honour.' Esper leaped to his feet. 'Objection under 404(b), Your Honour.'

'The objection is overruled,' said Judge Sparks. 'You placed all of this in evidence on your direct examination.' In other words, Esper had opened the door by calling Cox up to the witness stand, and now Gardner was going to tear the door off its hinges.

'On August twenty-sixth of 2011, were you aware that Chevo

Huitron was fined and suspended for doping, drugging two horses with clenbuterol at Retama Park?'

'Yes. I'm aware of those problems,' she said, now looking nervous.

'On June seventeenth, 2011, were you aware that Chevo Huitron was fined for doping a horse with polyethylene glycol?'

'I didn't know what the penalty was,' she said.

'Were you aware on July twenty-sixth of 2010 that Chevo Huitron was fined and suspended for obtaining fraudulent workouts through the bribery of track personnel?'

Gardner rattled off several more fines and suspensions filed against Chevo for doping horses. 'Were you aware that he applied batteries in a fixed horse race to Tempting Dash?'

'No.' She shook her head.

'You weren't aware of that?' asked Gardner. 'So again, being aware of all that, would that change your opinion as to whether he's an extremely honest person?'

'I still believe he's honest,' she said tentatively. 'Yes.'

'Pass the witness, Your Honour.' Gardner turned his back to the witness, and the judge excused Cox. The gallery was buzzing after the grilling that the witness had just endured. Bringing Cox to the stand had done Chevo Huitron more harm than good.

FIFTY-FIVE

ON THE FINAL DAY OF THE TRIAL, THE TENSION WAS VISIBLE IN THE FACES OF THE attorneys on both sides of the courtroom as they prepared to give their closing statements in a last effort to appeal to the jurors.

José's legal team had elected not to put him on the witness stand to testify. The other defendants had also remained silent throughout the trial. It would be up to José's lead counsel, David Finn, to speak for his client. Finn strode towards the jury box, then paced before the jurors, making eye contact with each one of them as he spoke. '. . . Remember the timing of all of this. This indictment got handed down one month before the Mexican presidential elections and three months before the US elections. Why presidential? Why is that important? Think back during that summer, what was going on in Washington. All hell was breaking loose about Fast and Furious and Mr Zapata, Agent Zapata getting killed, murdered by guns that were supplied by the ATF.'

Finn shook his head with a look of dismay. 'The Zetas they want are in Mexico. And ask yourself this: why do we have the war on drugs? . . . There's a problem here in the US. If demand dries up, then you don't need a supply. But there's also a problem in Mexico, isn't there? Corruption. Forty and Forty-two are supposedly in Mexico. They're not hiding in the hills of Afghanistan. It's not like it's Osama bin Laden. Don't you think that, if the Mexican government really wanted to find those guys, they could? But here we are. Can't get the brothers, let's get the clean brother.'

Now Finn tried to bolster his argument that José was nothing more than a scapegoat for his brothers' numerous crimes, that he was the real victim in this trial. 'José is either the smartest criminal on the planet or he's not guilty,' Finn said, looking at the jurors. 'The FBI was all over him and his family for years. And here we are. Zero plus zero plus zero equals zero. The burden of proof in a criminal case is on the government, and it's a high burden. That's why the government gets to sit close to you while we're sitting on the other side of the room. That's why the government gets to go first and the government gets the last word,' he said, shaking his head again. 'Because it's proof beyond a reasonable doubt, not maybe, not possibly, not even probably . . . Proof beyond a reasonable doubt is a high standard. I mean it's moral certainty because you've got to live with your verdict. And you are a group of individuals. You are not a team. Deliberation doesn't mean capitulation. Deliberation doesn't mean compromise because, I submit to you, folks, you'll forget about this trial. But two, three, four years from now in a quiet moment, maybe you've taken your family to Big Bend, you're going to think back about José and you're going to wonder, "Did I get it right? Did the government prove it beyond all reasonable doubt?"' Finn sat down, a look of solemnity on his face.

Doug Gardner would have the last word before the jury was finally excused to make its deliberation. He stood up and walked to the lectern, where his voice could be heard clearly over the mic in the courtroom. He showed, once again, the photos of each defendant on the screen for the jurors to contemplate. 'This evidence is here for you to go over on your deliberations. But what I want to do for a few minutes or so is go over a snippet to show that each one of these defendants knowingly participated in this conspiracy.' Gardner clicked through the slides showing image after image of key pieces of evidence: the wiretap transcripts, the photo of José's son and daughter making the signs of '40' and '42' with their hands in the winner's circle photo with Tempting Dash.

'It's about ego. It's about pride. It's about winning the horse race at all costs. It's about establishing the legacy for your family. It's about being the best trainer, regardless of whether the horse is doped, or batteries are applied to it to win, or money is applied to the gate starters to send it down the track,' he said, addressing the jurors directly. 'It's about pride. It's about having the best horse and it's about the money. It is not built on sweat, ladies and gentlemen. It's built on the money from his brothers. Who do you trust more than family? That's why José Treviño has the horses.'

After Gardner's final statement, Judge Sparks excused the jurors from the courtroom. Everyone sitting in the packed gallery watched as the twelve men and women slowly filed out of the courtroom and were ushered into a back room where they would deliberate for the next few hours or days. Neither Doug Gardner nor Michelle Fernald could guess how long the jury's deliberations might take but they felt good about the evidence they had presented and the number of witnesses who had testified. Even if the jurors decided they couldn't stomach the testimonies of men like Mamito, they would still have the testimony of Tyler Graham and other horse-industry insiders to consider, and the reams of financial evidence that Pennington and his task force had provided. Still, they anticipated it could be a long wait. It was early Wednesday afternoon and Judge Sparks was prepared to receive the verdict as late as Friday, or even Monday, if there were dissenting opinions among the jurors.

The team convened on the fifth floor of the courthouse in an office reserved for the US attorney's office. They ordered out for pizza and settled in for the long wait. It would be difficult to focus on other work or get much done with the pending verdict hanging over them. Lawson and Pérez played a game of trying to guess when the verdict might come down. Lawson didn't expect they'd hear anything that evening.

But much to their surprise, the phone call from Judge Sparks's clerk came in less than four hours. 'The jury is ready to deliver the verdict,' she told Gardner. The team rushed downstairs to Sparks's courtroom, still not believing the verdict had come so quickly. Fernald worried it could be a bad sign.

Judge Sparks banged his gavel down on the dais to settle the courtroom as the defendants' families, reporters and others quickly took their seats. Lawson felt a rush of adrenaline as he sat down at the prosecution table. Pérez was looking nervous, shifting in her seat in the gallery. Lawson also felt his nerves taking over as a member of the jury stood up to read the verdict.

'Guilty' – the word rang out in the courtroom.

Lawson gave Pérez a look of triumph across the room. There were times in the course of the investigation when they'd thought they might never see this day.

The jury had found each defendant guilty, with the exception of Jesse Huitron. The jurors had felt the evidence had not proved beyond a reasonable doubt that Jesse had knowingly been part of the conspiracy. His brother, Chevo Huitron, had not been so lucky. The family members in the gallery sitting around Pérez wept and hugged one another. José's mother bowed her head.

Jesse Huitron was caught between elation at having been freed and grief as his brother, Chevo, was escorted out a side door by US Marshals alongside José Treviño, who looked defiant. Lawson could tell that the jury's pronouncement hadn't sunk in yet. He still hadn't come to terms with the realisation that he was on his way to a jail cell and not his Lexington ranch.

Lawson had thought he'd feel a deeper sense of satisfaction. Here was the justice he had been chasing for so long. But he couldn't shake his disappointment that Miguel and Omar were still roaming free.

FIFTY-SIX

LAWSON AND PÉREZ RESUMED THEIR WORK IN LAREDO AND FOCUSED ON wrapping up the case. They still hoped to get their fugitives in Mexico but they knew their chances would be slim unless the men slipped back across the river into the States.

But two months after José's guilty verdict, Pérez received a text early in the morning on 15 July that gave her some hope. A source in Mexico reported that Miguel Treviño had been arrested. Pérez quickly shared her news with Lawson. They were cautiously optimistic but also doubted it was true. In the past, there had been other reports claiming Miguel had been caught, but he always managed to slip away, much to the embarrassment of law enforcement on both sides of the river. Still, throughout the morning the chatter grew louder along the border, all saying the same thing – Miguel Treviño had been captured. They began to hope it might be true.

By late afternoon, they were starting to believe it was another false rumour when an official law-enforcement bulletin was sent out in an email to the Laredo RA. Lawson and Pérez opened the email and saw a photo of a man surrounded by soldiers on a dirt road, his hands cuffed behind his back. They recognised the dark, menacing eyes. It was Miguel Treviño. According to the email, he'd been arrested early that Monday morning on a deserted highway outside Nuevo Laredo. He'd been travelling with his accountant and a bodyguard in his silver pick-up when a navy helicopter filled with soldiers carrying high-calibre rifles had cut them off on the road. Treviño was carrying loads of ammo, several weapons and $2 million in cash in case he had to bribe the military or law enforcement that weren't already on his payroll. Maybe he had tried to buy his way out this time too, like so many times before. But this time, it hadn't worked. Miguel's number had come up. Maybe he'd become too much of a liability, too volatile for the real men who moved Mexico to control. The soldiers arrested him without firing a shot.

A man considered by many to be one of the worst mass murderers in Mexican history was finally on his way to a jail cell in Mexico City. He'd risen to the top of the criminal underworld on a pile of bodies. Miguel had eluded them but Lawson and Pérez could still feel pride that his legacy would no longer be the Lexington ranch, the racing championships and expensive bloodlines. It would be mass graves and barrels of ash – these would be the only remnants of Miguel Treviño's legacy.

Later in the day, when the story broke in the news and they saw more photographs and video of Miguel being escorted by military men, their faces covered with black masks, towards a waiting helicopter, they knew there was no way the kingpin would escape this time. His face puffy and covered in red welts, he was no longer the slender killer he'd once been. Wearing a black polo shirt and military fatigues, he looked worn and out of shape, but his eyes still burned with the same intensity. For the first time in years, the two agents felt like the target on their backs had been removed.

As the day came to a close, Lawson, Pérez and the rest of the violent-crimes squad went to a nearby bar to celebrate. Raúl Perdomo raised a shot glass of tequila in the air and the others hoisted their shot glasses in a toast to Lawson and Pérez. Then they drank to the end of Miguel's criminal empire.

FIFTY-SEVEN

TWO MONTHS AFTER HIS BROTHER'S ARREST, JOSÉ TREVIÑO SAT ONCE AGAIN at the defence table in Judge Sparks's courtroom — this time for his sentencing. Instead of a new suit, he wore a red-and-white-striped prison uniform. His face gave away little emotion but he avoided looking at the crowded gallery, where his mother and sisters sat in the back row. Throughout the trial, he had remained silent, his defence choosing not to put him on the witness stand. After the guilty verdict, he had fired David Finn and hired another high-powered Dallas criminal defence attorney, Kirk Lechtenberger.

He was facing a maximum sentence of twenty years for money laundering and this was his final chance to argue for clemency. Francisco Colorado, in an orange prison jumpsuit, sat next to him. Unlike José, who kept his eyes on the judge and the prosecutors, Colorado scanned the gallery and smiled at his wife and two sons, Pancho Jr and his youngest, Antonio. Like José, Colorado was also facing a maximum sentence. But he didn't appear deflated like José as he sat at the defendants' table. Colorado had brought his business partner from Mexico to testify under oath before the judge that no drug money had ever passed through the coffers of ADT Petroservicios. A dealmaker at heart, he was still hoping to spin the wheel in his favour.

He would be the first to address the courtroom before the judge meted out his sentence. Colorado stood up from his chair and faced the judge and prosecution table.

'Throughout all of this, a lot has been said about me personally and about my company ADT Petroservicios but, unfortunately, we have still not gotten the whole truth . . .' he said in Spanish, shaking his head. '. . . ADT Petroservicios, throughout this period that it's been accused of all this, won public contracts. It wasn't given things, it won publicly tendered contracts for amounts of over $450 million for a period even before the Zetas came into existence. I am a person who, because I followed my instincts and my dreams, has been bankrupt on three occasions,' he said. 'Just like the phoenix, through hard work and perseverance, I have been able to take flight . . . I want you to know, Your Honour,' he said, now facing the judge directly, his eyes tearing with emotion. 'I've survived two very intense wars. The first one, I underwent seventeen years ago, and this is the war I waged against my addiction to cocaine and other character flaws I had. And the second war is the one I'm fighting now, trying to show that I am a good, decent man. And for that reason . . . I personally turned myself in, after having seen on – in the newspapers and on the Internet – my name linked to this shameful case,' Colorado said, looking defiant. 'But I'd also like to say there are many occasions, facts are not what they seem to be when you look at them, but they are circumstantial. And in this specific case, I find myself involved in a very big dilemma. I ask, what would you do if you find yourself at a sale or purchasing something and you get a phone call saying, "You do me the favour of buying this and/or your family will die like this and this and this." It's difficult.'

As Gardner and Fernald waited for the interpreter to finish translating Colorado's statement into English, they began to look alarmed. Colorado was trying to put forth an entirely new defence motive in his case by saying that he had been extorted at the point of a gun, like Alfonso del Rayo, into helping Miguel Treviño and his brothers. The extortion angle had never come up during Colorado's defence at trial, and now he was trotting it out during the sentencing phase, which was way out of bounds as far as the judge was concerned.

'Hold on,' Judge Sparks said, raising a hand. 'We'll take a brief recess and talk with your client.' The judge put on the noise-cancelling fan so that the gallery wouldn't hear what they were discussing up at the judge's podium.

After about five minutes, the judge called the hearing back to order. 'Ready to continue, Mr DeGeurin?'

'Yes, we are.' The attorney nodded, a contrite look on his face. 'Thank you, Judge.'

'Mr Colorado Cessa.' The judge gestured for Colorado to continue his soliloquy. Colorado talked about how he loved his family and gave them a smile once again in the gallery, and then he turned to the judge. 'And for you, Your Honour, with all due respect,' he said with some flourish, opening a book the size of a Bible to the appropriate page, 'I would like to quote a paragraph from *Don Quixote de la Mancha* . . .'

'I've read the book,' Judge Sparks said gruffly.

Colorado began to read in Spanish and a translator repeated the words in English. 'Sancho, he's talking to Don Quixote,' Colorado explained. '. . . "And fear not, my Lord, because in the face of your judgment, they have placed a wise man whose hammer, according to those people who know, works in favour of the Lord and not in favour of mankind." Thank you, Your Honour.' Colorado closed the book with an air of finality and went back to his seat.

Next up was Colorado's business partner, Ramon Segura. The handful of reporters in the room had expected the sentencing to be over quickly but now it appeared that Colorado was just getting started. Segura stood up and took the oath, then sat down at the witness stand. Segura was thin with a cavernous face and had the deep voice of a heavy smoker. As he testified about the sanctity of their business practices at ADT, Michelle Fernald and Doug Gardner looked as if they possessed some secret between them.

After he had finished, Fernald made her way to the lectern for the cross-examination. After peppering Segura with questions about the amount the Zetas had invested in ADT, she followed up with an unusual line of questioning that left everyone in the gallery wondering where she was headed.

'. . . When is the last time that you've had any contact with Francisco Colorado Cessa?'

'I have daily,' Segura said.

'And have since he's been incarcerated?'

'Yes.'

'. . . And Mr Segura, finally, have you ever been involved in any criminal activity with ADT Petroservicios, Francisco Colorado Cessa, or any activities on behalf of either the company or Mr Colorado Cessa?'

'No.'

'I remind you that you're under oath,' Fernald said with emphasis.

'Yes, ma'am.' Segura nodded.

'Pass the witness,' Fernald said. As she walked back to the prosecution table, it was difficult for her to hide a look of self-satisfaction. Lawson could see that the reporters sitting in the gallery looked perplexed. Something was going on, and no doubt they were hoping the prosecutors would clue them in soon, before their afternoon deadlines.

After the odd exchange with Colorado's business partner, it was José's turn to address the judge. He stood up and solemnly walked to the lectern. His delivery was plain spoken in contrast to Colorado's dramatic monologue. José told the courtroom that he was embarrassed to find himself in court, and that he was innocent. His change in fortune, he said, was all due to his purchase of Tempting Dash. 'The horse that I bought for my wife and myself and that, from there on, anything that I touch includes winnings from racetracks to a horse that I sold. It all includes winning $4.2 million . . . and of those $4.2 million, $2.6 million were race earnings,' he said, facing the judge. 'And like I said, I am very sorry. That it was in the trial that I'm a Zeta. It was proved in trial that I don't have any aggressive conduct to anybody . . .'

After José sat down, his new attorney made their case to the judge that José should only receive a sentence of ten years, not the maximum of twenty, which was what they feared the government was about to propose. After the defence attorney took his seat, Doug Gardner made his way to the lectern to address the judge. 'Mr Lechtenberger's right. The government is asking for two hundred and forty months . . . The ability of the defendant to take that money, knowing how it was earned and the price of blood in which it's covered with, fully justifies the court imposing a twenty-year sentence, the statutory max.'

Judge Sparks was silent for a moment, seeming to digest what Gardner had just said. He looked out at the courtroom, then turned his gaze towards José. 'Mr Treviño, nobody in this court has alleged that you are a Zeta . . . You're charged with moving money of the Zetas, and there's no question in my mind that that was done,' Sparks said. 'The evidence was pretty overwhelming . . . You had the opportunity to say no. You just didn't . . . And whether you knew about these murders or not, whether you knew about all the other things that were going on, you were the funnel for most of it, and you ended up with all of the horses, and it's just beyond comprehension that you could do all that on your own, as was the defence you put forward. I sentence you to two hundred and forty months in the custody of the Bureau of Prisons . . .'

There was a gasp from the back of the gallery where José's sisters, mother and extended family sat. But José didn't turn to acknowledge their shock. He kept his eyes on the judge as he read out the rest of his sentence. Whereas he had been defiant at the trial, Lawson now saw him as resigned. His expression gave away little as a US Marshal escorted him out of the courtroom. Colorado had also received a twenty-year sentence. And while José had accepted his fate stoically, a look of total surprise and shock had spread across Colorado's face as the judge read out his sentence. The reporters in the gallery would soon find out why.

Fernando Garcia received thirteen years and Chevo Huitron eight years for their roles in the conspiracy. José's wife, Zulema, was given three years' probation, and their daughter, Alexandra, now twenty-two years old and about to give birth to her first child in California, received two years' probation. Adan Farias and Felipe Quintero, the horse trainers from California, each received three years of probation. And the young Raúl Ramirez, who had created such a commotion at the Ruidoso auction, was sentenced to a year in jail.

The case finally felt like it was coming to a close, especially with Miguel in jail in Mexico. But five members in the money-laundering scheme, including Omar Treviño, Sergio 'Saltillo'

Guerrero, Luis Aguirre and two other men – Erick Jovan Lozano and Gerardo Garza Quintero, who had been added, along with Jesse Huitron, in a superseding indictment – still remained fugitives in Mexico. Lawson and Pérez worried that Miguel could still seek revenge. Together they had pierced the inner circle of the Zetas. They had arrested his elder brother, José, but Omar was still out there, the new leader of the cartel.

As Judge Sparks called the courtroom to recess, Gardner and Fernald told the reporters milling in the hallway to stick around because something unusual was about to happen. 'I think you'll want to be here,' said Gardner to the handful of reporters impatiently waiting to be let in on their secret. Lawson's mind was far away from the group, still focused on the drama that had just unfolded in the parking lot of the courthouse, which the press would learn about soon enough. But after a few minutes, Fernald and the rest of the team told the reporters to go home. 'Come back first thing in the morning,' Gardner promised with a knowing smile.

EARLY THE NEXT MORNING, their secret was finally revealed during a hastily called press conference outside the courthouse. Fernald and Gardner stood next to their boss, US Attorney Rod Pitman, who announced to the group of reporters assembled that, while Judge Sparks had been sentencing Colorado the previous day in court, his eldest son, Pancho Jr, and business partner, Ramon Segura, had been arrested in the parking lot of the courthouse on bribery charges.

Pancho Jr and Segura had planned to place a golf bag filled with $1.2 million in the trunk of Judge Sparks's car in exchange for a lighter sentence for Colorado Sr. Lawson could see it was all falling into place now for the reporters – Colorado's over-riding confidence yesterday and then his shock when the judge read out a maximum sentence of twenty years.

Pitman told the reporters that the FBI had first learned of the scheme back in August through recorded jailhouse phone calls between Segura, the elder Colorado and his son. The FBI's Austin office had set up a sting with an informant posing as a confidant of Judge Sparks who would act as a go-between for the bribe money. Pitman told reporters that Judge Sparks had been kept in the dark about the bribery attempt and the sting to catch Segura and Colorado's son in the act. 'He had no idea,' Pitman said. Now Michelle Fernald's line of questioning in the courtroom the day before about whether Segura had ever engaged in any criminal conduct with Colorado Sr made sense. She had caught Segura lying under oath.

Now the reporters, Lawson, Pérez and the other agents had the surreal experience of entering the courtroom across the hallway from Sparks for the arraignment of Pancho Jr and Ramon Segura, who was still wearing the business suit he had testified in the day before. Only now he wore ankle shackles with his loafers. Both men looked stunned as federal judge Andrew Austin ordered they be held without bond for two weeks until their detention hearings. Both men could receive up to five years in jail for attempting to bribe a federal judge, and now Francisco Colorado Sr would also face additional jail time on top of the twenty years he'd just received. Colorado had spun the wheel but he was all played out. The dealmaker had lost the game.

FIFTY-EIGHT

JOSÉ TREVIÑO HAD A DEAL WITH DOUG GARDNER AND MICHELLE FERNALD NOT to sell his most prized horses until it was certain he was going to prison. Prior to the trial, he had still believed he had a chance of walking out of the courthouse a free man. With the five horses, including Tempting Dash, Dashin Follies and Mr. Piloto, he could easily rebuild his horse-racing empire. But it hadn't worked out that way. He'd got twenty years instead. And now the last of the Treviños' horses would be sold to the highest bidder.

It would be a historic event. Not often did horses of this calibre get offered up at auction, and never all at the same time. Present at Heritage Place on 1 November 2013 were some of America's most prominent quarter-horse racing legends, including the now eighty-year-old Charles 'Doc' Graham in his signature tan Stetson. Wealthy Latin Americans and horse agents representing some of the industry's biggest US buyers circulated through the packed sales arena among the curious who'd come to have a look at the 'Zeta horses' from the news. It was hard for Lawson not to notice the young guys in rhinestone Ed Hardy baseball caps and jeans or leather Ferrari jackets, making hushed phone calls in Spanish on their Nextels. He knew that the Ferrari symbol had been adopted by the Zetas, since the sleek sports car was one of Miguel's favourites.

Lawson watched a groom lead the spirited Mr. Piloto around the sales ring. Pérez had stayed back in Laredo. She'd already spent too many months away from her family. Lawson wished she could have made it. This would be the finale of their investigation – their final chapter. Lawson wore a tan blazer to conceal his holstered Glock. The last of the horses up for auction, including Tempting Dash, were among Miguel Treviño's most prized possessions. And just because Miguel was in a Mexican prison didn't mean he no longer held any power. Lawson knew that, with Miguel's millions, he could buy almost anything, even his freedom. Many kingpins before him had run their operations from inside prison; some, like the Sinaloa leader Joaquín 'El Chapo' Guzmán, had even 'miraculously' escaped. He figured a man as ruthless as Miguel was capable of anything. And his brother Omar was still at large in Mexico and running the cartel now in his absence. They might send a *sicario* to settle scores. Or any number of Miguel's enemies might try to buy Tempting Dash and the other horses, to taunt the kingpin, inciting more death and destruction.

Tyler Graham stood not far from Lawson, appraising the horses in the sales ring. They made eye contact and Graham nodded. But he kept his distance. He looked calm as usual but Lawson knew he had much on his mind. If Miguel and his brothers would exact their revenge on anyone, it would be Graham. Lawson, Pennington and the rest of his task force were keeping a close eye on him and his grandfather. Lawson had established an easy rapport with Graham after working with him for two years but he also realised it was not a friendship but a partnership, forged out of necessity.

Brian Schutt, along with some deputies from Waco whom Pennington had enlisted for extra security, were camped out in folding chairs in front of Dashin Follies's stall. They worried the horses might be stolen by Treviño's men. To an outsider, the group looked like authentic horsemen in their cowboy hats and worn boots. But to regular auctiongoers, they were known as the 'boys from the IRS.' As Jeff Tebow, the manager of Heritage Place, had warned Pennington during his first visit so many months ago, 'There are no secrets at the racetrack.' Soon enough, he had discovered there were no secrets at Heritage Place either. Not that they didn't want their presence known: they hoped they were enough of an armed deterrent to prevent any cartel operative from making a bid. Steve Junker couldn't hide the urban cop that he was, as he scanned the crowd looking for anything unusual. Kim Williams, who walked alongside him in her beat-up cowboy boots, made a more convincing horse enthusiast.

On the other side of the sales ring from Lawson stood Steve Pennington. It would be his job to vet any of the winning bidders on the horses and make sure they hadn't inadvertently been sold back to the Zetas or some other cartel. It had taken painstaking years to uncover and document how the horses had been bought through a sophisticated network of straw buyers. With José's trial, they'd sent a message to the cartel world. But looking around at the groups of men in leather Ferrari jackets and rhinestone-studded jeans texting and photographing the horses up for bid, it was tough to say that their message had been received. If there was anything that Pennington had learned in his long career, it was that criminals had short memories. And as long as there were billions in black-market proceeds, they'd always be looking for places to wash it clean.

The auctioneer announced it was time to start the bidding for

Tempting Dash. Lawson noticed that Graham had moved in close to where the auctioneer stood on an elevated platform above the sales ring. But this time, there was no horse being paraded around the ring. Because of his contagious blood disease, Tempting Dash had to remain under quarantine back at the Southwest Stallion Station in Texas. The bidders would have to settle instead for two large screens that displayed photos of the champion stallion, alongside his race wins and earnings, as the auctioneer began the bidding.

Pennington and the rest of the task force had also drawn near to see what would happen. Tempting Dash had generated the most media coverage and the most attention of any of the horses throughout the long trial. For José and his brothers, the horse was a talisman, the foundation of Tremor Enterprises and the legacy they had built before it had all come crashing down in the early-morning raid.

Tyler Graham stood at the edge of the sales ring, his grandfather behind him, towering over him. Lawson had noticed the two in close conversation before the start of the bidding, which had made him suspicious. He didn't like surprises. Industry veterans had told him the stallion would be the sales topper of the two-day auction, maybe even of the year. The bids kept spiralling higher and higher, some of the winks and nods so subtle it was difficult for the untrained eye to tell who was bidding. But now Lawson could see that it was Doc Graham and Tyler who were bidding for the stallion, and the sum was already near the million-dollar mark. Lawson thought it was a reckless move, especially when Graham was already on Miguel Treviño's list for retribution.

Graham had never mentioned to Lawson that he planned to bid on Tempting Dash. Now he worried that Pennington and the others would think he'd withheld the information from them. He couldn't believe Graham's nerve. Maybe the breeder believed the horse was his due. Tempting Dash had been with him for nearly three years and the horse had brought a newfound prestige to his farm. Though there was no denying the horse's value, the six-year-old stallion had also brought him a lot of grief.

As the bidding went higher and higher, Lawson was playing through in his mind all of the potentially bad things that could happen if Graham and his grandfather prevailed. But then he noticed a look of anger come over Doc Graham's face and the old man turned away from the ring. Tyler Graham stood there silently, watching, now just a spectator like everyone else. The bidding had reached $1.7 million and the auctioneer, nearly breathless with excitement, announced the winning buyer, John Simmons. Lawson felt nothing but relief. The Grahams had lost Tempting Dash to a retired Texas banker.

The $1.7 million price tag for Tempting Dash was the most ever paid for an American quarter horse at public auction. José's other horses had gone for much less than Lawson had expected. Without the inflated prices that had been so common when José's crew was selling and buying horses to one another, the bids had gone back to a more realistic level. Dashin Follies, which José had purchased for $875,000, was sold for $260,000 to a Brazilian rancher, and Mr. Piloto got a paltry $85,000, surprisingly low for the winner of the prestigious All American Futurity. No doubt revelations about race fixing during the trial had something to do with the horse's deflated price.

Much to the team's relief, the last of the cartel's horses had been sold without incident. Maybe their presence at the auction had tamped down any plans for vengeance, or maybe the backlash from the Treviños and the Zetas was too high a price to pay for any Mexican bidder. Miguel Treviño was behind bars but he wasn't out of the game. And Omar was still on the run. The team had stopped the family's money-laundering scheme. But they knew the fast and loose world of quarter-horse racing was still too much of a temptation for anyone with millions to launder. And that someday soon they might be back again at Heritage Place.

But first they would celebrate. Lawson needed to feel some kind of closure after three years. He drove with Pennington and a couple of the deputies from the task force to a cavernous nightclub in downtown Oklahoma City called Cowboys. It was a Wednesday night but the place was nearly full. The bar had a bull-riding ring next to the dance floor, for patrons who preferred to cheat death on a live bull rather than risk a two-step. As Lawson and Pennington stood at the edge of the dance floor, a hostess brought them a round of drinks. The two men scanned the bar, looking for who might have sent drinks to two off-duty federal agents. Then Lawson noticed Tyler Graham standing in a dark corner nearby, surrounded by a group of friends drinking and laughing. Lawson wasn't surprised that Graham was celebrating too. The investigation was finally over and José and Miguel were in jail. In the end, Graham had lost Tempting Dash, but he'd had a good run while it lasted and now he was finally free of Lawson and the FBI. Lawson supposed that he'd never had any illusions about the world – Doc Graham had made sure of that. Neither did he, not anymore. He made his way over to Graham, who raised his beer in a toast as he drew near.

'I just want to thank you for everything,' Lawson said, shaking his hand. 'We did it.'

'Yeah, we did.' Graham smiled and took a draw off his beer. 'We sure as hell did.'

EPILOGUE

A MONTH AFTER JOHN SIMMONS BOUGHT TEMPTING DASH AT AUCTION, HE received an email at his office in Texas. The message, written in Spanish, threatened him with death if he didn't turn over all of the proceeds to Omar Treviño from the breeding of Tempting Dash. The email had another message too: Tyler Graham had better watch his back. Simmons immediately contacted the FBI.

The only surprise for Scott Lawson was that the threat hadn't come sooner. Miguel and José were in prison but Omar was still running the Zetas in Mexico. Lawson told Graham to take a vacation for a couple of weeks and not let anyone know where he was going. While he was away, Lawson and Pérez would work their sources in Mexico to see how serious Omar was about carrying out his threat. An FBI computer analyst traced the email back to the Mexican border state of Coahuila, where the Zetas still ruled with impunity. The cartel had been weakened by numerous arrests and from war with their enemies but Lawson didn't doubt that Omar would make good on his threat. Shortly after Simmons received the email, his ranch foreman's truck was shot at as he was returning to the stables one afternoon.

LUCKILY FOR TYLER GRAHAM and the new owner of Tempting Dash, Omar Treviño was increasingly consumed with keeping the volatile Zetas from further splintering. In March 2015, Omar was finally captured in one of Monterrey's most exclusive enclaves, San Pedro Garza Garcia, where he had been living for more than a year with his wife and children. In the video taken by the Mexican army of Omar being marched towards a waiting military helicopter, he looks worn out and diminished. He is thirty-eight but looks at least a decade older. For days afterwards, the television news would display the Zeta leader's numerous mansions in Monterrey, two warehouses filled with speedboats and luxury cars, and a sleek black Italian helicopter at a private airfield. For those living in the shacks on the margins of the cities and in the forgotten *barrios*, the drug lord's riches would offer a vision other than grinding poverty and a lifetime of hunger.

AFTER THE APRIL 2013 trial, Francisco Colorado, José Treviño, Fernando Garcia and Chevo Huitron immediately appealed their guilty verdicts. Colorado, sparing no expense, hired legendary lawyer and constitutional expert Alan Dershowitz to represent him before the 5th US Circuit Court of Appeals in New Orleans. In May 2015, the 5th Circuit granted a new trial to Colorado and overturned the eight-year prison sentence for Chevo Huitron due to insufficient evidence. The government hadn't shown definitive proof, ruled the 5th Circuit, that Miguel Treviño had channelled drug money through Colorado's ADT Petroservicios. The court, however, upheld the convictions of José Treviño and Fernando Garcia.

But Colorado's freedom was short-lived. In November 2015, the fifty-five-year-old received a second guilty verdict, this time before visiting judge Donald Walters in Austin. He was sentenced to twenty years in federal prison. During the trial, Carlos Nayen and Fernando Garcia testified for the first time in an effort to reduce their long prison sentences. Nayen's testimony was especially damaging for the man he considered a father figure, as he described truckloads of cash sent by Miguel Treviño to Colorado's ranch in Veracruz. In exchange for their testimonies, Garcia and Nayen were released from prison in 2017.

In a separate trial, Colorado received another five years for the bribery attempt with Judge Sparks. His son, Pancho Jr, and business associate Ramon Segura each served a year in prison. ADT Petroservicios is still in business in Tuxpan, Veracruz.

By the time of Colorado's second guilty verdict, the Zetas had become a weaker, splintered organisation. Kiko Treviño, the nephew of Miguel and Omar, became leader of a new group called El Cártel del Noreste and went to war with other factions of the Zetas. Said to be even more sadistic than his uncles, Kiko was arrested in Houston in September 2016. With many of its top leaders now dead or in jail, the Gulf Cartel also splintered but the violence hasn't ceased as the various factions tear each other apart in the Mexican border state of Tamaulipas, which has not seen peace in nearly two decades. In the rest of Mexico, the Jalisco New Generation Cartel, a paramilitary organisation created to fight the Zetas, is now devouring the cartel's former territory. The deaths in Mexico's drug war have already surpassed civilian casualties from the wars in Iraq and Afghanistan combined. As of 2017, Alfonso del Rayo and his family had not returned to Veracruz, one of the states hardest hit in the drug war. He is now seeking political asylum in the United States, which rarely grants protections to families fleeing violence in Mexico.

Both Miguel and Omar are currently being held in the maximum-security Altiplano prison outside Mexico City, infamous for the 2015 escape of Joaquín 'El Chapo' Guzmán, who was spirited out of the prison through a tunnel on a motorcycle on a built-in track. The United States has filed extradition orders for both Miguel and Omar, who are wanted on drug-trafficking and murder charges, but Mexico rarely extradites its cartel leaders. The extradition of a high-profile cartel leader like Guzmán has given the team some hope that the Treviño brothers someday might face justice in an American courtroom.

In December 2014, Scott Lawson finally got his transfer back to Tennessee. But he hadn't made that clean break from Laredo that he'd always bragged about to Alma Pérez. After the 2013 trial in Austin, he'd fallen in love with a native Laredoan. In November 2016, they were married. The couple bought a small homestead in the Tennessee countryside and plan on buying some horses. Now in the Lawson household there are jalapeños on the table at every meal and homemade tamales at Christmas.

Pérez could only smile at her prediction coming true. 'I told you a Laredo girl would get you after all,' she'd joked to Lawson after he'd announced his engagement. Pérez had her fourth child in 2015 and was promoted to border liaison, and collaborates whenever she can with her counterparts in Mexico. She also still works cases on the violent-crimes squad in Laredo. But she misses her former partner.

In 2015, another sorrel stallion thrilled the quarter-horse racing world. The horse's name was Kiss My Hocks, one of the first foals bred from Tempting Dash at Southwest Stallion Station. José Treviño had given Tyler Graham a handful of breedings with the champion in partial payment for boarding and breeding his horses. Kiss My Hocks won more than $1 million in purse winnings, double the amount of Tempting Dash, and put Southwest Stallion Station back on the map as a premier stud farm. In the end, Graham had got what he always wanted but he never could have imagined the price he would have to pay for his success.

Pennington and his Waco Treasury Task Force never stopped working. Four months after Omar's capture, the drug lord's father-in-law, Jesús Fernández de Luna, was arrested in Mexico City on criminal conspiracy and money-laundering charges. Fernández had been buying horses in the States all along for Omar, even as his brother José was on trial. Among his purchases was First Tempting Dash, the brother of racing champion Tempting Dash. The Waco Treasury Task Force was assigned to work the case in the States.

After the arrests of José and his network, and the Zetas' top coke wholesaler in Dallas, Brian Schutt and Steve Junker noticed it was impossible to find a pure gram of coke on the streets. They'd managed to disrupt Dallas's thriving cocaine market, which gave them some satisfaction. But they'd been in the game too long to believe it would last. Eventually, the market was flooded with heroin and meth, and Dallas's drug entrepreneurs got to work again concocting new deadly mixtures to meet the swelling demand. In October 2016, Schutt retired from the task force. Very soon, Pennington and Junker will face mandatory retirement. Kim Williams, who they hoped would run the task force along with Billy Williams, was taken off it in 2016 and promoted to sergeant at the Irving Police Department. The future of the Waco Treasury Task Force is uncertain.

After twenty-eight years fighting the drug war, Pennington sometimes felt like he was running in place. Lawson was having similar thoughts, especially after Chevo Huitron had been released and Colorado was given a new trial. As Lawson sat through Colorado's second trial at the federal courthouse in Austin, he realised the money-laundering case had taken five years of his life. Sometimes he wondered if the indictments had changed anything. There was too much money out there, the black market too big, too enticing, and there was too much demand. He was no longer the brash, naïve rookie in Laredo who thought that simply by exacting justice he could turn the tide in the drug war.

In July 2015, Lawson returned to Hardeman County with his elder half-brother to erect a sign in memory of their father, Mike Lawson, along a stretch of highway that had been dedicated to the former chief deputy of Hardeman County. Dozens of friends, neighbours, news reporters and local dignitaries turned out for the memorial. He could see that his father had made a difference in their rural community. As Lawson stood on a ladder, helping his brother make the final adjustments to his father's sign, he marvelled at the sea of faces that had come out to honour the local lawman, and couldn't help but feel the pull, once again, to follow in his father's footsteps.

ACKNOWLEDGEMENTS

I **FELL IN LOVE WITH MEXICO AS A CHILD GROWING UP IN SAN DIEGO, CALIFORNIA.**
The first time that I can remember crossing the border – maybe
at age seven, or even earlier – the food tasted better, the colours
seemed more vivid and the people were warmer than anything
I'd experienced in the United States. I felt I'd found my second
home.

I write this because I realise this book paints Mexico in a less
than favourable, even terrifying, light through the prism of the
drug war and the Zetas. But it is because I love Mexico so much
that I write about the devastating violence that has gripped it in
recent years. The years portrayed in this book from late 2009 to
2013 were some of the worst, as Miguel Treviño and the Zetas
reached their zenith of power. During these years, the violence
struck home for me personally as it devoured the Mexican states
of Nuevo Leon, Coahuila and Tamaulipas on the Texas-Mexico
border. As a reporter covering the region, I grew heartsick,
writing endless stories about gruesome killings, kidnappings and
mass graves that were never investigated, and the perpetrators
never brought to justice. And with the same heavy heart, I wrote

about my brave colleagues in Mexico, murdered in increasingly shocking numbers as they struggled to reveal the truth behind the violence, which is that the drug war is more about politics and corruption than drugs.

What drew me to the investigation of Jose Treviño and his brothers was the opportunity to understand the origins of the nightmare I had been reporting on for so many years. For the first time at José's trial, founding members of the Zetas testified in court about the inner workings of the secretive organisation and helped me understand how they became the de facto government in places like Coahuila and Veracruz. The federal agents who worked this case – especially Scott Lawson, Alma Pérez and Steve Pennington – were kind enough to entertain my hundreds, if not thousands, of questions over the three years I reported on the investigation. For their patience and for their trust I am deeply indebted. I also want to thank FBI special agent Michelle Lee, the media co-ordinator for the FBI's San Antonio office, who was always unfailingly helpful throughout the process of writing this book. If the bureau takes any issue with its characterisation within these pages, it is solely the author's doing and not Agent Lee's. I would also like to thank the Waco Treasury Task Force officers Brian Schutt, Steve Junker, Kim Williams and IRS special agent Billy Williams for their time and patience.

I would be remiss if I didn't thank former FBI special agent Art Fontes, former DEA supervisory agent Leo Silva, former DEA special agent Pedro Ayarzagoitia and DEA special agents Kyle Mori and Bill Johnston. I also owe a debt of thanks to FBI special agent Raúl Perdomo, FBI special agent Jason Hodge, Laredo PD homicide investigator Ernie Elizondo, FBI supervisory special agent David Villarreal and IRS special agent Michael Lemoine, as well as to my sources in Mexico who took the time to educate me about horse racing and organised crime.

I never could have written this book without the blessing of my employer, the *Texas Observer*, and my colleagues and friends at the magazine who gave me the time off to write this book, even though it meant more work for them. I also want to thank the Investigative Fund, especially Taya Kitman and Esther Kaplan, who have supported my work and kept me going through the hard times. I also owe much thanks to the Lannan Foundation, which has been an invaluable supporter of my work on the border. The team at Ecco, including my editor, Zachary Wagman, and his assistant, Emma Janaskie, also has my gratitude, as does my agent, Farley Chase.

I am also indebted to a number of friends who read various versions of the manuscript over the years and gave me much-needed insight to improve the book, including Karen Davidson, Karen Olsson, Athena Ponce and Dave Mann. The wonderful S. Kirk Walsh was an invaluable reader and editor who helped me immensely. Also thank you to my friend Jazmine Ulloa, who first started this journey with me when we wrote the magazine story in 2013, and to the incomparable journalist Ginger Thompson, who broke the story about Jose Treviño and Tremor Enterprises in 2012 and was a source of inspiration throughout the years of writing this book. I also owe a debt of gratitude to another formidable journalist, Cecilia Ballí, my *compañera*-in-crime, who travelled with me to racetracks and auctions. For their boundless support, I'd also like to thank Jordan Smith, Glynis Laing, Liz Pierson, Katie Wells, Jessica Montour, W. K. Stratton, Karen Tannert and Kim Sherman. I am indebted to Guadalupe Correa-Cabrera for giving me a deeper understanding of how organised crime functions in Mexico. *Y también muchísimas gracias à* Rebecca y Guadalupe Massey, and to Alfredo Corchado, Angela Kocherga, Jason Buch *y toda la banda en los Camineros* for staying true to Mexico and the border, despite the toughest of times in journalism.

And finally, to my family, who endured my long absences, even when I was at home, and who made my happiness and the writing of this book possible. *Los quiero mucho.*

A NOTE ON THE SOURCES

THIS BOOK IS BASED EXTENSIVELY ON INTERVIEWS WITH FEDERAL AGENTS FROM the FBI, IRS and DEA, as well as federal prosecutors. I also consulted thousands of pages of court transcripts, not just from the José Treviño trial, but also from dozens of others involving members of the Zeta cartel.

The name Alma Pérez is a pseudonym, which the FBI agent requested that I use for the safety of her family. Accordingly, the names of her family members have also been changed. For privacy reasons, the name Veronica Cárdenas is a pseudonym, as well as the name of Scott Lawson's former girlfriend. All other names in the book are real.

Tyler Graham, who was the key source for the FBI in the investigation, declined to be interviewed for this book, as did José Treviño. To reconstruct the scenes and events surrounding them, I relied on court testimonies, accounts from agents and others who interacted with them, wiretap recordings and other investigative documents. For anything in quotation marks, I relied on the agents who were present, court transcripts, wiretap recordings, investigative documents and media reports, which are cited in the endnotes section. In addition, I interviewed various quarter-horse racing experts and a law-enforcement official in Mexico, all of whom requested anonymity because they feared retribution.

NOTES

ONE

1 *Special Agent Scott Lawson:* Author interview with FBI special agent Scott Lawson.

2 *Back then, in 2005:* Alex Chadwick, 'Drug Cartel Battles Escalate in Nuevo Laredo' (interview with *Dallas Morning News* correspondent Alfredo Corchado), NPR, 26 July 2005, http://www.npr.org/tem plates/story/ story.php?storyId=4771483.

3 *Every day, more than twelve thousand:* 'International Trade', Laredo Development Foundation, http://ldfonline.org/site-selection/inter national-trade/.

4 *The Zetas were a new kind of cartel:* George Grayson and Samuel Logan, *The Executioner's Men: Los Zetas, Rogue Soldiers, Criminal Entrepreneurs, and the Shadow State They Created* (New Brunswick, NJ: Transaction, 2012).

TWO

5 *They'd narrowly escaped:* 'Aterroriza la balacera,' *El Mañana de Nuevo Laredo,* 22 October 2009.

6 *Villarreal picked up his Nextel:* DEA wiretap, 21 October 2009.

7 *As the illicit drug economy:* Jason Lange, 'From Spas to Banks, Mexico Economy Rides on Drugs', Reuters, 22 January 2010, http://www.reuters. com/article/us-drugs-mexico-economy-idUSTRE60L0X120100122.

8 *Generals, law enforcement, and politicians:* June S. Beittel, 'Mexico:

Organized Crime and Drug Trafficking Organizations', Congressional Research Service, 22 July 2015, 7–9.

9 *But by 2000, the old arrangements:* Ibid.

10 *The cartel's military founders:* George Grayson, 'Los Zetas: The Ruthless Army Spawned by a Mexican Drug Cartel', Foreign Policy Research Institute, 13 May 2008, http://www.fpri.org/article/2008/05/los-zetas-the-ruthless-army-spawned-by-a-mexican-drug-cartel/#note5.

11 *Nearly half of the trade between the two countries:* Port of Entry: Laredo Impact on the Texas Economy, 2015, https://comptroller.texas.gov/economy/docs/ports/overview-laredo.pdf.

12 *By 2008, Lazcano had also tasked:* George Grayson and Samuel Logan, *The Executioner's Men: Los Zetas, Rogue Soldiers, Criminal Entrepreneurs, and the Shadow State They Created* (New Brunswick, NJ: Transaction, 2012).

13 *The Zetas were training:* Alfredo Corchado, *Midnight in Mexico: A Reporter's Journey Through a Country's Descent into Darkness* (New York: Penguin Press, 2013).

14 *But by 2010 there was little:* Molly Molloy, 'The Mexican Undead: Toward a New History of the "Drug War"', *Small Wars Journal*, 21 August 2013, http://smallwarsjournal.com/jrnl/art/the-mexican-undead-toward-a-new-history-of-the-%E2%80%9Cdrug-war%E2%80%9D-killing-fields.

15 *Even more troubling:* 'Transcript: Janet Napolitano Sits Down with CNN's Wolf Blitzer', *The Situation Room with Wolf Blitzer,* 19 March 2009, via AZCentral.com, http://archive.azcentral.com/news/articles/2009/03/19/20090319brewertranscript0319.html.

16 *In one month:* Court testimony of Mario Alfonso Cuellar.

17 *They were a large and sprawling family:* Treviño family background from FBI intelligence brief.

THREE

18 *Homeland Security Investigations:* Melissa del Bosque and Patrick Michels, 'Homeland Insecurity', *Texas Observer,* 7 December 2015, https://www.texasobserver.org/homeland-security-corruption-border-patrol/.

19 *Two months into his new job:* Author interview with FBI agent Scott Lawson.

20 *An American had bid:* Ben Hudson, 'Highest Selling Broodmare Ever

Brings $875,000', *Track,* February 2010, http://www.heritageplace.com/sales_2010/Winter2010/HighestSellingBroodmare.pdf.

21 *Hodge had found the interview:* Author interview with FBI special agent Jason Hodge.

FOUR

22 *Graham's grandfather Charles 'Doc' Graham:* Brooke Prather, '"Doc," an American Dreamer', Department of Animal Science, Texas A&M University, 4 February 2015, http://animalscience.tamu.edu/2015/02/04/doc-an-american-dreamer/.

23 *Bred from small, sturdy Spanish horses:* Robert Moorman Denhardt, *Quarter Horses: A Tale of Two Centuries* (Norman: University of Oklahoma Press, 1967).

24 *Tyler Graham was just breaking:* Cynthia McFarland, 'If I Ruled the Horse Business', *Track,* March 2014, http://tqha.com/wp-content/uploads/If-I-ruled-the-horse-business-Tyler-Graham.pdf.

25 *Inside, Graham appeared unruffled:* Description of office from author's visit to Southwest Stallion Station in July 2013.

26 *Graham gestured for Lawson:* Author interview with FBI special agent Scott Lawson.

27 *Graham explained that his friend:* Tyler Graham court testimony, April 2013.

28 *He'd even dropped $12,000:* Ibid.

29 *There was the Dallas drug bust:* Court transcript for trial of Juan Francisco Treviño, December 1995.

30 *At one time, Miguel:* Jason Buch, 'Trial Exposed Zetas' U.S. Ties', *San Antonio Express-News,* 29 January 2012, http://www.mysanantonio.com/news/local_news/article/Trial-exposed-Zetas-U-S-ties-2798216.php.

FIVE

31 *Pérez had spent the last five years:* Author interview with FBI special agent Alma Pérez.

32 *But in 2005:* Marla Dickerson, 'Mexican Police Chief Is Killed on His First Day', *Los Angeles Times,* 10 June 10 2005, http://articles.latimes.com/2005/jun/10/world/fg-chief10.

33 *The two cities:* US embassy and consulates in Mexico, https://mx.usembassy.gov/embassy-consulates/nuevo-laredo/nuevo-laredo-history/.

34 *Of the more than 13,500 FBI agents:* Figures provided by the FBI, 15 March 2017.

SIX

35 *Working his first kidnapping case:* Author interview with FBI special agent Scott Lawson.

36 *With five years already:* Author interview with FBI special agent Alma Pérez.

37 *Graham said that that morning:* Tyler Graham court testimony, April 2013.

SEVEN

38 *There were only two things:* Author interview with FBI special agent Scott Lawson.

EIGHT

39 *He called a meeting:* Carlos Nayen court testimony.

40 *In Nuevo Laredo, convoys:* Blanche Petrich, 'Nuevo Laredo Campo de Battala entre los Carteles', *La Jornada,* 14 June 2011. http://www.jornada.unam.mx/2011/06/14/index.php?section=politica&article=004n1pol.

41 *And even worse, Miguel:* Court testimony of Jesús Rejón Aguilar.

42 *The asking price of $21,500:* Court testimony of David Finn.

43 *Mario Alfonso Cuellar:* Court testimony of Mario Alfonso Cuellar.

44 *Colorado and Barradas were so intertwined:* Court testimony of Carlos Nayen.

NINE

45 *Lawson sat at the conference table:* Author interview with FBI special agent Scott Lawson.

46 *The DEA's Houston headquarters:* Houston DEA website, www.dea.gov/divisions/contacts/hou_contact.shtml.

TEN

47 *Last time, they'd met:* Author interview with FBI special agent Scott Lawson.

48 *'The All American Futurity':* Ruidoso Downs website, http://www.all american-ruidoso.com/.

ELEVEN

49 *After they checked into their room at the Best Western:* Author interview with FBI special agent Raúl Perdomo.

50 *Graham answered the door:* Author interview with FBI special agent Scott Lawson.

51 *A world speed record:* Ruidoso Downs website, http://www.allameri can-ruidoso.com/.

52 *It had been Ramiro Villarreal:* Testimony of IRS special agent Steve Pennington at José Treviño detention hearing, July 2012.

53 *The LLCs were easy to incorporate:* Stephen Fishman, 'How to Form an LLC in Texas', Nolo.com, http://www.nolo.com/legal-encyclo pedia/texas-form-llc-31745.html.

TWELVE

54 *Ramiro Villarreal mopped the sweat:* Author interview with former DEA supervisory agent Leo Silva.

55 *In the past three years:* Court testimony of IRS special agent Steve Pennington.

56 *With the help of a man:* Author interview with Mauricio Paez.

57 *The day after the auction:* Court testimony of DEA special agent René Amarillas.

58 *Miguel had been on the DEA's radar:* Author interview with former DEA supervisory agent Leo Silva.

59 *Villarreal begged to be let go:* Author interview with Mexican law-enforcement official, granted with agreement that the official remain anonymous for security reasons.

THIRTEEN

60 *By now, they were working:* Author interview with FBI special agent Scott Lawson.

61 *A Mexican police commander:* 'Investigator in Missing Jet Skier Case Beheaded', CBS News, 12 October 2010, http://www.cbsnews.com/news/investigator-in-missing-jet-skier-case-beheaded/.

62 *She'd stuck out the surveillance:* Author interview with Alma Pérez.

FOURTEEN

63 *Ramiro Villarreal had kept his end:* Author interview with anonymous Mexican law-enforcement official.

64 *They'd even hung giant banners:* Diego Enrique Osorno, *La guerra de los Zetas: Viaje por la frontera de la necropolítica* (Grijalbo, 2013).

65 *The cartel also stockpiled weapons:* Court testimony of Jesús Rejón Aguilar.

66 *Special Agent Amarillas:* Author interview with anonymous Mexican law-enforcement official.

67 *A few days after the failed operation:* Ibid.

68 *But when Miguel directed:* Court testimony of Carlos Nayen.

69 *In Nuevo Laredo, he waited:* Author interview with former DEA supervisory agent Leo Silva

70 *Miguel greeted Villarreal:* Ginger Thompson, 'A Drug Family in the Winner's Circle', *New York Times,* 12 June 2012, http://www.ny times. com/2012/06/13/us/drug-money-from-mexico-makes-its-way-to-the-racetrack.html.

FIFTEEN

71 *He explained that Graham:* Author interview with FBI special agent Scott Lawson.

72 *At Don Martin's:* Author interview with FBI special agent Alma Pérez.

SIXTEEN

73 *By the end of 2010:* E. Eduardo Castillo and Katherine Corcoran, 'Two Powerful Cartels Dominate in Mexico Drug War', Associated Press, 1 October 2011, via Fox News, http://www.foxnews.com/world/2011/10/01/2-powerful-cartels-dominate-in-mexico-drug-war.html.

74 *In early December, del Rayo:* Author interview with Alfonso del Rayo.

SEVENTEEN

75 *Lawson had been living in Laredo:* Author interview with FBI special agent Scott Lawson.

76   *He invited Pérez over for dinner:* Author interview with FBI special agent
     Alma Pérez.

EIGHTEEN

77   *When Lawson returned:* Author interview with FBI special agent Scott
     Lawson.

78   *But he did find a brief mention:* 'Escándalo de Pancho Colorado salpica
     campañas en Veracruz', *Proceso,* 15 June 2012, http://www.pro ceso.
     com.mx/310996.

79   *He'd looked into Chevo Huitron:* Court testimony of prosecutor Doug
     Gardner.

100 *Injecting racehorses with everything:* Ray Paulick, 'Horse Dies After
     Winning Ruidoso Futurity; Trainer Banned', *Paulick Report,* 13 June
     2013, http://www.paulickreport.com/news/ray-s-paddock/horse-dies-
     after-winning-ruidoso-futurity-trainer-banned/.

101 *The doped-up horses broke down:* Walt Bogdanich, Joe Drape, Dara L.
     Miles and Griffin Palmer, 'Mangled Horses, Maimed Jockeys', *New York
     Times,* 24 March 2012, http://www.nytimes.com/2012/03/25/us/
     death-and-disarray-at-americas-racetracks.html?pagewanted=all&_r=0.

102 *One of the industry's most famous studs:* Lazy E Ranch, http://lazye ranch.
     net/stallions.asp.

NINETEEN

103 *Alfonso del Rayo had spent his Christmas holiday:* Author interview with
     Alfonso del Rayo.

104 *He'd served as a senator:* 'Fidel Herrera Beltrán', Red Política, http://
     www.redpolitica.mx/yopolitico/perfil/fidel/herrera-beltran.

105 *Lawson was sitting at his desk:* Author interview with FBI special agent
     Scott Lawson.

TWENTY

106 *Alfonso del Rayo took the first flight:* Author interview with Alfonso del
     Rayo.

107 *Blues Ferrari had a top-of-the-line pedigree:* Court testimony of Russell
     Stooks.

108 *'Sold for 310!':* 'Heritage Place 2011 Winter Mixed Sale Is Highest Grossing in History', Stallion eSearch, 15 January 2011, http://stallionesearch.com/default.asp?section=21&story=8875.

109 *Jason Hodge and one of the task force officers:* Author interview with FBI special agent Scott Lawson.

110 *Tebow had gone from being excited:* Court testimony of Jeff Tebow.

111 *'The International demand':* 'Heritage Place 2011 Winter Mixed Sale Is Highest Grossing in History', Stallion eSearch, 15 January 2011, http://stallionesearch.com/default.asp?section=21&story=8875.

TWENTY-ONE

112 *After the Heritage Place winter auction:* Author interview with FBI special agent Scott Lawson.

113 *The breeding of the champion:* Court testimony of Tyler Graham.

114 *Lawson still hadn't brought up:* Author interview with FBI special agent Scott Lawson.

115 *The lobby of the Omni Hotel:* Ibid.

TWENTY-TWO

116 *Graham had lost Tempting Dash:* Author interview with FBI special agent Scott Lawson.

117 *Lawson picked up the vibrating mobile phone:* Ibid.

118 *The historic and imposing:* 'History', La Posada Hotel, http://laposada.com/history/.

119 *Lawson sat nearby:* Author interview with FBI special agent Scott Lawson.

120 *'I'll go talk to CBP':* Author interview with FBI special agent Raúl Perdomo.

121 *Stocky and in his late twenties:* Surveillance photos provided by the FBI.

TWENTY-THREE

122 *The Laredo division:* Statistics provided by Laredo US attorney's office, 8 May 2017.

123 *But without a federal prosecutor:* Author interview with FBI special agent Scott Lawson.

TWENTY-FOUR

124 *It was hard for Lawson:* Author interview with FBI special agent Scott
     Lawson.

125 *Hodge briefed Gardner:* Author interview with prosecutor Doug Gardner.

126 *The program had been created:* 'Organized Crime Drug Enforcement
     Task Forces', US Department of Justice, https://www.justice.gov/
     criminal/organized-crime-drug-enforcement-task-forces.

127 *called the Waco Treasury Taskforce:* Author interview with IRS special
     agent Steve Pennington.

TWENTY-FIVE

128 *In twenty-two years:* Author interview with IRS special agent Steve
     Pennington.

129 *The IRS had fewer than:* 'Our Legacy & Importance to America', *History
     – IRS-Criminal Investigation (IRS-CI),* http://www.fleoa.org/downloads/
     history_irs-ci.pdf.

130 *especially after the passage:* Glenn Kessler, 'History Lesson: More
     Republicans Than Democrats Supported NAFTA', Fact Checker,
     Washington Post, 9 May 2016, https://www.washingtonpost.com/news/
     fact-checker/wp/2016/05/09/history-lesson-more-republicans-than-
     democrats-supported-nafta/.

131 *Williams had subpoenaed:* Author interview with IRS special agent Billy
     Williams.

132 *In the late 1980s:* Mutual Legal Assistance Cooperation Treaty with
     Mexico, 16 February 1988, https://www.oas.org/juridico/mla/en
     /traites/en_traites-mla-usa-mex.pdf.

TWENTY-SIX

133 *At his office in Waco:* Author interview with IRS special agent Steve
     Pennington.

134 *Over the years:* Author interview with Waco Treasury Task Force officer
     Brian Schutt.

TWENTY-SEVEN

135 *Lawson phoned Graham:* Author interview with FBI special agent Scott
     Lawson.

136 *They had a wire room:* Author interview with FBI Special Agent Alma Pérez.

137 *Graham told him to look:* Author interview with FBI special agent Scott Lawson.

138 *But if she took on the investigation:* Author interview with FBI special agent Alma Pérez.

139 *She didn't think Villarreal:* Ibid.

TWENTY-EIGHT

140 *Lawson's frustration was only heightened:* Author interview with FBI agent Scott Lawson.

141 *After searching for a few minutes:* Clau Viernes, 'Muere sujeto calcinado tras accidente automovilístico', *RN Noticias,* 11 March 2010, http:// www.rnnoticias.com.mx/nuevo-laredo/muere-sujeto-calcinada-tras-accidente-automovilistico.

142 *Chevo answered after a couple of rings:* Author interview with Eusevio 'Chevo' Huitron.

TWENTY-NINE

143 *Horse racing in Mexico:* Author interview with Mexican racetrack official on condition of anonymity.

144 *Top cartel leaders:* Court testimony of Carlos Nayen.

145 *One rancher from Monterrey:* Author interview with former supervisory DEA agent Leo Silva.

146 *So it was a lucky break:* Author interview with FBI special agent Scott Lawson.

147 *About twenty minutes into their meeting:* Author interview with FBI special agent Alma Pérez.

148 *The grooms, hot walkers, and exercise riders:* Patricia Leigh Brown, 'Behind the Racetrack, a Tough Existence for "Backstretch" Workers, *California Watch,* 4 September 2011, http://californiawatch.org/dailyreport/behind-racetrack-tough-existence-backstretch-workers-12174.

THIRTY

149 *Once Pennington and the Waco Treasury Task Force:* Author interview with FBI special agent Scott Lawson.

150 *Pennington, sitting next to Brian Schutt:* Author interview with IRS Special Agent Steve Pennington.

151 *If the idea had come:* Author interview with prosecutor Doug Gardner.

152 *Lawson put down his pen:* Author interview with FBI special agent Scott Lawson.

153 *They got into Lawson's Chevy:* Author interview with FBI special agent Alma Pérez.

154 *His mobile phone wouldn't power up:* Author interview with FBI special agent Scott Lawson.

155 *Pérez would have to work the case:* Author interview with FBI special agent Alma Pérez.

THIRTY-ONE

156 *He and Billy Williams:* Author interview with IRS special agent Steve Pennington.

157 *Junker wouldn't be working:* Author interview with Waco Treasury Task Force officer Steve Junker.

158 *Just thirty-two, Williams:* Author interview with Waco Treasury Task Force officer Kim Williams.

159 *Two weeks after Lawson:* Author interview with FBI special agent Scott Lawson.

THIRTY-TWO

160 *Tyler Graham had worked:* Author interview with FBI special agent Scott Lawson.

161 *But José would put none:* Ibid.

162 *A devastating drought*: Consensual wiretap recording provided by FBI.

THIRTY-THREE

163 *When Alfonso del Rayo:* Author interview with Alfonso del Rayo.

164 *In mid-July, Graham:* Consensual wiretap recording provided by FBI.

165 *In Veracruz, del Rayo:* Author interview with Alfonso del Rayo.

166 *In the first week:* Consensual wiretap recording provided by FBI.

THIRTY-FOUR

167 *Gone were the scuffed work boots:* Author interview with FBI special agent Scott Lawson.

168 *Graham found it hard to believe:* Court testimony of Tyler Graham.

169 *The next afternoon:* Author interview with FBI special agent Scott Lawson.

170 *Pérez hoped he was right:* Author interview with FBI special agent Alma Pérez.

THIRTY-FIVE

171 *In September 2011:* Author interview with FBI special agent Jason Hodge.

172 *At home, Pérez had talked:* Author interview with FBI special agent Alma Pérez.

173 *Lawson glanced at the front-page news story:* Author interview with FBI special agent Scott Lawson.

THIRTY-SIX

174 *Not long after their meeting:* Author interview with FBI special agent Scott Lawson.

175 *José asked Graham:* Court testimony of Tyler Graham.

176 *Again, José asked Graham:* Court testimony of IRS special agent Steve Pennington.

177 *The media covering the race: Track,* July 2011.

178 *José could scarcely contain his pride:* Court testimony of IRS special agent Steve Pennington.

179 *The Sinaloa cartel responded:* 'Los "Mata Zetas" reivindica la matanza de Veracruz', *El País,* 30 September 2011, http://internacional.elpais.com/internacional/2011/09/28/videos/1317209317_454012.html.

180 *On November 23:* 'Las autoridades de Sinaloa localizan 23 cadáveres en tres municipios', CNN Mexico, 23 November 2011, http://expansion.mx/nacional/2011/11/23/las-autoridades-de-sinaloa-localizan-20-cadaveres-en-dos-municipios.

181 *The next day, the Zetas:* '26 cadáveres son abandonados en vehículos en una avenida de Guadalajara', CNN Mexico, 24 November 2011, http://expansion.mx/nacional/2011/11/24/cadaveres-en-tres-camio netas-son-abandonados-en-un-avenida-de-guadalajara.

182   *In July 2011, the Mexican army:* 'Top Zetas Drug Boss "El Mamito" Captured', NBC News, 4 July 2011, http://www.nbcnews.com/video/nbcnews.com/43633033#43633033.

183   *When Jaff arrived at his office:* Court testimony of Arian Jaff.

THIRTY-SEVEN

184   *Pennington thought of every investigation:* Author interview with IRS special agent Steve Pennington.

185   *Pérez and Lawson drove up:* Author interview with FBI special agent Scott Lawson.

186   *In Dallas, IRS special agent:* Author interview with IRS special agent Billy Williams.

187   *While people above their pay grade:* Author interview with IRS special agent Steve Pennington.

188   *Working with Tyler Graham:* Author interview with FBI special agent Scott Lawson.

THIRTY-EIGHT

189   *It was like the DEA:* Author interview with FBI special agent Scott Lawson.

190   *Six months after Pennington:* Ibid.

191   *Pérez found it difficult:* Author interview with FBI special agent Alma Pérez.

192   *Cuellar explained that, in 2007:* Court testimony of Mario Alfonso Cuellar.

193   *Miguel and Omar had killed:* Author interview with FBI special agent Alma Pérez.

194   *After the interview:* Ibid.

195   *Vasquez said his main point of contact:* Court testimony of José Vasquez Jr.

196   *Cuellar's warning about Miguel:* Author interview with IRS special agent Steve Pennington.

THIRTY-NINE

197   *When Lawson and Pérez:* Author interview with FBI special agent Scott Lawson.

198   *'The way I look at it':* Author interview with FBI supervisory special agent David Villarreal.

FORTY

199   *The investigation was finally:* Author interview with FBI special agent Scott Lawson.

200   *López had briefly met José:* Court testimony of ICE special agent Ed O'Dwyer.

FORTY-ONE

201   *But as they moved into the spring:* Author interview with FBI special agent Scott Lawson.

202   *Pérez was also having problems:* Author interview with FBI special agent Alma Pérez.

203   *When itseemed like things:* Author interview with FBI special agent Scott Lawson.

204   *As the raid had progressed:* Author interview with DEA special agent Kyle Mori.

205   *With so much law-enforcement heat:* Author interview with FBI special agent Scott Lawson.

FORTY-TWO

206   *After the raid, Carlos Nayen:* Court testimony of Carlos Nayen.

207   *With Nayen off the grid:* Court testimony of Felipe Quintero.

208   *Fernando Garcia, who had not been:* Court testimony of Fernando Garcia.

209   *José had grown increasingly suspicious:* Author interview with FBI special agent Scott Lawson.

FORTY-THREE

210   *Since January 2010, Pennington:* Author interview with IRS special agent Steve Pennington.

211   *Three weeks passed:* Author interview with FBI special agent Scott Lawson.

212   *Unbeknown to Lawson and the team:* Author interview with Ginger Thompson.

213   *Steve Pennington took the news:* Author interview with IRS special agent Steve Pennington.

214 *After a tense month:* Author interview with FBI special agent Scott Lawson.

FORTY-FOUR

215 *Pennington and Billy Williams:* Author interview with IRS special agent Steve Pennington.
216 *For several weeks, supervisors:* Ibid.
217 *Pérez's three kids:* Author interview with FBI special agent Alma Pérez.
218 *After their conversation:* Author interview with FBI special agent Scott Lawson.

FORTY-FIVE

219 *But Lawson couldn't resist:* Author interview with FBI special agent Scott Lawson.
220 *With the wedding:* Author interview with FBI special agent Alma Pérez.

FORTY-SIX

221 *The night before the raid:* Author interview with FBI special agent Alma Pérez.
222 *Lawson was pacing:* Author interview with FBI special agent Scott Lawson.
223 *The U.S. Department of State:* Jason Buch and Guillermo Contreras, 'Agents Go After Zetas in Raids', *San Antonio Express-News,* 13 June 2012, https://www.mysanantonio.com/news/local_news/article/Agents-go-after-Zetas-in-raids-3628244.php224 *In San Antonio:* Author interview with FBI special agent Alma Pérez.
225 *Even though they had indicted:* Author interview with FBI special agent Scott Lawson.
226 *It was still dark outside:* Author interview with Laredo task-force officer Ernie Elizondo.
227 *As they left the outskirts:* Author interview with FBI special agent Alma Pérez.
228 *It made him feel better:* Author interview with FBI special agent Scott Lawson.
229 *He pulled out a check:* Author interview with IRS special agent Steve Pennington.

230 *'I want you to just listen':* FBI 302 report provided during trial, April 2013.

231 *Lawson could see he wasn't:* Author interview with FBI special agent Scott Lawson.

FORTY-SEVEN

232 *In Oklahoma City, Lawson:* Author interview with FBI special agent Scott Lawson.

233 *While Pennington worked with Lawson:* Author interview with Waco Treasury Task Force officer Brian Schutt.

234 *Billy Williams, Steven Junker:* Author interview with Waco Treasury Task Force officer Steve Junker.

235 *The task force had left:* Author interview with Waco Treasury Task Force officer Brian Schutt.

236 *'If it's one Suburban':* Author interview with Waco Treasury Taskforce officer Steve Junker.

237 *Brian Schutt had his own:* Author interview with Waco Treasury Task Force officer Brian Schutt.

238 *As soon as they returned:* Author interview with FBI special agent Scott Lawson.

239 *Alfonso del Rayo had been living:* Author interview with Alfonso del Rayo.

240 *But del Rayo had never:* Author interview with FBI special agent Scott Lawson.

241 *José's winning streak:* Steve Andersen, 'Top Quarter Horse Owners Indicted in Connection with Mexican Drug Cartel', *Daily Racing Form,* 15 June 2012, http://www.drf.com/news/top-quarter-horse-owners-indicted-connection-mexican-drug-cartel.

FORTY-EIGHT

242 *In yet another entanglement:* Author interview with FBI special agent Scott Lawson.

245 *Pennington had no such outlet:* Author interview with IRS special agent Steve Pennington.

246 *For Pérez, it was growing:* Author interview with FBI special agent Alma Pérez.

247 *Two weeks after Lawson spoke:* Author interview with FBI special agent Scott Lawson.

FORTY-NINE

248 *Through co-operating witnesses:* Author interview with IRS special agent Steve Pennington.

249 *The next morning, Fernald:* Author interview with IRS special agent Michael Fernald.

250 *Lawson's friend, DEA special agent:* Author interview with DEA special agent Bill Johnston.

251 *The one downside:* Author interview with IRS special agent Steve Pennington.

FIFTY

252 *In October 2012, Heriberto Lazcano:* Randal Archibold, 'Mexico Kills a Drug Kingpin, but a Body Gets Away', *New York Times,* 9 October 2012, http://www.nytimes.com/2012/10/10/world/americas/mexico-zetas.html.

253 *The agents hadn't received:* Author interview with FBI special agent Scott Lawson.

254 *A dedicated horsewoman:* Author interview with IRS special agent Steve Pennington.

FIFTY-ONE

255 *The police and the sheriff's department:* Author interview with Waco Treasury Task Force officer Steve Junker.

256 *IRS special agent Bob Rutherford:* Author interview with federal prosecutor Michelle Fernald.

257 *He'd argued for larger courtrooms:* Ken Herman, 'Our New Federal Courtroom: Too Big and Too Small', *Austin American-Statesman,* 11 May 2013, http://www.mystatesman.com/news/opinion/herman-our-new-federal-courthouse-too-big-and-too-small/SyQmFaPj0oRFZIouD47BVL/.

258 *This would be the most complex:* Author interview with FBI special agent Scott Lawson.

259 *But by now, Finn:* Ibid.

260 *'This case is really':* Doug Gardner opening statement at trial.

261 *Scott Lawson sat across:* Author interview with FBI special agent Scott Lawson.

262 *'There's more to this story':* David Finn opening statement at trial.

263 *Gardner moved in closer:* Court testimony of Mario Alfonso Cuellar.

264 *Vasquez explained to the jury:* Court testimony of José Vasquez Jr.

265 *Michelle Fernald stood up:* Court testimony of José Carlos Hinojosa.

266 *Lawson watched the noted defence attorney:* Author interview with FBI special agent Scott Lawson.

267 *Bliss explained to the jury:* Court testimony of Dr Shalyn Bliss.

FIFTY-TWO

268 *On Monday morning:* Author interview with FBI special agent Alma Pérez.

269 *Del Rayo walked down the aisle:* Court testimony of Alfonso del Rayo.

270 *This had been one:* Author interview with FBI special agent Scott Lawson.

271 *Fernald discovered that Colorado:* Author interview with IRS special agent Michael Fernald.

272 *First, Fernald broke down:* Court testimony of IRS special agent Michael Fernald.

FIFTY-THREE

273 *Alma Pérez, sitting:* Author interview with FBI special agent Alma Pérez.

274 *Now he was going to testify:* Court testimony of Jesús Rejón Aguilar.

275 *As Doug Gardner prepared:* Author interview with FBI special agent Scott Lawson.

276 *Lawson hadn't seen Doc Graham:* Ibid.

FIFTY-FOUR

277 *Steve Pennington had spent:* Author interview with IRS special agent Steve Pennington.

278 *The next morning, as they assembled:* Author interview with FBI special agent Scott Lawson.

279 *Earlier in the morning:* Author interview with FBI special agent Alma Pérez.

280 *It would be Lawson's job:* Court testimony of FBI special agent Scott Lawson.

281 *When Esper called Shae Cox:* Court testimony of Shae Cox.

FIFTY-FIVE

282 *Finn strode towards the jury box:* David Finn closing statement at trial.

283 *Doug Gardner would have:* Doug Gardner closing statement at trial.

284 *Neither Doug Gardner nor Michelle Fernald:* Author interview with federal prosecutor Michelle Fernald.

285 *The team convened:* Author interview with FBI special agent Scott Lawson.

FIFTY-SIX

286 *But two months after:* Author interview with FBI special agent Alma Pérez.

287 *By late afternoon:* Author interview with FBI special agent Scott Lawson.

FIFTY-SEVEN

288 *He was facing a maximum sentence:* Author's own observation at sentencing.

289 *'Throughout all of this':* Court testimony of Francisco Colorado Cessa at sentencing.

290 *Colorado's business partner, Ramon Segura:* Court testimony of Ramon Segura at sentencing.

291 *His change in fortune:* Court testimony of José Treviño at sentencing.

292 *As Judge Sparks called:* Author's own observation.

293 *Early the next morning:* Melissa del Bosque, 'Businessman's Son, Partner Arrested for Bribery in Zeta Money Laundering Trial', *Texas Observer,* 6 September 2013, https://www.texasobserver.org/businessmans-son-partner-arrested-outside-zeta-money-laundering-trial/.

FIFTY-EIGHT

294 *It was hard for Lawson:* Author interview with FBI special agent Scott Lawson.

295 *As Jeff Tebow, the manager:* Author interview with IRS special agent Steve Pennington.

296 *Lawson had noticed:* Author interview with FBI special agent Scott Lawson.

297 *The $1.7 million price tag:* Jason Buch, 'Zetas Horse Sells for $1.7 Million', *San Antonio Express-News,* 1 November 2013, http://www.mysanantonio.com/news/local/article/Zetas-horse-sells-for-1–7M-4947460.php.

298 *But first they would celebrate:* Author interview with FBI special agent Scott Lawson.

EPILOGUE

299 *A month after John Simmons:* Author interview with FBI special agent Scott Lawson.

300 *In March 2015:* Katy Watson, 'Mexico Arrests Zetas Cartel Leader Omar Treviño Morales', BBC News, 5 March 2015, http://www.bbc.com/news/world-latin-america-31731842.

301 *Colorado, sparing no expense:* Jazmine Ulloa, 'Mexican Businessman Seeks to Withdraw Plea in Judge Bribery Case', *Austin American-Statesman,* 4 December 2014, http://www.statesman.com/news/crime-law/mexican-businessman-seeks-withdraw-plea-judge-bri bery-case/EHr1nktODohZLU3bW45DUO/.

302 *Nayen's testimony was especially damaging:* Court testimony of Carlos Nayen.

303 *The deaths in Mexico's drug war:* Jason Breslow, 'The Staggering Death Toll of Mexico's Drug War', *Frontline,* 27 July 2015, http://www.pbs.org/wgbh/frontline/article/the-staggering-death-toll-of-mexicos-drug-war/.

304 *Four months after Omar's capture:* 'Mexican Authorities Arrest Father-in-Law of Former Zetas Cartel Boss', *San Diego Union-Tribune,* 19 July 2015, http://www.sandiegouniontribune.com /hoy-san-diego/sdhoy-mexican-authorities-arrest-father-in-law-of-2015jul19-story.html.

305 *After the arrests of José:* Author interviews with Waco Treasury Task Force officers Steve Junker and Brian Schutt.